CHANCERS

CHANCERS

SCANDAL, BLACKMAIL AND BUYING THE ENIGMA CODE

BARBARA JEFFERY

AMBERLEY

First published 2019

Amberley Publishing
The Hill, Stroud
Gloucestershire, GL5 4EP

www.amberley-books.com

British Library Cataloguing in Publication Data.
A catalogue record for this book is available from the British Library.

ISBN 978 1 4456 8978 4 (hardback)
ISBN 978 1 4456 8979 1 (ebook)

Typesetting by Aura Technology and Software Services, India.
Printed in the UK.

Contents

PART TWO: The Worldwide Adventures of Newton and Lemoine

PART THREE: The Spymaster who Bought the Enigma Code, the Traitor who Sold Them and his Brother – Hitler's Favourite General

PART ONE

Maud, the Rajah and the Mayfair Mob

The Truth behind the Blackmailing of Sir Hari Singh – a tale of Riches and Love, Sex and Snobbery, Crime and Betrayal

Preface

London at the end of the First World War – the Great War – was almost out of control. The old order of society had collapsed: young women had cropped their hair and thrown away their corsets, enjoying a new independence, but the men were crippled, mentally and physically, by the war. People just wanted to forget its horrors and have fun any way they could: cocktails, card games and crazy parties. Into this charged atmosphere stepped a young man from a far-off, feudal world, ready for adventure. He found entertainment in royal palaces, on battleships – and in brothels. During his few months in London, high society and affairs of state were to collide with a city's underworld and a ring of globe-trotting conmen. The scandal that followed rocked the world and its aftermath remains to this day. The young man was Rajah Sir Hari Singh, heir to the Maharajah of Kashmir. His downfall was to meet an adventuress called Maud, and her associates, the Mayfair Mob.

When the Rajah came to London in 1919, his first time in Europe, between visits to the King and Queen and the Prince of Wales he was introduced by his *aide de camp* to Mrs Maud – Maudie – Robinson. They became lovers and spent Christmas in Paris, where they were 'discovered' in bed together. The Rajah parted with cheques for the equivalent today of fourteen million pounds in hush money to stop Maudie's husband citing him in a divorce action The plot was planned by his trusted friend and *aide*, Charles Arthur, an Irish nobleman, with Monty Newton, a notorious card sharp, and William Cooper Hobbs, a crooked solicitor's clerk and the Mr Big of the London underworld. But were Maudie and her husband also in on the plot? And if so, how were they cheated out of all but £21,000 of the blackmail pay-out? When they found out, the ensuing court case gave Sir Hari a nickname that haunted him forever: 'Mr A'.

The British Government imposed the greatest secrecy on the case, keeping files closed for seventy and a hundred years rather than the usual thirty. Records only recently released by the National Archives throw new light on the court case that gripped the world for eight days in 1924. The affair was to turn a high-spirited and impulsive young prince into a wary, suspicious man and a tyrannical ruler, a change which was to have repercussions that last to this day in the fraught relations between India and Pakistan over Kashmir.

The strange case of the Rajah, his mistress and the Mayfair Mob as they set about 'plucking the pigeon' proves that the whole truth does not always come out in court.

Dramatis Personae

Florence Maud Robinson. Maudie. A working-class woman with the chutzpah to pass as a society lady and indulge her expensive tastes in clothes, jewellery and houses. She lived, partly, on the profits of a patent medicine business inherited from her grandmother in 1916.

Charles Robinson. Maudie's husband. A bankrupt bookmaker, known as Butcher because he had worked as one in Australia; Maudie said he looked like one, too. 'Known' to the police for his racecourse con tricks, although they had never been able to pin anything on him.

William Cooper Hobbs. A solicitor's managing clerk and *very* well known to the police as adviser and fixer to the criminal classes. The 'Mr Big' of the London underworld.

Montague Noel Newton. A loveable rogue and card sharp. Suave and elegant, much admired by the police for his skill and audacity; they called him 'the daddy of all conmen'.

Rodolphe Lemoine. Newton's long-time partner in crime and London flat-mate; he plays a behind-the-scenes part in this story. German-born, he is also star spy recruiter for France and is our main character in Part Three of this narrative. He seems to have recruited Newton, too.

Sir Hari Singh. Mr A. Heir to his uncle, the Maharajah of Kashmir. Married four times, he outlived three wives.

Charles William Augustus Arthur. Singh's *aide de camp*, who inherited a run-down Irish estate in childhood; also a lady-killer.

Khusru Jung. Sir Hari's military secretary, and a nawab, or prince, from Hyderabad. Despite the nickname of Mahboob, another ladies' man.

Lyllian Bevan. Maudie's housemate, the widow of a Brighton wine merchant.

Detective Inspector W. C. Gough. A Scotland Yard man who kept a close eye on Monty Newton's career for twenty-five years.

Detective Sergeant Percy J. Smith. A member of a Scotland Yard squad set up to clear London of the influx of conmen causing havoc in the West End after the war; the first person to get a whiff of the blackmail plot.

Lord Justice Darling. A dandy and joker who injected a lot of fun into the 'Mr A' Case.

Money Matters

Sir Hari's two £150,000 cheques would be worth more than £14 million today. But that does not give the full picture; it is easier to compare what things cost in those days with current prices: a new semi-detached house in the London suburbs cost at least £1,000 and a family of four spent £3 a week on food. A cleaner earned two shillings (ten pence) for a morning's work and a solicitor or accountant earned £800 or £900 a year. A four-course dinner in the West End of London could be had for four shillings (twenty pence) and a diamond-and-platinum watch cost £80. Sir Hari's eleven-month tour of Europe for his party of seven cost £55,000 not counting the hush money.

CHAPTER ONE

After the Ball – London, November 1919

There was an air of reckless gaiety in the city in the months after the end of the First World War, the Great War. While the provinces were having a hard time – landowners complained that because the value of sterling had halved since 1913 they could no longer keep up their stately homes and many were demolished – London was booming. It was the biggest city in Europe. Living standards had risen during the war because there was plenty of work. Although Mayfair was still full of mansions that needed thirty people to staff, between 1901 and 1921 the number of female servants in London fell by more than a third; there were better jobs to be had in offices and the big stores that were springing up – plans to rebuild Regent Street were well underway.

The West End was bubbling with life. It was teeming with demobbed officers with fat gratuities in their pockets, doing their best to forget the horrors of war. Pre-war emigrants who had made good in the United States and Australia were coming back to visit the old country and then to 'do' a rather macabre tour of the battlefields, just as they did on the centenary of the end of the war. And where there's money, there's crime. A new wave of conmen had arrived in London. Most came from Australia where they learned their trade on the racecourses and at the card tables, Australians being as fond of a punt then as now. These colonial boys, as the police called them, took over from the English and American conmen on the London scene and were successful because they did not *look* like conmen. They played the part of simple country boys: tanned, blue-eyed with sun-bleached hair and an open manner that seemed utterly unsophisticated and trustworthy. London was almost out of control, and the police had set up a special squad to try to clear out these crooks.

A non-stop dancing craze was one of the more innocent pursuits among Londoners. There was a dance hall in the Strand where you paid a shilling to enter and there were two bands, one at each end of the room. When one band finished its set, the other started. The other crazes were card games and cars. The first 'Motor Car Show' since before the war opened at Olympia on 7 November 1919. The next day, a Saturday, more than 33,000 people went through the gates. There were queues to get in and queues to get out. The streets were jammed with traffic for a square mile round Olympia. There were not enough hotel rooms for all the visitors so some slept in the bathrooms and in billiards rooms and others took the train to Brighton for a bed. There were two-year waiting lists for cars and people were complaining about the high cost of petrol and of car dealers making outrageous profits.

There was a question asked in the House of Commons about a female refugee being allowed into the country because she said she had come to marry a soldier; when she didn't produce the marriage certificate she faced deportation but was allowed to stay because she had found a job and was maintaining herself in 'respectable surroundings'. There was a newspaper story about 'mystery millions' being offered to the Prime Minister by a Mr Ian Robertson for investment in what is now called 'affordable housing'. Where does it come from? asked *The Daily Telegraph*. One young woman wanted to be a football referee. The concerns of the time were not very different from our own.

In the middle of this celebration of consumerism came the first anniversary of the end of the fighting in the Great War. It was a bittersweet occasion; the King had ordered two minutes' silence to mark the signing of the armistice at the eleventh hour of the eleventh day of the eleventh month. The nation's grief was monumental. Thirty-five thousand war memorials had been erected. Every town, every village, every street, every family had been touched by the war. There were no Flanders poppies – they were not introduced until 1921 – and a wreath of rosebuds from the King and Queen was laid at the new cenotaph in Whitehall, designed by Sir Edward Lutyens. The street was crammed with weeping crowds. The Prime Minister, David Lloyd George, laid a bouquet of red roses and lilies. Piles of simpler flowers mounted up: country bunches of autumn leaves, chrysanthemums and potted plants. A card on one spray bore the scrawled message: 'To Billy, our brother'. But there was victory to be celebrated, too, and Lady Hulton, wife of the proprietor of the *Daily Sketch* newspaper, had helped to organise a fancy dress Victory Ball at the Royal Albert Hall for that evening.

The first snowflakes of the winter fell on London that day. There was gridlock on Kensington Gore with cars coming into the West End from Olympia competing with horse-drawn hansoms making for the Albert Hall from Mayfair and Knightsbridge. Inside, the Southern Syncopated Orchestra was playing jazzy tunes and people were dancing shoulder to shoulder, their costumes making a constantly changing dazzle. There were pierrots and pierrettes, a Russian prince, Bolsheviks, Egyptian princesses; French onion sellers were a centime a dozen.

One gallery was full of wounded soldiers, and two hundred nurses in uniform watched from another. At midnight the crowds parted to allow a chariot drawn by six women to pass through. Upon the padded seat of the chariot sat a woman dressed, the newspapers said, as Peace. It was Lady Hulton. She stood up, parted her flowing white and gold cloak dramatically and three white doves flew from her bosom. The lady had been an actress before her marriage and the urge to perform never left her; she still had many theatrical friends but devoted her time now to raising funds for charity – the Victory Ball was in aid of the Central Council of the Infant Welfare Work. She had attracted *la crème de la crème* to her party. Lord Birkenhead, the Lord Chancellor, was with Lady Birkenhead; the Prime Minister's wife, Lady Lloyd George, was in Sir Edward Hulton's box. The other newspaper proprietors, Lords Rothermere and Beaverbrook, were there; all people who would be touched by the train of events which was to begin that night.

In one of the three tiers of boxes that surround the vast circle of the Albert Hall sat Sir Hari Singh, the twenty-four-year-old heir to the Maharajah of Kashmir, Sir Pratab Singh. He was splendidly garbed, not in fancy dress but in the traditional style of his own country, which was pretty fancy: billowing jodhpurs and a high-collared scarlet silk tunic. His chest sparkled with jewels and five ropes of huge pearls reached almost to his waist. His fleshy face was topped by an intricately folded silk turban that supported a waving feather secured by a jewelled clasp. With him was his entourage of five Indians and Captain Charles Arthur, his *aide de camp*. They were enjoying an elaborate late-night supper. In the next box sat two women, one of them Maudie Robinson. Maudie wore a flimsy green gauze outfit and an enormous headdress emblazoned with the word 'grasshopper'. A woman of thirty-two, she was ahead of her time. She lived apart from her husband and survived on the income from a small patent medicine business inherited from her grandmother in 1916.

With her mousy hair and prominent teeth, Maudie was not a conventionally beautiful woman but she was what the French call *jolie laide*, a lively woman who was very attractive to men. Her medicine business was called Grasshopper Ointment and the ball was a good opportunity to advertise it. Her companion, Lyllian Bevan, was a widow who was living with her in a rented house in Chapel Street. Chapel Street is between Buckingham Palace and Belgrave Square. It was modest compared with the huge stuccoed mansions in the square, but it was a very good address – the closer to the palace the smarter – and the rooms were nicely furnished. It was also well beyond Mrs Robinson's means.

The ball was an informal affair and there were comings and goings between the two boxes, Maud said she wasn't introduced to the Rajah at the time but she thought he looked splendid. She was too kind; another woman described him as 'unhealthily stout and unattractive with a listless, indolent air, moving heavily and without grace'. Photographs bear this out and show a man looking more like forty-four than twenty-four. By this time Hari Singh was already on his second marriage – he would marry four times. His first wedding was in 1913 when he was sixteen and straight from Mayo College in Rajputana, the Indian Eton. This bride died of consumption within a year. Two months later he was betrothed again and remarried in 1915, ten months or so after the death of his first wife. Sir Hari had left his second wife at home in Kashmir and now he was about to embark on a liaison which was to bring him worldwide notoriety and ridicule. In view of their later relationship it would be logical to assume that Maudie was introduced to Sir Hari during the Victory Ball, but she insisted this was not so, although she met several of his party. She bumped into one of them again a few days later as she and Lyllian Bevan were leaving the Savoy Hotel after lunch and he offered her a lift home. In the light of the etiquette of the day, driving off with a 'black man' was a racy thing to do; in fact, having lunch at the Savoy without your husband was a pretty racy thing to do. Maudie's reputation would have suffered less had she said she was introduced to Sir Hari at the Albert Hall; meeting as neighbours at a smart social function would have been seen as a respectable introduction.

After Sir Hari's friend had driven them home, Maudie invited him in for coffee and a liqueur. The friend told her his master had noticed her and Mrs Bevan at the Ball and would very much like to meet them. Curzon Street, where Sir Hari was living, was not far away and soon the couple met and a 'great and true' affection sprang up between them. Before long – by the first week in December, in fact – they were lovers. Not to be outdone, Lyllian had become the special friend of the Military Secretary, Khusru Jung, who was known as Mahboob. He was a nawab, or prince, from Hyderabad and a fine-looking fellow with an imposing presence, a rich voice and a reputation as a ladies' man. The four often had dinner at Maudie's house and played cards afterwards, much to the annoyance of the parlour-maid, who was rather shocked at 'men of colour' entering the house.

By Christmas the four were in Paris together. Hari spent the days buying jewels – one of his major interests in life. Sapphires and other precious gems were discovered in Kashmir in the 1880s and his family had an interest in the mines, which made them immensely rich. Hari's income at the time was said to be £12,000,000 a year, rather an exaggeration as it turned out. When he acted as page to the Viceroy, Lord Curzon, at the age of six he wore a gown of gold cloth and a rope of pearls worth a million pounds. At the 1911 Durbar when King George V visited India, he was arrayed even more extravagantly in robes of shimmering gold embroidered with diamonds, emeralds, rubies and pearls, the whole estimated to be worth about three million pounds.

On his first visit to Europe he was certain to have attracted the attention of those conmen who had made London their centre after the war – his jewels were the talk of the town – but for the moment he was having a thoroughly good time. Maudie and Lyllian had arrived in Paris on 20 December and checked into a suite Sir Hari had reserved at the Hotel Brighton on the Rue de Rivoli, overlooking the Tuileries Gardens. Sir Hari had official business in London and arrived the following day with Mahboob. The two couples talked about the future. Sir Hari and Mahboob wanted the women to return to Kashmir with them. They pored over plans for the houseboats Maudie and Lyllian would live in on Lake Dal in Srinagar, the summer capital of Kashmir. Maudie had just about decided to accept the proposal. Although she was a little dubious about a public relationship with a 'man of colour', she said, 'Some of them can give a woman a little more happiness than white men.' And she had come to enjoy Sir Hari's unusual way of making love.

Then, inexplicably, the women moved into the St James and Albany hotel, just up the road, on 23 December. Maudie said it was because the ADC was unexpectedly joining them on Christmas Eve and Sir Hari did not want him to know about their *affaire*, so he kept the suite at the Hotel Brighton for himself, Mahboob and Captain Arthur, Hari's minder.

The two couples and Captain Arthur dined together at the Cafe de Paris on Christmas Eve. They spent Christmas night together, too, wining, dining and dancing. It was six o'clock in the morning before the lovers got back to their hotel, leaving Captain Arthur, who must surely have realised what was going on, to return alone to the grand suite at the Hotel Brighton.

* * *

If the story so far has something of the Ruritanian musical comedy about it, with the Prince falling in love with the society lady and her lowlier friend becoming involved with his secretary, here our story moves first into the realm of bedroom farce and then into something darker.

Hari and Maud were not to get much rest. An hour and a half later, their bedroom door opened and in burst a man. Maudie and Hari (in mauve silk pyjamas) were in one of the two single beds in the opulently furnished room. Hari sat up, clutching the bed covers round him, too startled to speak. Maudie leapt out of bed, screaming, and pummelled the man in the chest. Hari tried to calm her, saying: 'Maudie, Maudie, don't make a scene. After all, it is your husband.'

It was not her husband. It was Montague Noel Newton, the cosmopolitan conman, who left as quickly as he had arrived. Hari dressed and rushed to the Hotel Brighton to rouse Captain Arthur and confess all. Arthur, whose job it was to keep the young heir out of trouble, advised that Mr Robinson would almost certainly sue for divorce on the grounds of his wife's adultery and when Sir Hari was named as co-respondent it would place him in a very difficult position in Kashmir and his uncle Sir Pratab Singh might well disinherit him; the India Office in London might rescind their approval of his right to inherit the throne. A pederast in his youth, there had been doubts at the India Office about Sir Pratab Singh's suitability for the job of Maharajah, but by 1919 he was seventy-four and a reformed character, a strict vegetarian and Hindu who often fasted and lived for his religion first and his country second. He was utterly disdainful of Europeans and felt that they contaminated his race by their presence, refusing to shake hands with them unless he was wearing gloves. The Maharajah's only son had died in infancy and he was forced to accept his nephew, Hari, as heir. In spite of his youthful predilection for boys, Sir Pratab was said to have 350 concubines, 200 of his own and 150 inherited from his brother, Hari's father, who had been murdered, rather extravagantly, by having powdered rubies dropped into his drink. Despite his harem, Sir Pratab never produced an heir acceptable to the British, the sons of concubines not being Maharajah material. Several times he produced 'borrowed' baby boys whom he said were his sons but the British would have none of it and insisted on Hari being named heir.

Sir Hari knew there was some feeling against him in Kashmir so he took Captain Arthur's advice to buy off the wronged 'husband'.

He gave the Captain two blank cheques, signed but not dated, and a letter to take to his lawyers in London:

> Dear Sir, I am giving Captain Arthur, whom you know, two signed blank cheques, numbered B204561 and B204562. He has my instructions to fill in these cheques and he will inform you at the time the amount for which he is to draw them. Will you be kind enough to see that they are immediately honoured?[1]

Sir Hari was content to leave the matter entirely to Arthur, who advised him to remain in Paris until all was settled. Arthur returned to London that night by rail and boat with Maudie and Lyllian. Sir Hari saw them off at the station. Maudie remembered his parting words: 'I know there is something wrong somewhere but I know you are innocent and I will stand by you to the end.'

CHAPTER TWO

Who *is* Charles Arthur?

Sir Hari's trip to London had been a last-minute affair and the Foreign Office was cross they were not given enough notice to arrange a suitable programme for him. Captain Arthur caused a ripple of curiosity, too. Sir James Dunlop Smith, political assistant to the Secretary of State for India, wrote a memo saying he could not get from Arthur what his exact status was, only that he was married and his wife appeared to be a guest of the Rajah – in Kashmir, presumably. The India Office sent a coded telegram to the Viceroy asking what to do with the unexpected visitors. The Viceroy replied a fortnight later in telegramese:

> Hari Singh no special recommendation but good offices may be extended to him as heir apparent of Kashmir. He would no doubt appreciate advice, help and introductions. Arthur is his ADC. Hari Singh pays him rupees one thousand five hundred a month plus travelling and hotel expenses arrangement can be terminated at three months' notice on either side.

1,500 rupees would be about £150 at the time, the equivalent of around £5,500 today, so Captain Arthur was not doing badly.[2]

Charles William Augustus Arthur, an Irish nobleman, was in the Vale of Kashmir in the Himalayas when the Great War broke out, hunting black bears and wild boar, shooting duck, fishing for trout in the mountain streams and playing polo with Rajah Hari Singh, the young heir. Beautiful and isolated, the happy valley, as it was known, was the playground of the east. Green and fertile, it is a mile high, twenty wide and eighty long, surrounded by snow-capped mountains which have earned it another extravagant description: an emerald set in pearls. Today's air travel – it is an hour and a quarter's flight north of Delhi – makes you forget how remote it is, but there is no railway and a century ago visitors had to travel overland from Rawalpindi, in what is now Pakistan, which could take six days in a horse-drawn landau.

The capital of the Vale, Srinagar, was known as the Venice of the Orient. It is built round Dal Lake, one of a network of lakes and canals that run into the Jhelum River that winds through the town. This kingdom, which is about the size of the British mainland, was never part of British India but was a princely state, ruled over by the Maharajah, Sir Pratab Singh. The British never approved of the Maharajah for the reasons already given, but by 1914 Hinduism and cricket had become his main interests. In his turn the Maharajah was deeply suspicious of Europeans and decreed that they could not own immoveable property in his state; so the resourceful colonial British had houseboats built of sandalwood and pine and took to the waters of Srinagar for their holidays. They did their sight-seeing by *shikara*, skiffs with upholstered seats and awnings to keep the sun off.

The biggest houseboat on the lake, the *Diana*, was more than a hundred feet long and fourteen wide and had a staff of fifteen, including two tailors and two cooks. 'It looks like a gentleman's boat,' said one European visitor when an American archaeologist took the *Diana* for the summer of 1914. The choice of food was wide: there was lamb and mutton, chicken, duck and geese, as well as trout from the mountain streams. (Queen Victoria provided the original stock with a tankful of baby trout in return for a gift of two Kashmiri pashmina goats.) Apples, peaches and apricots were bought from the kitchen garden at the Europeans' club – thought to be more hygienic than those you could buy in the floating market. If you sat on your houseboat veranda for long enough all the world would come to you, from Messrs Wonderful and Marvellous with their skiffs piled high with flowers massed together like a giant Victorian posy, to the carpet sellers, the jewellers, the *papier-mâché* merchants, the walnut carvers and the man selling fizzy drinks.[3]

Bordered by Afghanistan to the west, Tibet and China to the east and with only a narrow strip of Afghan territory separating it from Russia, the Maharajah's kingdom was an important listening post for the British, who were afraid that Russia would invade India through Kashmir. The kingdom consists of three parts: Jammu in the south, the Vale of Kashmir, 5,000 feet above sea level, and Ladakh, a 12,500-foot-high mountainous desert to the north-east. Two or three hundred British spent the whole year in the Vale but the summer population rose to about 3,000 with families coming up from the plains to escape the heat. The Maharajah and his court spent July and August at Gulmarg in the foothills of the Himalayas. Tennis, golf and polo were the morning routine with tea parties and garden fetes in the afternoon. Social life centred round the Club and the Residency, the home of the British resident officer whose job was to keep track of the central Asian political situation. He also had to make sure the European visitors behaved themselves and observed the strict Hindu dietary laws; one family was asked to leave after importing Oxo beef cubes to a country where the cow was sacred.

Charles Arthur arrived here in 1914 with his wife, Rose Violet, and their son, leaving behind a story of family conflict that perhaps foreshadowed future troubles. Charles had a younger brother, Desmond, an early member of the Royal Flying Corps. The two boys, orphans, were like chalk and cheese: Dessie, methodical and businesslike; Charles, wild and fun-loving. The family story was that Charles got into debt after going on drinking sprees with his young footman. The brothers were estranged and Dessie spent most of his time with the Ropner family, West Hartlepool shipbuilders, who treated him like a son. Dessie died when his plane disintegrated near Montrose airfield in Scotland in May 1913. When his body was recovered he was wearing a locket with a miniature portrait of a thirteen-year-old girl next to his heart, the daughter of the Ropner family. On their last meeting she had given him her favourite rag doll, Clare, as a mascot.[4]

A romance between a daredevil flyer of twenty-nine and a little girl would raise eyebrows today. In 1913, her family saw it as an innocent affection likely to lead to marriage. The romance caused absolute fury in *his* family when it was revealed. Dessie left his estate – mainly property in Dublin – to the little girl, Winsome. It was worth £12,500 and more than £7,000 of it was owed to him by his brother. Charles contested the will, saying it was not properly made, complaining: 'It was not right for my brother to leave money away from his own family which needed it, to the Ropner family, which did not.'[5]

He soon abandoned his claim, accepting £1,000 from Mr Ropner, and by the time the legal affairs came to an end Charles Arthur was on board the SS *Elysia* en route to Bombay with his wife, Rose, and baby son. They were bound for the Vale of Kashmir and a new life. He wrote to Mr Ropner on 19 January 1914: 'I am compelled to go to India or I would miss an appointment I am getting.'

Presumably the appointment was not for lunch but a new job, but I have found no record of this. What is certain is that the summer of 1914 found Charles in Kashmir and firm friends with Sir Hari; Charles was thirty-two and Sir Hari nineteen. Hunting, shooting and polo united them – but had Charles Arthur already targeted the young Hari for something more? Charles Arthur was a rich man by European standards but when he saw the dazzling wealth of his young friend, the famous Kashmiri sapphires, the palaces, the opulent royal barge rowed by a hundred oarsmen, did he feel a twinge of envy or, indeed, spot an opportunity?

The Arthurs had first visited the Vale in 1909. They arrived by car, which attracted much attention because there were only two other cars in the state. They fell in love with the valley and stayed much longer than the few weeks they had originally planned. As well as being an expert duck shot and horseman, the Irishman proved to be one of the best card players in the Valley. He was full of Irish charm and was an immediate success in Srinagar. Six feet tall with a round, chubby face and a dimpled chin, he was handsome and had a fund of rude stories. He'd kissed the Blarney stone all right, and charmed all who met him.

Charles went to Kashmir for the big game hunting: there were black bears and brown bears, wild boar, snow leopards and stags, He could have found these more easily in other places. So what attracted him to Kashmir? It is tempting to think he had read *Lalla Rookh*, a poem about Kashmir written by a fellow Irishman, Thomas Moore, in 1817. It was a huge success, translated into every

European language and most eastern ones, and famous composers based operas on it. Moore wrote that 'if there be paradise on earth, this is it, this is it, this is it', but he had never visited Kashmir. He produced his epic after long talks with earlier travellers; a fantasy, really, like much of Charles Arthur's life.

The Arthurs were an old Limerick family, descended from the Vikings. The family is credited with rebuilding the city in the eighteenth century on the Georgian grid pattern and there are still references to the Arthurs in the city today: Arthur's Quay Park on the bank of the Shannon and Arthur's Quay Centre, a shopping complex, were opened in the 1980s. The names of forty-eight Arthurs are listed as mayors of the city and they provided bishops (Catholic as well as Protestant) and members of parliament. Charles Arthur was born in 1882 and his father died when he was only six, so he inherited the family estate, Glanomera, in County Clare. There were debts then, which Charles increased for he couldn't live on his share of the rents from their forty-odd houses in Dublin, which brought in about £7,000 a year.

He was an absentee landlord, living in London as a gentleman in a grand flat in De Vere Gardens, opposite Kensington Gardens. He returned often to Ireland for the sport: the Glanomera estate was famous for its duck and pheasant shooting and he had horses to race. He didn't even bother to collect the paltry rents from the poor farms on the estate.

The well-to-do Irishman impressed in Kashmir. A woman who met him there said 'his conversational powers are exceptional ... he is the sort of man who gives one the impression that life is a great big joke.'[6]

In July 1914, like the Maharajah and the British officials, he drove up through the pine forest to Gulmarg, twenty-eight miles away, for the summer holiday season. A marg is a large, grassy down in a clearing among the pine forests where hill people graze their ponies, buffalo, sheep and goats. Gulmarg was the Court's hill station – as the Indian summer resorts were called – where the Maharajah and his entourage lived in wooden bungalows. It is twenty-eight miles from Srinagar and in Sir Hari's time the last three miles had to be negotiated by pony, dandy (a light, sprung cart) or on foot. The marg is two miles long and half a mile wide; there is a sheer drop to the Vale of Kashmir on three sides and on the other side the mountains rise steeply. The summer weather is cool and wet and holidaymakers often needed to keep fires burning in every room for twenty-four hours a day, but it didn't deter those who couldn't find a hut, as the cottages were called, to rent. They would happily pitch a tent in the meadow, so that the place took on the look of a huge encampment. It was worth it, for the scenery is magnificent with beautiful views down to the vale and up to the snowy peaks of Nanga Parbat, clearly visible although ninety miles to the north. Of course, there was the inevitable club plus a sports centre with tennis courts, cricket and polo grounds and two golf courses, one for men and one for women, which were regarded as the best in the sub-continent. There was even a stone church, for there were missionaries in Kashmir, a Church of England Mission school in Srinagar with eighty teachers and 250 pupils, the Presentation Convent, also in Srinagar, run by Irish nuns, and a Moravian school in Leh – all still in operation and extremely popular.

This paradise is where the young Hari Singh aimlessly and languidly whiled away his summers – his uncle liked to keep power to himself despite his age and Sir Hari had only a little work each day as Commander-in-Chief of the state army. He played golf and tennis and captained his polo team against the Europeans. He was not without a sense of humour and could be a boisterous companion. There was a competition at a gymkhana one day: he had to write the first line of a limerick, ride up to a point where his partner was waiting and hand it to her. She had to complete it and Hari had to gallop back to the judges with it. Hari's first line was: 'In Gulmarg the gossips all say...' His partner added:

> It is ripping when hubby's away
> But one came up in June
> Just a fortnight too soon
> And now there's the devil to pay!

And there was a devil of a row about those harmless lines. It's easy to see how Hari longed to escape to the more liberal attitudes of Europe. He enjoyed the company of the British and American holidaymakers, he had an English tutor and spoke excellent English with an Oxford accent. Hari Singh was still a boarder at Mayo College when the Arthurs first visited Kashmir, but when they returned in 1914 with their ten-month old son the two men soon became friends in spite of the difference in ages: Hari was nineteen and Charles thirty-two. Hari loved to play cards with his western friends and hear their stories of life in cities with luxurious hotels, cinemas, theatres and that new development of Mr Selfridge, the department store in Oxford Street. Just to get away from the intrigues and politics of his uncle's court was a relief to the teenager.

When war broke out in August that year Charles Arthur's interlude in paradise ended and he returned to Europe to join up, leaving his wife and son behind in Srinagar. Although Hari was in theory the commander-in-chief of the Kashmir army, which had been put at the disposal of the British government, he was not allowed to fight in Europe. Most Maharajahs encouraged their princes to travel but Pratab Singh was against the idea. 'I shall never see your country,' Hari moaned when his friends went off to fight and he was left behind in his palace.

Hari was married straight from Mayo College. His bride was fifteen and the niece of the Maharana of Dharampur. The young bridegroom weighed her down with jewels. She was taller and fairer of skin than the average Englishwoman, with beautifully manicured fingernails painted crimson. Her feet were always bare and diamonds and rubies glistened on every toe. She wore a white muslin shirt beneath a jacket of purple and gold, studded with all manner of precious stones. An enormous ruby blazed from the centre of her forehead, surrounded by yet more diamonds. Row upon row of priceless pearls hung from her neck to her knees; diamonds, emeralds and rubies flashed from every finger and her earrings were so heavy with jewels that they had to be suspended by gold thread passed round the ears. Her neck was encased in a 'dog collar' of diamonds at least three inches deep that was tight and uncomfortable. These were not her best clothes; she wore them to entertain her European friends; she spoke no English but excellent French and read French novels all day.[7]

Hari was already fat and growing fatter. No surprise there, if the menu at the State dinner to celebrate the wedding is anything to go by. It was written in French and the food was French, too, which suggests the Maharajah was not quite as anti-European as most people said. There were ten courses and six wines were served, including 1904 Bollinger champagne as well as two ports, four liqueurs and cognac:

Mixed hors d'oeuvres
Mock turtle consommé *or* cream of asparagus soup
Poached trout with Hollandaise sauce
Quails with a red wine sauce
Lamb cutlets with stuffed mushrooms *or* roast saddle of mutton
Seasonal salad
Duckling with green peas
Pyramid of macaroons with chocolate sauce *or* peach Melba
Grilled ham with Madeira sauce
Dessert

Another of the wedding celebrations was a garden party held in the *Nishat Bagh*, or the garden of gladness, one of the most beautiful of all the gardens belonging to the Maharajah, built in the seventeenth century. There are nine huge terraces, supported by terracotta painted walls and shaded by immense chinar trees. The view from the terraces, sloping down to the Dal Lake and across to the panorama of mountain peaks beyond, rising above twenty thousand feet and covered with snow throughout the year, is magnificent always but best in the evening when the changing colours of the sunset turn the snowy mountains from white to pink to gold, then purple and grey, and the lake looks like liquid silver and gold. Just about all of the British residents of the Valley attended this party, as well as the Maharajah's nobles, staff and important citizens – thousands of people – to wonder at its beauty. Leading off from the formal central section with its canals, waterfalls and waterslides are quiet orchards, colourful summer houses, temples and pagodas.[8] Another garden Sir Hari would have known was that of the British Residency on the bank of the River Jhelum in Srinagar.

They are everyone's dream of an English garden: shady trees, informal planting, lots of honeysuckle and sweet peas, alleys of rambling roses leading to secret, leafy corners. The hospitality was famous and guests often remarked they felt as if they were in the grounds of Windsor Castle rather than two hundred miles from the nearest railway. After Sir Hari's wedding the Maharajah softened his attitude to Europeans and would often attend events at the Residency. His own home was a palace on the river bank. Inside, the sofas and chairs were covered in crimson velvet emblazoned with his coat of arms in gold. Precious stones studded the walls but the plaster that held them was crumbling, the velvet hangings were faded and rotting and the magnificent marble entrance was grimy, which puzzled the English and American visitors, who could never understand why this richest of men, who would happily spend thousands of pounds on diamonds and pearls, was too mean to maintain his palace properly. The India Office in London noted that the state was wealthy, 'although unsatisfactory reports upon the condition of the people have lately reached this office'. The people were, indeed, poor, reduced to poverty by the high taxes imposed to fund the Maharajah's shabby but extravagant life.

A few months after Charles Arthur went off to war, Hari's young wife died childless of consumption during pregnancy, eighteen months after their wedding. Hari knew his duty; another bride was quickly found, and he was engaged within six weeks and married again eleven months later. Again, there was no baby. Hari was restless and lethargic, and by 1917 the Government of India in Delhi was showing some concern about his future. The Viceroy, Lord Chelmsford, head of the government, tried to persuade the Maharajah that Hari, now twenty-two, should be given some experience of the world outside Kashmir, and his Political Secretary, Sir John Wood, had a chat with the young man about his future. On 17 November 1917 he wrote rather despairingly to Colonel Arthur Bannerman, the British Resident in Kashmir, saying Hari Singh 'did not display any particular keenness to go to the front, nor did he show any anxiety to obtain other employment in the state. What he was keen about was that he should have an opportunity of travelling and seeing the world as early as possible.' Colonel Bannerman replied:

> Hari Singh, I think, wishes for some more work but at the same time is evidently not at all desirous of having any considerable amount of work which would keep him busy for more than three and a half or four hours a day. The military work, if he really would go into it thoroughly and do it himself, would give him almost sufficient employment. But, as it is, he does not go into any of the details. The papers are put to him by the secretary when matters have been enquired into and worked out and Hari Singh has not often more to do than perhaps ask a few questions and then affix his signature.

Hari suggested going to the war in France after visiting England but his mother and three aunts were against the journey; they were worried about German submarines in the Mediterranean and his mother also thought that the Maharajah might change his mind about the succession if Hari left the State. In the face of such opposition, Hari caved in. 'There will be no peace in the family if I go on pushing,' he said miserably, abandoning the idea of travel until after the war.[9] So there he was, rich, bored, and lazy. His spirits perked up when he was made Knight Commander of the Order of the Indian Empire in the New Year's Honours list of 1918; he was proud to be called Sir Hari, and now even more determined to travel. As soon as the Armistice was signed he began planning his trip. The question of a travelling companion, an *aide de camp* or ADC, arose and several names were put forward.[10]

Arthur had reappeared early in 1918, and Sir Hari suggested him. Enquiries were made from the Army Department that did not give a satisfactory account. There was a feeling he had been insubordinate and unreliable as an officer. In fact, he had an undistinguished if not terrible war. He enlisted in the City of Limerick Royal Garrison Artillery and obtained a temporary commission with the rank of captain. He served in France, was blown up during the Battle of the Somme and was invalided back to England with shell shock. He was given a teaching job at the Royal Artillery cadet school at Trowbridge but was unable to concentrate. He was sent for light duties in India but complained that the heat made his condition worse and at the beginning of 1918 asked for permission to resign his temporary commission and return home. On 16 March 1918 he was given permission to return to England at his own expense, but instead of going to Bombay to catch a ship he went AWOL to Kashmir with his wife and son to renew his friendship with Hari Singh. This was only discovered when the War Office in London, expecting Captain Arthur to report to them, wondered what had happened to him. He was finally traced to Srinagar from where he sent a telegram to the army asking for his pay to be sent to his bank in Rawalpindi. The army thought it a bit rich that he should ask for pay while he was absent without leave and he was taken to Rawalpindi for another medical on 3 September, which found him in a highly nervous condition, suffering from insomnia and lack of concentration. The doctors did not consider him fit to travel to England and recommended that he should stay in Rawalpindi for two more months. So he was there until probably the end of October, when he went back to Kashmir rather than to England to resign.[11]

He resumed his friendship with Sir Hari and landed a plum job; Sir Hari was soon making clear his desire to take him as ADC on his trip to Europe. The British officials thought Arthur was not suitable but decided that Sir Hari was old enough to look after himself.[12]

So Hari got his way, and packed a trunkful of jewels. A telegram from the Viceroy dated 30 April 1919 arrived in London the next day, announcing that he had sailed for Europe on the SS *Loyalty* accompanied by Captain Arthur, Nawab Khusu Jung, Major Hoshiar Singh, Babu Gian Chand, Moti Ram and Hari Chand.[13] The Viceroy was tardy with his news for the *Loyalty* left Bombay on 5 April and arrived at Marseille on the 23rd. Sir Hari and his party took a train to Paris where they settled into a hotel for a few days, sending Captain Arthur on to London to tell the India Office of his impending arrival. The news caused irritation and agitation in the India Office because, according one official's memo, 'according to the rules, ample notice of the visit should have been given'. Another noted crossly on the 29th that Sir Hari had arrived in Marseille the previous week and would arrive in London that very night.

'This is the first intimation I have received of the visit. Captain Arthur says he is attached to the Rajah but has no particular plans and asks for advice and assistance. I shall help àll I can but I think we have a right to expect a letter from the Government of India as to how the Rajah may most profitably spend the "six or eight months" he is to be in Europe.'

The party booked into the Hyde Park Hotel in Knightsbridge and told the India Office the purpose of the visit was to study methods of government, transport and industry. An audience with the King was arranged and the India Office set to work on an improving programme for the Rajah. It was brief: according to the Court Circular, on 15 July he flew to Paris with a Captain Zuloaga, Assistant Military Attaché of the Argentine Legation. On 8 December he visited Portsmouth dockyard and was shown the warship HMS *Renown*. Four days later the Prince of Wales received him at St James's Palace. Between such events, he devoted himself to the pursuit of pleasure. He went to the theatre, visited grand hotels, went to the races and gave lavish dinner parties where he showed off his jewels, which became the talk of the town.

He bought three cars – jumping the queues, for most people had to face a two-year waiting list – including a 60-horsepower model suitable for the steep climb from Jammu to Srinagar. Although he spent prodigiously, he could be mean and a bad loser; a friend said he sulked – almost wept – for days after losing a ten-pound bet at Ascot. Horses were Sir Hari's great love and Captain Arthur was a racehorse owner himself. He escorted the party to Ireland for the Dublin horse show in August. Sir Hari spent thousands of pounds on horses and installed them with a well-known trainer in County Kildare. Then he set about recruiting staff to take back to Kashmir to look after the horses and the cars. Permission was given rather reluctantly: a hand-written 'I wish he would take British boys instead of Irish' implied that someone suspected that this was an attempt by Sinn Fein to get one of their emissaries into India. The India Office grumbled: 'Whether it is advisable for the Rajah to start a racing stable is another question, the old Maharajah will be very angry but we have no grounds for interfering.'

Enchanted by Ireland, Sir Hari even thought of buying an estate there, as several Indian princes had already done, but at the beginning of September the party moved on to Scotland where he rented Douglas Castle in Lanarkshire, then the home of the Douglas-Home family, for the grouse, partridge and pheasant shooting. (Sir Alec Douglas-Home was Prime Minister in 1963–4.) There were lavish house parties for the many British friends he had made in Kashmir. The house party would usually total ten or twelve. The new cars were parked in the drive and one day while driving a woman guest, Sir Hari put his foot down to show how fast the new machine would go. She was terrified and asked him to slow down; instead he turned the car on to rough ground and headed for a tree stump. Roaring with laughter, he told her the car could withstand anything and drove it into the stump. Nobody was hurt but it cost more than £400 to repair – that would be £8,000 today. It meant nothing to Sir Hari. Then came the winter and Sir Hari and his party returned to London and rented No. 27 Curzon Street, right in the heart of Mayfair.

It was not always easy for Captain Arthur to keep tabs on his young master, who, it was said, would sometimes sneak out with Khusru Jung and pick up prostitutes in Shepherd Market, Mayfair's red light district, just down the road from the Curzon Street house, now Aspinall's club.

Captain Arthur had his outings, too. He was a gregarious man and liked to drop in to the bar at the Hyde Park Hotel where Sir Hari's party had stayed when they arrived in London. Here one evening, by chance or not we will never know, he fell into conversation with Maudie Robinson, a meeting which was to change his life forever. Maudie was captivated by Captain Arthur's stories of life in Kashmir and of his employer's huge wealth.

CHAPTER THREE

Oh! Mr Robinson

Maudie's real husband, Charles Ernest Robinson, was a bookmaker. He learned his trade in Australia, where his parents took him in 1889 at the age of fifteen to join his brothers, who were butchers. Charlie worked for them as a cashier but the business got into trouble, with the brothers spending their time and money at the racecourses. They introduced Charlie to the excitement of a flutter, to the horror of their father, a respectable vet. The time in Australia left Charlie with his nickname, Butcher. When he returned to England in 1898 with a couple thousand pounds in his pocket, he set up as a bookmaker in London under the name Bloomfield so that his father would not be upset at the family name being besmirched by a connection with gambling. His father returned to England in 1907 and lived with Charlie in some style in a large house in Hendon with three acres of land and seven servants. The father died the next year, a few days before Charlie married Maud, on 14 December. Despite inheriting about £1,500 from his father, by the following year Robinson was made bankrupt, owing £4,000, having lost money gambling.

Charlie Robinson's trade did not prosper during the war as horseracing was suspended. At this time Charlie became known to the police as an associate of confidence tricksters. Detective Sergeant Percy J. Smith, one of the team set up to clear the West End of London of the influx of conmen that had been causing havoc since the end of the war, believed Charlie Robinson was Australian, one of a gang of nine 'colonial boys' he had identified.

He had a couple of minor convictions and, long before the 'Mr A' Case, Percy J. Smith knew that the 'colonial boys', including Robinson, had relieved a supposedly astute and canny Scottish landowner and businessman of a total of £147,000 by a series of scams that stopped only when the hapless man drowned himself.[14]

Maudie's war was no happier. She had three serious internal operations in 1914; Charlie took her on a voyage to Egypt to recover. They decided to return overland and Charlie left her in Switzerland to enjoy some clean, invigorating air while he returned to London; as a result, Maudie was alone in Switzerland when war was declared in August. She managed to get back to England before the fighting began.

* * *

Charlie Robinson allowed himself to be bought off by his wife's lover. His story, as told at the Royal Courts of Justice in the Strand, was that Monty Newton, whom he had known slightly since 1917, came to him on 27 December 1919 to tell him that Maudie was 'not conducting herself as she ought and she was carrying on in Paris with a black man'. Robinson decided to start divorce proceedings and next day went with Newton not to his usual solicitor but to Appleton and Co., a firm managed by William Cooper Hobbs, who gave him the details. Fifty-five-year-old Hobbs had known Robinson for several years; Robinson had passed him a dud cheque for £25 nine or ten years before. Hobbs was also known to the police as the Mr Big of the underworld, although he had never been arrested. Whenever a card sharp or a conman got into difficulties with the law, he called on Hobbs, who, although he never qualified in law, instead calling himself an accountant, knew how to exploit the legal system, particularly the law of libel. Hobbs was the son of a respectable barge owner from Battersea and started his career working for a firm in Smithfield Market, but was dismissed for dishonesty and moved on to work with a man who had a great knowledge of the underworld. Hobbs was an able pupil and soon, showing enterprise and imagination, he became one of the first 'ambulance chasers'.

This was in the early days of motoring. The streets were crowded with buses, pedestrians and horse-drawn carriages and naturally there were accidents. Hobbs would trace the victims, maybe even visit them in hospital, offer to deal with their insurance claims and then cheat his clients of their award. If, for instance, he succeeded in getting an award of £300 for damages, he might invite his unfortunate client into his office; sitting behind a pile of bank notes, he would present a list of his expenses: '£200 for my costs,' he would say, '£50 for my fee and £50 for you.'

Robinson went back to Hobbs a couple of days later to say he had spoken to his wife and couldn't believe her guilt. 'There's no doubt about it,' Hobbs told him, adding that the man's solicitor had admitted it. When Robinson next saw Hobbs on 10 January it was to hear for the first time the identity of his wife's lover and his position in Kashmir and that the great man's solicitor had said they didn't want a scandal so they had offered £20,000 if he would drop divorce proceedings. This was much, much more than what he might be awarded in damages if Sir Hari were named as co-respondent. When the offer was increased to £25,000 he agreed and signed a document to say he would abandon the divorce proceedings. On 17 January he took Maudie to Hobbs's office to collect the money. Hobbs produced a newspaper bundle which he said contained £25,000. Robinson said he wanted nothing to do with the money and, agitated and upset, stormed out of the office.

According to Maud, Hobbs took four £1,000 notes from the pile on the table as his costs (an enormous fee, worth more than £20,000 now). He wrapped up the rest of the money and gave it to Maudie, who claimed to have taken it to her room at the Mandeville Hotel in Mandeville Place, just north of Oxford Street. Since her return from Paris she had taken against the house in Chapel Street and went with Lyllian Bevan to stay at the Adelphi Hotel in Liverpool on 31 December. She splashed out on a very good New Year's Eve dinner, which was bold, as the rent for Chapel Street was due and she was already six pounds in the red at the bank. They returned to London on 9 January and booked into the Mandeville Hotel.

While Maudie was sitting on the bed, wondering what to do with the money – 'I wanted to give it back to Sir Hari somehow' – a servant came to announce that Captain Arthur had arrived. 'Send him up,' she said, but when she opened the door in walked Newton, again. He tore open the parcel and grabbed a bundle of notes, and when she tried to stop him he flung her across the room saying, 'If you mention this to any living soul, I'll have you done in.'

For the first time, Maud counted the money; there was £11,000, so she deduced that Newton had taken £10,000. She wanted to leave London as soon as possible, but first took a taxi to Golders Green where her mother lived in a modest but newly built semi in Russell Gardens. She gave her mother three £1,000 notes: £2,000 was to put in Maud's private account, £500 was for her mother to keep and £500 was to pay any of Maudie's own small debts. She returned to the hotel, put another three £1,000 notes into an envelope for her husband with a note asking him to place £2,000 in her business account and to settle up any debts she might have in connection with the house in Chapel Street. The next day, 18 January, Maud and Lyllian packed up, Maud carrying the remaining £5,000 in her hold-all, and left for Paris where they stayed for a week before going on to Menton to stay with friends. They usually went into Monte Carlo in the evenings for dinner and to play the tables at the casino, but Maudie became terrified of the drive along the corniche in the dark, so they moved to the Hotel de Paris in Monte Carlo, where she had time to kill, having arranged, she said, to meet Sir Hari in Nice on 14 February, believing they were to embark from Marseille for India immediately.

They drove to Nice on the fourteenth; it was Valentine's Day, the day when a young woman was traditionally allowed to approach the man she had set her heart on (this was long before it became a retail opportunity between Christmas and Easter). It was carnival time in the fashionable winter resort. In the streets the decorated floats and the marching bands pushed slowly through the crowds. The casino, a confection of tiled domes and minarets, stood apart on a pier over the sea, framed by the glitter of fireworks exploding offshore. Maud crossed towards it from the Westminster Hotel where she was staying. She had lost at the casino at Monte Carlo; this place would be luckier for her, she knew. This day would be the beginning of her new life. She paused at the double doors of the gaming-room and immediately saw who she was looking for. Sir Hari had not seen her – he was with another woman – but one of his party had. He told Sir Hari's solicitor later that Maudie and Lyllian 'attempted to come up to us but having ladies in our party, I suppose they thought better of it'. Maudie turned and left but she did not give up. When Sir Hari and his friends went on to a restaurant for supper, Lyllian sent in a note asking her lover to see her and enclosed a note to Sir Hari from Maudie asking the same. Both were returned without a reply. A little later, there was a telephone call that Sir Hari also refused to accept. There was a telephone message at their hotel, the Savoy, asking the men to call. This was ignored. Next morning Sir Hari received a note from Maudie, which was also ignored.

The women stayed at the Westminster Hotel on 14 and 15 February, perhaps hoping for a change of heart from their men; but it was not to be. On the sixteenth, Charles Arthur saw the Chief of Police at Nice and complained that the women were harassing Sir Hari and asked if he could do anything about it. He could, and before the day was out Maudie was accosted in her hotel lobby by a man who handed her a note. 'What's going on?' she demanded. 'It's a letter to say you and Mrs Bevan are requested to leave here at once,' came the reply. There was one more letter to Sir Hari from Maudie, telling him they had been asked to leave and asking 'why this indignity was put upon us'.

St Valentine, patron saint of lovers, had not looked kindly on Maudie. Considerably upset, the women returned to Paris but Maudie found no pleasure in life. She would not eat. She was wilting, and Lyllian became anxious about her friend's state of mind as well as her health. She suggested returning to London.

Back in Chapel Street, Maudie took to her bed where she remained for three months – alone. The woman famed for her *joie de vivre*, the woman who had charmed the Rajah of Kashmir, dined with diplomats and played bridge with the gentry, was so depressed she could not lift her head from the pillow. Lyllian did her best: she persuaded Maudie to do a little shopping and she went to Bravington's jewellers in Wardour Street and spent £755 on a long string of pearls, but she was irritable with the assistants and picky about the colours of the pearls, so the outing was not a great success.

The doctor came every day and recommended a live-in nurse to make sure Maudie took some nourishment. It didn't help. Finally, she was admitted to a nursing home in Ascot on 15 May suffering from a 'serious condition of nerve exhaustion', as the proprietor of the home, Dr Herbert Challis Crouch, described it; this was in addition to a touch of gonorrhoea. Discharging her after five weeks, the doctor advised her to live quietly for some months and to keep away from her old associates. Despite that, four days later she went to Ostend with her husband and Lyllian. They stayed until the end of July, walking on the beach, shopping, gambling and taking occasional trips to Brussels for long lunches. Maudie and Charlie Robinson assumed a platonic relationship after the tumult and he continued to manage the Grasshopper Ointment business. Maudie took a flat in Knightsbridge and tried to forget her disappointment.

Monty Newton upgraded, too, and moved from Half Moon Street to No. 4 Down Street, three streets away, off Piccadilly. He complained that he was not very comfortable, 'for the furniture is more to look at than to use'. His love life took a turn for the better, and on 7 October 1922 he married Elizabeth Helen Wotherspoon, who was twenty-three and the daughter of a merchant from West Norwood in south London. He gave his age as forty-nine but he lied – he was born on Christmas Day 1871, making him fifty-one. He described himself on the wedding certificate as a bachelor and gave his profession as 'gentleman'. He had promoted his late father from turf accountant to stockbroker. The couple divided their time between London and Paris, and Newton vowed to abandon his life of crime. Things were looking good.

CHAPTER FOUR

Captain Arthur Spills the Beans

Sir Hari sailed from Marseille for Bombay on 28 March 1920 and arrived home in Kashmir in May to much rejoicing for his safe return. Not a word of his adventures in London and Paris had leaked out. No one had been hurt except in the pocket. It looked like the perfect crime, a great caper, as they would have called it. But partners in crime often fall out, and Captain Arthur's extravagant ways would lead to disaster. He remained in France, spending and womanising. His wife sued for restitution of conjugal rights and when that did not happen, Monty Newton provided the evidence for her divorce, bursting yet again into a hotel room, this time in Folkestone, to find Captain Arthur with a woman. Arthur travelled regularly between London, Paris, Vienna, India and the Far East, money running through his fingers like water according to Newton: 'He surrounded himself with lady friends and lived a hectic life. The rate at which he lived would have brought financial disaster to a millionaire.'

Newton was right, and by 1923 Arthur was broke and his tailor was threatening to bankrupt him over unpaid bills. One day in July he turned to the only man he knew who was financially secure, William Cooper Hobbs, and told him he hadn't had breakfast and he didn't know where his lunch was coming from.

'I'm due rents from my estates in Ireland,' he said. 'I just need something to tide me over.'

'My boy,' said Hobbs. 'My position is worse than yours. I have a father, wife and children to support. I'd like to help you, though,' he told the Irishman. 'The best thing I can do is to send you to a firm of money-lenders I know. But take my advice, my boy, and look a little more cheery when you talk to them. Leave that woebegone expression behind. Try to give yourself an air of prosperity and explain in as natural a way as possible that you are temporarily embarrassed.'

Arthur went to the moneylenders, who weren't impressed by his story. 'Look here,' they said, 'Mr Hobbs is a very rich man. If your tale is not good enough for him, it is not good enough for us.' Realising he had been fobbed off by Hobbs and barely able to contain his anger, Arthur returned to the man. Swallowing his pride, he made another appeal for a loan.

Hobbs strung him along, enjoying his power over this Irish toff who was begging for his help. In the end he said his heart was touched by the fact that Arthur was actually hungry.

'It's very difficult,' he said, pulling a handful of pawn tickets from his pocket. 'I had to borrow money myself this morning to pay the rent but it's up to me to make a sacrifice for you,' and he counted out £15. But before handing over the money he said: 'My boy, I shall want a post-dated cheque for £25.'

Boiling with rage, Arthur wrote out a cheque, knowing it was not worth the paper it was written on. He was still furious when he told Monty Newton the story a couple of days later. Thinking of the £4,000 fee Hobbs took for arranging to pay off Robinson, he said: 'After the money we made for him, I never expected such shabby treatment. But I'll get up a little trouble for Hobbs.'

And he did. He immediately went to Charlie Robinson and revealed the truth. The truth was that Sir Hari's payment for Robinson's abandoning the divorce proceedings three-and-a-half years before was not the £25,000 he was told but £150,000, the balance of which had been paid into an account at the Midland Bank in Kingsway in Robinson's name. What is more, there was a second cheque for the same amount that had not been cashed. Those cheques were for the equivalent of fourteen million pounds in today's money.

Imagine Robinson's feelings; a man of the world, taken in by three men, two of whom he knew to be conmen. Grabbing Arthur by the arm, he went to his solicitor, Mr Hyam Davies, and on

23 August 1923 he issued a writ against William Cooper Hobbs and his employers, Appleton and Co., claiming, '£129,000 moneys had and received by the defendants for and on behalf of the plaintiff'. This represented the £150,000 received by Hobbs less the £21,000 paid to Robinson.

Appleton and Co. put in a defence denying all knowledge of the matter. Hobbs also filed a personal defence and said he never gave Robinson £21,000 or any other sum. He then filed a notice in the High Court directed to Mr M. Newton of No. 4 Down Street, Piccadilly, claiming: 'You informed this Defendant that you were Charles Robinson and the husband of Maud Robinson and that you had a matrimonial complaint against your wife and the said Hari Singh and all that this Defendant did in the said manner was done on your instructions.'

Since Newton and Hobbs were old acquaintances and Hobbs had witnessed Newton's second wedding in 1922, this was an audacious move; but he knew Newton was living in Paris and was not likely to come to England now that the truth was out. Hobbs's attempt to shift the blame on to Newton was to have disastrous results.

Robinson and his solicitor next went to the Kingsway branch of the Midland Bank and discovered that Hobbs had opened an account there for a Mr C. Robinson by post, enclosing a sample of his signature, and paid in a cheque for £150,000 on 6 January 1920. The cheque was made out to Appleton and Co. and endorsed on the back 'C. Robinson', which Robinson said was a forgery. On 7 January, Hobbs had returned to the bank with a cheque for £130,000 signed C. Robinson, and asked for it to be cashed over the counter. He explained that Mr Robinson was in Paris and needed the money for a business transaction. This was irregular and the bank refused to pay, saying they did not have that much cash in the safe. Hobbs was asked to return in two hours' time. This time he managed to bully the manager, Edwin Biggs, into letting him have the money.

It was and is astonishing that Mr Biggs cashed a cheque of this size; at this time, when there were so many conmen in London, a prudent bank manager would query the withdrawal of even £10,000. Mr Biggs's explanation was that Hobbs had a substantial account at the branch, had introduced a number of good clients and threatened to take his money elsewhere if he did not oblige. Hobbs cashed another cheque for £17,000 a week later. The bank continued to honour all the cheques drawn on the account and returned the used cheques to Hobbs. It was the custom in those days to return cashed cheques to the account holder, but as the bank did not have an address for Robinson, statements and used cheques went to Hobbs – all most irregular.

Meanwhile, Robinson's solicitor realised that even if they won their case against Hobbs he would be most unlikely to pay the £129,000 and he thought they had a better chance of suing the Midland Bank for negligence. This they did. On 8 December 1923, Robinson took out a writ against the Midland Bank claiming from it £150,000 less the £21,000 he and Hobbs had shared.

The Midland Bank officials were horrified to receive Charlie Robinson's writ; they had no idea what lay behind it. They knew nothing of Maud Robinson and Sir Hari and the denouement in Paris. They consulted their solicitors, Messrs Coward, Chance and Co., and their lawyer, Malcolm Hilbery, and set out on a quest to discover the story behind the vast cheque, unravelling a tale of intrigue and dishonesty that had the newspaper readers of the world agog when the case came to court eleven months later. The solicitors believed the bank was the victim of forgery and went to Scotland Yard for help. Quite by chance, Detective Sergeant Percy J. Smith heard of the problem. He was one of that team set up to clean up the West End, and he recalled that nearly four years earlier an informer had given him a tip-off. The man had told Percy J. that some 'swell mobsmen' had pulled off a great coup and fleeced an Indian potentate of £300,000.

Percy J. knew from the size of the job that some of the best brains had been at work and he guessed his informer was probably acting out of revenge for not being included in the scheme. The informer had not known the name of the potentate, nor did he say who had done the job, but it did not take long for the detective to discover the essential facts of what was to become the Mr A Case. The names of Newton and Hobbs soon came up. Montague Noel Newton he knew as a 'first class confidence trickster and one of the cleverest crooks who has ever operated'.

Although it was his job to catch conmen, Percy J. often expressed admiration for them. He regarded them as the gents of the underworld. 'The specialist *par excellence*, the paramount operator and glamorous intriguer' is how he described this kind of fraudster in his memoirs. He particularly admired Monty Newton. 'He was the "daddy" of all conmen. Tall, distinguished and polished to the last degree, he could be more entertaining than a theatre of actors.' Monty worked hard at his trade. Apart from keeping his clothes in perfect order, his valet, who had worked for an English duke, schooled him in the social graces so that his modest beginnings would not betray him. He rehearsed chat-up lines for hours until he was word perfect. He pored over the financial and social columns of the newspapers to follow the movements of millionaires and their money. He would spend months and money sizing up a victim; once marked out, he would put him on his list of future pigeons or pass him on to someone else in the trade. He had beaten the systems in a round-the-world crooks' tour of casinos and gambling dens: the USA, Mexico, Peru, Australia, China, Indonesia, France, Spain, and Hungary.

William Cooper Hobbs had no criminal record but Percy J. knew he was a receiver of stolen property, the organiser of many big jobs and robberies and an all-round villain, although working as the managing clerk of a perfectly respectable firm of solicitors. Percy also knew Charlie Robinson as a conman who specialised in horse-race betting swindles. He knew Maudie associated with criminals but the police had nothing on her.

Percy J. found that Newton and Hobbs had plotted to blackmail the Rajah over his association with Maudie by catching them together in her house in Chapel Street, but that the trap was finally sprung in Paris and the cheques were handed over there. What is more, he discovered that Sir Hari's trusted friend and ADC, Captain Arthur, was the instigator of the plot. As the British police have no jurisdiction over crimes committed abroad, he abandoned the case and filed his notes.

The story of Maud, the Rajah and the Mayfair Mob might have remained a secret forever had not Captain Arthur and then

Monty Newton fallen out with Hobbs, and had not Robinson discovered his partners in crime had tricked him.

Percy J. Smith realised that if the £150,000 cheque paid into the Midland Bank by Hobbs could be proved to be part of the money taken from Sir Hari, the fact that it was cashed in England gave him the chance of bringing criminal proceedings. He handed all his information to the Midland Bank's solicitors and, although Robinson's case was a civil action, Scotland Yard shadowed the bank's enquiries and Percy J. was in court holding a watching brief on 19 November 1924 when the case of Charles Ernest Robinson v Midland Bank opened before Lord Justice Darling in the King's Bench Division of the Royal Courts of Justice in the Strand.

Lord Darling was seventy-four and had retired a year before but returned to help clear up an arrears of cases. For twenty-six years he had been trying *causes célèbres* and now, at the very end of his career, he was to preside for eight days over the most amazing of them all. All over the world newspapers were saturated with accounts of a story that fascinated and repelled, titillated and disgusted, amused and shocked their readers. Even the Judge was appalled, remarking scathingly in his summing-up: 'The facts are so notorious all over London by this time that I need not recapitulate them. I do not know the religion of this man but this is Mrs Robinson's way of keeping the Christian festival of Christmas.'

Lord Darling could kill with a look but in reality he had a very happy nature. He wrote poetry and essays, as well as leaders for the *Pall Mall Gazette*, and he liked to joke from the bench. Most called him witty, others a buffoon; he was once rebuked in Parliament for the chaos that overtook his court following some of his remarks in a libel case. He was described variously as dapper, dainty and debonair (strange, then, that he went under the nickname of Doggo).

Appearing before him for the Midland Bank were four men who were destined for great careers. Sir John Simon, KC, had already been Home Secretary in 1915 and served in government from 1931 until 1945 as Foreign Secretary, Home Secretary, Chancellor of the Exchequer and Lord Chancellor. He led the bank's team and proved a ruthless cross-examiner. He threw himself into the case, even travelling to Paris to seek a solution to a question that puzzled him: why Maudie and Lyllian checked into a suite at the Hotel Brighton reserved by Sir Hari and then moved a couple of days later to the Hotel St James and Albany. He confided to his biographer, C. E. Bechhofer Roberts, who was a private secretary to Lord Birkenhead, by now the Secretary of State for India and deeply involved in the background of the case, that he thought the bank did not have a chance of winning. His fellow KC was Rayner Goddard, who was to become Lord Chief Justice in 1946. Malcolm Hilbery, the bank's counsel, became a High Court Judge, as did Roland Oliver.

Robinson's team was Lord Halsbury, the son of the 1st Earl of Halsbury, and John Paul Valetta, a barrister with great charm, experienced in criminal and civil law. But neither was quite up to the power of the bank's team.

In the pre-television age the law courts were the soap operas of the day, giving glimpses into other, richer, more glamorous and permissive worlds. People would queue for hours to get into the gallery for a juicy case; sometimes tickets were issued to avoid unseemly jostling for seats. Word had got out about Robinson's action, and people started arriving at daybreak. There were queues, four deep, stretching for 250 yards on each side of the main entrance to the Law Courts. Fur-coated women and smartly dressed men had breakfast on the pavement. Those who had thought ahead had folding stools that they paid messenger boys to guard while they went to a café to eat. The surging crowd pushed the attendants at the double doors back several times until they finally retreated inside and locked the doors. Even the Judge found it irresistible and his private gallery in court was filled with his guests. The courtroom was so packed that witnesses had difficulty getting through the crowd to the witness box.

Every day, *The Times* and *The Daily Telegraph* devoted a full page to the proceedings. Newspaper magnates like Rothermere, Beaverbrook and Sir Edward Hulton must have been astonished to hear what had begun under their noses at the Victory Ball. Throughout the case Sir Hari was referred to as Mr A and described as an eastern potentate. The Judge, explaining why he was allowing anonymity, said: 'He is a person of high rank. It is for reasons of State, not connected with rank at all. It is very important that scandal should not be caused where this potentate lives and it is for that reason – absolutely for that reason only – that I am allowing the name to be omitted.' It was reported that he had travelled to Europe with an entourage in which there was an English ADC and the Judge allowed his identity to be concealed too, and he was to be referred to as the ADC. None of this pleased the hundreds of other Indian princes who felt they might be under suspicion.

CHAPTER FIVE

The Mr A Case Begins

Lord Halsbury opened the proceedings for Robinson and explained his case: he claimed £125,000 from the Midland Bank, which was the balance of a sum of £150,000 being money received for his use; he alleged negligence by the bank. The bank denied they received the money for the plaintiff's use; they also denied negligence and astonished the court by saying Robinson had been concerned with others in a conspiracy to obtain money by blackmail and that under the circumstances he was not entitled to recover the money. Lord Halsbury replied that normally it would be enough for him to show that the bank had actually received the money on Robinson's behalf, either paid directly into the bank or paid in by his agent. But the bank had alleged the most hideous case of a blackmailing conspiracy that the jury had probably ever heard. The question was whether Mr Robinson had anything to do with the conspiracy, which the bank must prove, and the jury would have to consider Mr Robinson and whether he was likely to be a party to such a conspiracy.

Robinson, a well-dressed, portly figure with a pompous turn of phrase, was Lord Halsbury's first witness and spent the whole of that day and half of the next in the box. He said he managed his wife's Grasshopper Ointment business without a regular salary, just taking expenses of £5 or £6 a week. He described his strained relationship with his wife and how they had lived more or less separately since 1914. He had a flat in Panton Street in 1919 when Maudie took a house in Chapel Street and he joined her there for a short time. He said he left in September after a disagreement about her extravagant way of life. Now we come to the events leading up to the Mr A Case.

Lord Halsbury: Now I want to know about Newton. When did you first meet him?

Robinson: I first met Newton when he was in uniform in 1917; that was my first knowledge of Newton.

Lord Halsbury: Did you see much of him?

Robinson: No.

Lord Halsbury: Do you remember in 1919 dining with your wife at the Berkeley Hotel?

Robinson: I remember it quite well.

Lord Halsbury: Was Newton there?

Robinson: He was.

Lord Halsbury: Did you introduce Newton to your wife?

Robinson: I did.

Lord Halsbury: At that time did you know anything against Newton?

Robinson: Nothing whatever.

Then Robinson told how Newton telephoned him on 27 December 1919 and asked to see him. They met at the Royal Automobile Club where Robinson was then living. 'He stated that my wife was not conducting herself in the manner in which she ought to, or words to that effect, and related the incident of the party whom we have spoken of as Mr A.' Sir John Simon intervened: 'Don't be too quick. "My wife was not conducting herself as she ought to?"'

Robinson: And inferred an affair was taking place with the party in question mentioned.

Lord Halsbury: Pausing there for a moment – don't say it – did he, in fact, tell you the name of Mr A?

Robinson: He did not.

Lord Halsbury: When did you first learn the name of Mr A?

Robinson: I first heard of it from Mr Hobbs.

Lord Halsbury: Now may I go a little farther? Did he give any description of Mr A?

Robinson: He described him as a black fellow.

Lord Halsbury: Upon that, what did you reply?

Robinson: Well, I was naturally very upset and asked him if he had any proof of it and so on and he said it was common property in London prior to going to Paris.

Robinson told Lord Halsbury that he telephoned the Chapel Street house and was told that Maud had returned from Paris that morning. 'It upset me very greatly, naturally, at the time and I said to Newton that I should go for a divorce procedure.'

Lord Halsbury: What did Newton say?

Robinson: He suggested that I should go to Hobbs with him – that was, to Appleton and Co.

Lord Halsbury: Had you any transaction with him before?

Robinson said he was introduced to Hobbs, whom he understood was a solicitor, at the Café Royal in 1901 or 1902 after a bad day at the races and Hobbs had lent him £40, which he was finally sued to repay, so he did not like the idea of consulting him now.

Lord Halsbury: What did Newton say with regard to going and seeing Hobbs?

Robinson: He stated that in view of his having some other business with Hobbs at the time and in view of his having to give evidence that would be required, it would suit his purpose better for me to go to Hobbs.

Next day they went to see Hobbs who asked for details of what Newton knew and asked Robinson to sign a paper saying Hobbs was to act for him. Then he told how Maud came to see him two or three days later and told him she had done nothing wrong. After thinking about it he went back to Hobbs on New Year's Day and said he doubted very much whether she was guilty.

Hobbs told him: 'There is no question, Robinson, about her guilt. As a matter of fact, I have already had an intimation from Mr A's solicitor to that effect, confessing guilt in her direction.' Robinson told Lord Halsbury that in view of this he told Hobbs to proceed with the divorce proceedings but the next time the two met, on 10 January, Hobbs told him he had an offer from the solicitors of Mr A stating that they did not want exposure and so on and that he thought it would be better if he accepted, mentioning at the same time who the party was. 'That was much to my astonishment, you see, when he mentioned that.'

Lord Halsbury: Was any sum mentioned?

Robinson: £25,000.

Lord Halsbury: What did you say to that?

Robinson: Well, I was naturally very much surprised at it.

Robinson said he told Hobbs he disapproved of any settlement and would prefer to go on with the case. He said Maud called on him a couple of days later at the Royal Automobile Club and he told her about the offer. 'She stated that I ought not to take it and I had no right to it.' But when he next saw Hobbs he finally agreed to it. He told Lord Halsbury: 'I practically agreed to hush the matter up, at the same time saying that I had no desire to participate in the matter and he stated at the same time that there was no reason to keep the money, that if I wanted to I could settle it on my wife.'

When he saw Hobbs two days later, on Friday, 16 January, he signed an undertaking not to proceed with the divorce. Next day he and Maudie went to Hobbs's other office in Bedford Street, off the Strand, where he conducted his private business. Hobbs produced a large parcel.

Robinson: He put it on the table and said there was £25,000 which he had received from the solicitors in settlement of the divorce proceedings. I stated to him that I had no desire to participate in the money, that it did not interest me and instructed him to give it to Mrs Robinson.

Lord Halsbury: Then what happened?

Robinson: With that – I was very agitated – I left the office.

Lord Darling: Did you see him give it to her?

Robinson: No. It was put on the table.

Lord Halsbury: Was anything said about who was to pay the costs of the solicitor, Mr Hobbs?

Robinson: Not in my hearing.

Lord Halsbury: Now, did you get, I think that same day, a letter from your wife?

Robinson: I did.

Lord Halsbury: Was there an enclosure in that letter?

Robinson: There was.

Lord Halsbury: What was that enclosure?

Robinson: £3,000.

Lord Halsbury: Were there any instructions from your wife as to what was to be done with the £3,000?

Robinson: There were.

Lord Halsbury: What were they?

Robinson: Asking me to place £2,000 to the credit of her business. The other £1,000 was to pay certain debts for her, which she owed, and at the same time stating that she was going abroad. That was the purport of the letter, the letter that I did not keep.

Lord Halsbury: Can you remember exactly how much of her debts you paid?

Robinson: Out of that £1,000, roughly speaking, I should think £350.

Lord Halsbury: And the remaining £650 did you spend on your own living?

Robinson: I should think in all probability I did.

Lord Halsbury: Let me just clear that up. As far as you are concerned, apart from that £650, which you have spent on your own living, is there a penny piece of this money, which you have touched?

Robinson: Not one penny piece.

He said the next time he saw his wife was in early March when her doctor telephoned him to say she was very ill and she was admitted to a nursing home for two or three months with a nervous breakdown.

Lord Halsbury: Up to the month of July 1923, had you any knowledge that anything more than £25,000 had been paid?

Robinson: Not the slightest knowledge.

Lord Halsbury: Did you see the person that we have agreed to call the ADC?

Robinson: I did.

Lord Halsbury: Had you ever seen him before?

Robinson: Never.

He then recounted how he consulted his usual solicitor, Mr Hyam Davies, went to the bank and came to be taking the current proceedings. There was a short adjournment before Sir John Simon began his cross-examination; a most rigorous, penetrating, elegantly worded cross-examination but there was no doubt about what he was suggesting about Mrs Robinson; that she was a woman of very easy virtue. He had been through her bank passbooks and noticed cheques to Paquin, Gray, Redfern, Revillon, all expensive dressmakers. He could see she dealt extensively with jewellers and had some real pearls, and when she travelled she stayed at the very best hotels.

Sir John: I think you and she and a man named Young were all at Ostend in 1914.

Robinson: Yes.

Sir John: She and Mr Young stayed at the Hotel de Phare, didn't they?

Robinson: I believe so.

Sir John: And you, her husband, stayed at the Hotel Splendide?

Robinson: Not at the same time.

Sir John: She is evidently an expensive lady. You didn't provide her with the money to do all that, did you?

Robinson: She has been able to provide for herself.

Sir John: As a matter of fact, from time to time, you got money from her, didn't you?

Robinson: Never.

Sir John: Do you mean to say you have never received money from your wife?

Robinson: Never one penny.

Slowly, the state of Robinson's finances emerged. A month before his marriage a judgment was given against him for £626 and 6 shillings, which he had borrowed from an antiques dealer, and a few months later he went bankrupt for around £4,000. He never repaid the money and was bankrupted again in June 1919. Florid-faced Robinson grew pinker as he blustered his way through the cross-examination. He finally admitted he was discharged from bankruptcy in January 1920, just after Mr A's money was paid. He first denied then admitted that in his public examination of bankruptcy he had said his income averaged about £150 a year from his winnings as a professional backer of horses.

His own lawyer, Lord Halsbury, interrupted to quote another paragraph from the bankruptcy examination: 'The debtor says that his occupation is that of a betting man but for the past three or four years he has been supported by his wife from her separate estate.'

Sir John must have been delighted by this support for his line of questioning and said: 'And you have, have you not, been supported by your wife for a good many years?'

Robinson denied this.

Sir John: Why did you swear just now that you had never had one penny from her, when you told the Official Receiver in bankruptcy that your wife supported you?

Robinson: When I related that to the Official Receiver I intended it to mean that it was the question of my managing the business. I just took it as a living wage out of the business. That is all.

Sir John remarked sarcastically that it was just after the second bankruptcy that 'your pretty wife fell in with Mr A'. And within less than two months of the first bankruptcy his wife took 'this expensive and fashionable house'. Robinson admitted that he lived there with her for 'a short period'. He added that he stayed for no longer than six weeks and left in September but he was vague about the exact dates. Sir John wanted to know about the rent; the first ten weeks' or so, £245, was paid in advance.

Sir John: Was the second instalment due from your wife on 20 January?

Robinson: From memory, I couldn't say.

Sir John: I suggest to you, sir, that she had got through her money and you had not got any and that at the end of the year, 31 December, she even had an adverse balance at her bank. She had no money. Wasn't it a fortunate thing that just then she fell in with Mr A and there was a large sum of money?

Robinson: It was a most unfortunate thing.

Sir John: Suppose it is proved in this case that your wife used five £50 notes, the proceeds of Mr A's money, in order to pay the second instalment after it was due, though she could not pay it on the due date, don't you think it was a fortunate thing she fell in with Mr A?

Robinson: I don't think anything about it. It doesn't concern me at all in that respect.

Sir John's questions became even more personal and showed the extent and the determination of the bank's enquiries. He forced Robinson to admit he had been seeing quite a lot of his wife since the action started, at her flat at No 45 Knightsbridge.

Sir John: Do you know you have been watched?

Robinson: I had an idea that I was, yes.

Sir John revealed what the watchers had seen every day since 1 November and Robinson agreed with him. The routine was this: Robinson went early every evening to Maud's flat where he was joined by one or another of two men, a Mr Mackersey, who had a flat in the same building as Robinson, in Denman Street, just by Piccadilly Circus, and a Charles Young. The Robinsons and whichever man was visiting that evening would leave the flat together about ten o'clock and walk to the Ritz Hotel when Robinson would go on alone and leave Mrs Robinson to return to her flat with the man, who would stay there till the early hours.

Sir John: It is your view of what an honest husband does, that he leaves his wife, his unprotected wife, in a flat she occupies and allows men to return to her after he, the husband, has gone home?

Robinson: If he has every faith in their good intentions, yes, it is my view.

Even the Judge appeared to join in Sir John's character assassination of the Robinsons. He put in here: 'Do you mean to say that you have every faith in your wife being left alone with men late at night now you know what happened in Paris?'

Robinson: To escort her home, my Lord, I say yes. With these men in particular, I am in business relations with one and the other man is her manager and it would naturally never dawn on me, the question of anything wrong.

Lord Darling: Although you know what she is?

Robinson: I don't think she is as bad as she is painted.

Lord Darling: Did you believe truly that she was, and is, leading a virtuous life?

Robinson: For the past twelve months, yes.

Lord Darling: Why didn't you live with her?

Robinson: For the simple reason that we have not had an opportunity to take a flat together. There is no reason I should not live with her because she is leading an honest life.

Lord Darling: Do you mean to say you could not get one flat between you?

Robinson: Yes, my Lord, that is so.

Lord Darling: In all London?

Robinson: I have been so unsettled regarding this case and so on that I have wanted more or less to be alone. As a matter of fact, that is so.

He said that the meetings at the Knightsbridge flat were a sort of family gathering where they could discuss matters and his wife could see the only friends she had. Questioned further by Sir John, he admitted that Maudie and Mr Young had stayed in the same hotel in Ostend three times that summer and during one of these visits he himself stayed at a different hotel.

Going back to when Maud was renting the house in Chapel Street, Robinson said he moved out after a quarrel about her way of life. Lord Darling interrupted again: 'Did you believe she had become a dissolute woman?' Robinson replied: 'Not exactly but I disapproved of her mode of life, my Lord.'

Lord Darling went on interrupting and asked about Maud and Lyllian's visit to Paris.

Lord Darling: Your own case is that these conspirators, of whom you were not one, got these two women over to Paris and that one of them slept with the master while the other one slept with the secretary, both of these people being of a different race, a coloured race. That is your case.

Robinson: That is stated.

Lord Darling: The common sense is that they are disreputable women, both of them isn't it?

Robinson: No. I should not say that. I think a woman can make a misdemeanour and I think she can be forgiven for a misdemeanour.

He insisted that he knew nothing about the trap planned for Paris and agreed that £25,000 was an enormous sum of damages in a divorce case but repeated that he wanted none of it and had told Hobbs to give the money to Maud and told Maud he never wanted to see her again.

To back up his story that he and Maud knew nothing about the conspiracy Robinson had to show that there was no share-out of the money between the six: the Robinsons, Mrs Bevan, Newton, Hobbs and the ADC. He said Hobbs took £4,000 for his fee and gave him £21,000 which he immediately gave to Maud. His ploy failed because he did not know that the bank had kept a record of the numbers of every note paid out to Hobbs.

There was a gasp of excitement in court when Sir John went on to tell how the bank had traced all the notes given for the £150,000 cheque by their numbers.

Sir John: As regards Hobbs, £40,000 can be traced to him. £40,000 can be traced to the ADC, £40,000 can be traced to Newton; another £1,000 cashed in Paris by Hobbs can be traced and another £1,000 shown to be cashed at Cox's bank in Paris. That makes out of the first £130,000 no less than £122,000. And when I come to 17 January what you will find is that, of the notes that were left, you get this: Hobbs gets £4,000, the ADC gets £5,000, the plaintiff, Mr Robinson, gets £4,000, Mrs Robinson gets £4,000 and Newton gets £4,000. Mrs Bevan was not there at the share-out but her amount was handed to the plaintiff, £4,000 and she was so fortunate as to get £3,000 of it. Now, Mr Robinson, I will ask you this. I quite appreciate your contention that you are not in any conspiracy but there is no doubt that there was a conspiracy?

Robinson: Everything points to that.

Sir John: Now that we know what rascals there were in this, everything points to the fact that they had arranged to trap Mr A, does it not?

Robinson: It is suggestive of that.

Sir John: Let us look at it from the ADC's point of view. Can you suggest any honest service that the ADC could have rendered to entitle him to any part of Mr A's money?

Robinson: I can't suggest anything about it.

Sir John: And he has got £45,000 out of his own employer?

Robinson: That seems quite plain.

Lord Darling: Well, he must have been mustn't he, the worst of the whole lot because he was a gentleman, or he was supposed to be a gentleman, attached to this potentate as an *aide de camp* to protect him. And, instead of that, he sold him to a lot of sharpers and got £45,000 for doing it?

Robinson: Yes, apparently.

Sir John went on: And is one of the persons that he must have arranged this with your wife, Mrs Robinson?

Robinson: No.

Lord Darling: You say you were innocent of this. Do you say your wife was innocent, too?

Robinson: Yes, innocent of any conspiracy, hence my taking this action to prove her innocence.

Mr A's solicitor, Mark Waters, was in court and was asked to produce the two £150,000 cheques endorsed 'C. Robinson', which Robinson said were forged signatures.

The Judge sat there with the two pieces of paper in his hand and studied them intently. He read out the figures dramatically: 'Pounds: one hundred and fifty thousand only' to great laughter. 'Then, two dashes to show that there are no shillings and no pence.' More laughter. That concluded the first day of the hearing.

* * *

Charlie Robinson had been in the witness box all day Wednesday and he was back again the next day when Sir John Simon resumed his cross-examination, probing relentlessly, asking the same question over and over. The Judge regularly intervened. Robinson blustered pompously and usually ended up contradicting himself. He was not as stupid as he made himself sound, though. He would not commit himself to an answer because he knew Sir John would never ask a question to which *he* did not know the answer; Robinson's problem was that he was not sure what Sir John knew. Sir John started the morning's questioning by asking Robinson to elaborate on his account of what happened when Newton rang him up on 27 December, the day after Mrs Robinson and Mr A were caught in bed in Paris. 'Didn't you tell her, when you met her that the accusation was that she was misconducting herself with a black man or a nigger?' Robinson admitted that he had.

He said he did not know Maud had been found in Paris with Mr A until the case started; he had never asked her about it. He had never asked Newton to explain the where and when of his wife 'misconducting' herself in Paris. Sir John opined sharply that Robinson had no reason to ask for more details because he knew exactly what had gone on.

CHAPTER SIX

Sir John's Bombshell

It is hard to believe but Britain's theatres were subject to censorship until 1968. On the second day of the trial a comedian called Albert de Courville submitted a sketch to Lord Cromer, the censor. It was called 'Mr A, or a Matter of State.' Mr A did not appear on the stage at all, and all the characters were indicated by their initials only. Nevertheless, Lord Cromer's verdict was that 'no mention of this disgusting case is to be made in any sketch or play.'

'Why should my sketch be treated like this?' demanded Mr de Courville. 'Every music hall comedian in the country is joking about the case. And references to £150,000, Mrs Robinson and all sorts of things creep into nearly all the reviews.' Lord Cromer replied that he couldn't follow every comedian about and he couldn't go to every revue every night but he could stop this sketch. The jokes continued: a husband in Tottenham, summonsed for arrears of maintenance, said: 'I can't pay. I'm not Mr A.'

Maud Robinson was photographed arriving at the Court with Mr Mackersey. She sat next to Lyllian Bevan while her husband gave his evidence. She was wearing a mink coat and a handsome rope of pearls – perhaps the pearls she bought at Bravington's – when she took her place in the witness box to tell Lord Halsbury the story we have already heard. He took her gently through it. She described how she and Charlie drifted apart after her several operations, including a hysterectomy; her health was delicate and her husband's bad temper made him difficult to live with. She told how she invited Lyllian Bevan to share the Chapel Street house because she was lonely and also to protect her from Newton, whom she didn't want to see alone. Her husband had introduced her to Newton when they were lunching at the Berkeley Hotel at the beginning of 1919. She met him again in August when he came to dinner and finally he seduced her. He wanted her to sell her business and go away with him; when she refused he became violent and insulting and she was frightened of him because she thought he would tell her husband of their affair. She denied that before and after the Paris incident she had been leading 'an immoral life promiscuously with men' and that her husband was living on her immoral earnings.

Talking about the visits of Mr Mackersey and Mr Young to her flat she agreed with her husband's evidence that she had walked with him to the Ritz Hotel and sometimes she had left her flat at half past ten or eleven at night with Mr Mackersey or Mr Young and gone to sit in the lounge of the Hyde Park Hotel, after which the man would walk her home and take her up to her flat – she was nervous, there were a lot of stairs up to her flat and it was very dark. It was not true that they stayed any length of time in her flat. Mournfully, she told Lord Halsbury that had she gone to India with Mr A: 'I suppose I should have had everything in the world that a woman could desire.'

Lord Halsbury: There was no motive, then, as far as you were concerned, for blackmailing him by this plot?

Maudie: Oh, it is too ludicrous. It is ridiculous.

Lord Halsbury: And the fact that it did take place evidently put an end to all your schemes of going out to India?

Maudie: It finished everything.

Sir John Simon listened intently to Lord Halsbury's questioning of Maud. His own cross-examination was rigorous. He had rubbished her husband's story, now he was rubbishing hers. He wanted to know how she could afford the huge sum of twelve guineas a week rent when she was drawing only £6 a week from Grasshopper Ointments. She said this was because she had borrowed £2,000 from an uncle and was paying eight per cent interest to him. He asked about payments to her husband, implying that she was a prostitute and he was living off her immoral earnings but she insisted the payments were related to her Grasshopper business. He made her admit that she didn't have the £250 to pay the second instalment of the rent when it was due on 9 January, yet she was spending large sums of money a couple of weeks later.

She was asked how Newton got into the locked suite at the St James and Albany Hotel and replied: 'I don't know how he got in. I have been wondering for the last five years.' Sir John suggested – how did he know? – that when Newton entered the room she shouted: 'My husband. My brute of a husband,' which would show she was part of the conspiracy. She denied it and said she told Mr A: 'I must get back tonight before that brute reaches my husband.' She said that until then she had no idea that Newton knew about her relationship with Sir Hari and she had no idea Newton was in Paris.

She told Lord Halsbury that when she heard about the hush-money pay-out she twice telephoned the Carlton Hotel in Pall Mall where Mr A was then staying, he was out so she left messages with his secretary.

Asking about the payout, Sir John said: 'Do you know that, instead of your having as you said, £11,000, the notes that can be traced to you are £4,000?'

She replied: 'I think you are wrong. I think we can trace more.'

She John asked if she knew, or if she had ever heard of, a man called Hope Johnstone and Maudie said she had heard of him but she didn't know him

Sir John: He has a magnificent name, George Granville Hope-Johnstone. He is an unmitigated blackguard, isn't he?

Maudie: I don't know. I heard he was a great dope fiend. That is all I heard.

Sir John: You know enough about him to know that he is an utter blackguard, don't you?

Maudie: I don't know anything about him.

Lord Darling: I don't know exactly what a dope fiend is but I should suppose that, if he is a simple fiend, he is a blackguard.

Sir John: Did this Mr Hope-Johnstone learn that there was this scheme in foot?

Maudie: I haven't the slightest idea. I don't know the man.

Asking about the share-out of the £25,000 at Hobbs's office, Sir John suggested that as Mrs Bevan was not there, Robinson had taken charge of her £4,000 but Maudie said this was rubbish, there was no share-out. Sir John said that when the notes were traced, only £3,000 of the £4,000 could be traced to Mrs Bevan but Maudie insisted that the only person who gave any money to Mrs Bevan was herself. This was after their return from Nice when she gave her £2,500 paid with three £1,000 notes, with Mrs Bevan giving her a cheque for £500 as 'change'.

Maudie: Here was a woman without a penny in the world and I thought it was my duty to give her something because I had been the cause of her losing a brilliant future.

Sir John: Let us understand her brilliant future. You told me that the plan was, or the hope was, that Mrs Bevan would go to the east and live as a kept mistress. Is that the brilliant future you are talking about?

Maudie: Well, some of those people can give a little more happiness than white ones.

Sir John squirmed with embarrassment and the court hummed with anticipation and seethed with disappointment when he said that he needed to ask Mrs Robinson an 'intimate' question and to spare her feelings would write it down, then the question and her written answer would be passed to the jury. Lord Halsbury read it, the Judge read it and Lord Halsbury objected: 'We have two women on the jury.'

Lord Darling was indignant: 'I can't help there being women on the jury. The law was altered at their own wish, and there they are.'

In the end, four written questions were put and the replies seen by the lawyers before being given to the jury. The questions were never revealed in public but they referred to nothing more shocking than Sir Hari's request for Maudie to shave off her pubic hair – a full Brazilian was the custom of his country.

Maudie told Sir John how once when Newton was dining at her house the ADC arrived unexpectedly with a message from Mr A and she 'unfortunately' introduced them. She denied she and her husband, Lyllian, Newton, the ADC and Hobbs were in a plot to catch Mr A in bed with her, with Newton pretending to be her husband. And she also denied that there were a number of meetings between herself, Newton, Mrs Bevan, Hobbs and the ADC at the Chapel Street house.

* * *

Next morning, day three, Lord Halsbury recalled Maudie to the witness box for more questions; he knew that her former parlour-maid, Nelly Cadney, was in court and he foresaw danger. Maudie now admitted Hobbs had been to the Chapel Street house once. It was the first time she had seen him and he had come to see Mrs Bevan and, after being introduced, she left them alone. Sir John was on this bit of information like a flash:

Sir John: This is the first time you have ever told the Judge and jury that, before ever you went to Paris with Mr A, Hobbs saw you at Chapel Street.

Maudie: I was never asked.

Sir John: He asked if Mrs Bevan would confirm that if she went into the witness box.

Maudie: Absolutely, of course she can.

Sir John: So it turns out that all the six people whom I allege to be in this plot were all at Chapel Street before you and Mr A went to Paris?

Maudie: Apparently so.

Sir John: Had you really overlooked the importance of that until you were recalled just now?

Maudie: I do not see any importance attaching to it at all.

Sir John: Until you knew that Nelly Cadney, the parlour maid, was in court?

Maudie: She has been here every day.

Sir John: Had it struck you how important that was?

Maudie: No.

Lyllian Bevan was never called as a witness. Sir John Simon had been to Paris and now suggested the reason for the hotel change during the Christmas trip was that the St James and Albany Hotel had two entrances, one on Rue de Rivoli, the other on Rue St Honore, so if a man who had no business to be in the hotel were seen entering by one door early in the morning, the concierge could assume that he was a guest who had gone out of the other earlier.

After cross-examining Robinson's other witnesses, Sir John opened his case for the bank. He had already had a distinguished career as a lawyer and in government but this was surely his finest hour. No one in court doubted that the conspiracy the bank alleged had happened but nobody in the crowded room had the slightest idea how he was going to prove it. Robinson's team was equally in the dark.

Sir John had a secret weapon, but so clever was he that not the slightest hint of its existence was revealed. He began by asking the jury if they could conceive a more appropriate victim for blackmail than Mr A. He was a man who was so much concerned that there should be no disclosure that he gave two signed but otherwise blank cheques capable of being drawn for any amount and handed them to the ADC before he had consulted a legal adviser.

'What man or woman outside a lunatic asylum would not say that the man had been exposed to the menace of exposure in the extreme degree?'

It was not now disputed by Mr and Mrs Robinson that there must have been a plot and the submission of the Bank was that it was a conspiracy of six people – Mr and Mrs Robinson, Mrs Bevan, the ADC, Newton and Hobbs. Every one of the six had received substantial amounts from the proceeds of the conspiracy; the banknotes had been traced to them.

Sir John felt he had to give credit where it was due and went on: 'There is one person in Mr A's suite, to which not a single banknote has ever been traced. Out of all this £150,000 there is one person in Mr A's suite who cannot be shown to have received six pence. Who is it? It is not the ADC. It is a terrible infliction on every British subject who has looked into this case to think the story is that Mr A had in his service a man who was of a white skin who was a traitor and a Judas. He also had in his service a man with a black skin – the native secretary. The native secretary had been faithful, the Britisher had cheated and, whatever else is true about this case, it is a humiliating reflection for every one of us.'

He said every one of the banknotes could be traced but not a single £5 note could be traced to the native secretary – who was, you will remember, Mahboob, the highborn nabob from Hyderabad, Mr A's military secretary and Lyllian Bevan's lover. Clearly, there had been no careless pillow talk from Mrs Bevan.

Sir John then coined a phrase with which we have become familiar. He said that the Robinsons were 'economical in regard to the truth' until they realised that unless they admitted a bit more they might be landed with a piece of evidence that would blow them sky high. He regarded it as a striking thing – although it was not admitted until Mrs Robinson was recalled – that every one of the six people was at Chapel Street before she left for Paris. Mr Robinson, the jury was asked to believe, had left the house for some substantial time but Sir John would show that this was not true and that he left the house only after his wife had made the acquaintance of Mr A, which was a necessary step if the conspiracy was going to be carried through. Mr Robinson was there, Mrs Bevan was there, Newton was there, the ADC was there and, last of all, Hobbs, as Mrs Robinson admitted, was there. Why should Hobbs be there? He was not the solicitor who ordinarily acted for Mr and Mrs Robinson; Mr Davis was their solicitor. Mr Robinson knew Hobbs and Newton knew Hobbs, a most suitable instrument for such a plan. Mrs Robinson, at the eleventh hour, revealed the fact that Hobbs was there. The jury would see why: suppose the parlour maid had come into the witness box and said things that Mrs Robinson had not admitted? Mrs Robinson admitted it at the eleventh hour, with a fantastic explanation, that he came to attend to business for Mrs Bevan. Sir John commented on the fact that Mrs Bevan, who had sat faithfully by Mrs Robinson in court, had never been called as a witness. He asked the court to reject utterly the belated explanation that Hobbs was there on business for Mrs Bevan, who dared not go into the witness box.

He asked how Newton knew which room of the Paris hotel suite Mrs Robinson and Sir Hari were in, unless Mrs Robinson was in the plot, or Mrs Bevan, or both. The native secretary discharged his duty to his master and bolted the door of the suite. Sir John suggested that Mrs Robinson unfastened the door because she was a party to laying the trap. If that were the case, away went the whole of the elaborate construction put before the jury, that the lady was the poor victim of circumstances whose brilliant future had been destroyed by the unfortunate fact that she had been found out in adultery with Mr A.

The ADC admittedly went back to London with the lady; they were on the same train. Mrs Robinson did not deny that Newton returned to London at the same time and by the same route. If that were true, what was the good of pretending that Mrs Robinson was the victim of circumstances and that there were just three conspirators? He did not see why Mrs Robinson went back to London if she and Mr A had any affection for each other, as alleged, and if it had been decided that she should live as Mr A's mistress in Asia.

'If it were true that she was deeply and passionately attached to the man and he was honestly devoted to her and they had planned for the future in some other world, what was the use of her going back to London? If, however, she was a party to the plot to rob him, then it was necessary to get back to London, where the spoils were to be divided.'

He said that while that was to be done among the six people, there were three of them who were cheating the other three. He divided the six into 'the big three' and 'the little three' and the 'big three' adopted an ingenious trick whereby they shared £120,000. Out of the first £130,000 cheque drawn, £120,000 was taken to Paris at once by Hobbs, put into a bank there and transferred into various French securities, £40,000 going to Hobbs, £40,000 to Newton and £40,000 to the ADC. 'No doubt the big three were swindling the little three. They were taking off the cream before they distributed the skimmed milk.'

The tense onlookers were still mystified as Sir John approached his final, dramatic climax. He mused that the jury might wonder how he came to be in a position to put the story he had to Mrs Robinson and he explained that last summer the solicitors instructing him had learned that Newton was prepared to make a statement. They obtained this from him in France and that statement had primed him to put many of his questions. It had been planned to read his statement at the trial – Newton not wanting to risk arrest in London – but Robinson's lawyers objected to this.

Sir John paused, savouring the drama of the moment, before dropping his bombshell, which must have struck terror into the hearts of the Robinsons and Hobbs. He went on: 'We are a bank and you must remember and, if you believe me, the Midland Bank and their solicitors who appear for them are deeply concerned in this matter, that they may do what is their duty here to the Court and the Judge and that is all. We conceived it to be our duty, and I think we were quite right, to see if there was any means of getting Newton here. It was not a question of getting his evidence; we had it. The question was, "could we get him here?"'

The doors of the Court room opened and a man was ushered to the solicitors' table as Sir John moved to his peroration: 'Newton, after some reflection, decided he was prepared to run the risk – and it is a very great risk – of coming to this country, if promised a certain payment and the bank had promised him £3,000.'

He raised his arm and pointed to the man at the solicitors' table. 'There,' he said, 'is Mr Newton and I call him into the witness box.'

So skilfully had Sir John managed his opening speech and so efficiently had the bank's solicitors conducted their case that nobody had any idea that Newton had come from France and been at his flat in Mayfair throughout the trial.

CHAPTER SEVEN

What the Parlour-maid Saw

Newton became the star of the show. He was tall, with thick, black hair, a suave manner and a line in snappy repartee. He wore a different, immaculate suit every day; his valet travelled everywhere with him. His black moustache was neatly clipped and his polished fingernails, filed to an oval shape, shimmered under the Court's lights. Speaking in a quiet, cultured voice with a slight drawl he told his version of the story as Sir John questioned him and it was very different from Maudie's.

He explained that he had agreed to be a witness for the bank because Hobbs had tried to wriggle out of his part in the scam by claiming that Newton was the one who had signed all the cheques taken from the Robinson account at the Midland Bank.

He told how Maudie telephoned him in November 1919 to say she had met the ADC to Mr A, a man of great wealth, and he was very dissatisfied with the way he was treated by Mr A on account of his meanness and it was suggested that money should be got out of him. The ADC had a plot to do this by finding him in bed with a woman and then demanding money to prevent a divorce action. Maudie was to be the woman but she felt that Charlie Robinson would not pass as the husband of a society lady because he looked like a butcher, so she asked Newton to play the part. There were originally to be five people in the plot: the Robinsons, Mrs Bevan, the ADC and himself. Hobbs was added later because they would need a solicitor.

He said there were no locked doors when he went to Maudie's hotel suite. 'If a coloured man can turn green, Mr A did when he saw me. Maudie jumped out of bed shouting: "My brute of a husband. It's just the sort of thing you would do" and endeavoured rather to maul me about and scratch me and so on and I had to tell her in an undertone to stop or she'd tear the clothes off my back. Mr A tried to calm her by saying: "Maudie, after all, it is your husband."'

Monty then told the couple: 'Now I have the evidence I want and I will bid you good morning, sir.'

When he returned to London Robinson told him there had been a lot of gossip while he was away: Scotland Yard had been told about the sting and was making enquiries, Lewis and Lewis, a well-known firm of solicitors, knew something, there was a lot of danger and he wanted out. The others were happy to take him at his word, but Newton said they couldn't leave the women out as they had played their parts so well. They decided to tell Robinson that £25,000 had been offered, which would be shared between the six of them and the balance of the £150,000 would be divided between Hobbs, the ADC and himself.

He told how he later went to India twice to try to get the second cheque, which the ADC held, cashed, but couldn't see Sir Hari who was in mourning because another of his series of wives had died. But the ADC was so sure of it being paid that he bought Newton's share for around £17,000.

He denied seducing Maudie. It was a 'physical impossibility because she was without most of her insides.' Quite what he thought a hysterectomy involved is not clear. And he denied stealing £10,000 from her. 'Why? I had just got £4,000 and £40,000.'

The Judge quipped: 'You had enough to be going on with for a bit' and when Newton said he thought he played the part of the husband well, the Judge joked: 'Isn't the proof of the pudding in the eating? Very few actors, as far as I know, make £150,000 in one piece.'

Sir John wanted to ask Monty about another 'intimate' matter and once again went through the rigmarole of writing notes and passing them round. It was a question about Mr A's wish for Maudie to remove her pubic hair: 'Did you learn anything about the instrument used and did you subsequently take any action having regard to the instrument used?'

Lord Darling solicitously suggested to Newton: You had better sit down and write it; you will write so much better.

Sir John: Can you tell me the name of the shop where you ordered what is described in the answer to the last question?

Newton: Longman and Strongi'the'arm.

Sir John: They are well-known people at the bottom of Regent Street. Did you order one article or two?

Newton: Two.

The Court was never told what the mystery objects were. Newton went on to tell Sir John that after he had disturbed Maudie and Mr A in bed he returned to his hotel where he was joined by the ADC and told him what had happened.

He told how he, the Robinsons, the ADC and Hobbs all met at Hobbs's office in Bedford Street on 17 January for the split. 'So far as I know, everybody received £4,000 with the exception of the ADC who got £5,000. Robinson took care of Mrs Bevan's £4,000.'

Lord Halsbury then cross-examined Newton and asked about his past career.

Lord Halsbury: Have you been living on blackmail all your life?

Newton: No.

Lord Halsbury: How many people have you blackmailed?

Newton: Nobody and it won't help you at all to bully me, either, I may say.

Lord Halsbury: Not even Mr A?

Newton: I took the part that I did take.

In fact, Newton had led a life of crime for at least twenty-five years. He had been round the world three times, card-sharping with a partner called Lemoine, otherwise known as the Baron, but he had been convicted only once. Lord Halsbury reminded him of the occasion. It was in 1908, when he was sentenced at the

Old Bailey to twenty months' hard labour for copying a sheet of headed writing paper from the solicitors Lewis and Lewis, who were now taking an interest in the Mr A plot, and then forging a letter purporting to come from Sir George Lewis on it. This said that a Mrs Violet Fraser was due some money shortly and asked to borrow against her expectations. He had done the same thing before for her with no problems. From letters found in his room, Newton and Mrs Fraser – Brownie – were very close friends. They had been involved in some shady card games in London and Germany. Had it not been for her ill health, she would have been prosecuted, too.

Brownie wasn't Monty's only love interest. Detective Inspector W.C. Gough, who arrested him, told the Court that Monty had been arrested in Boston, Massachusetts, accused of swindling, by promise of marriage, a widow he met on an ocean liner, but he was never charged. Afterwards he was arrested in New York for desertion of a woman he had married. Mr Gough did not know the details.

Lord Halsbury rather rattled the usually calm Newton by saying: 'You said you were an honest man. Was that forgery on Sir George's notepaper an honest thing to do?'

Newton said plaintively: 'Don't turn and twist my answers. I did not say I was an honest man. I wish to God I could. I said I was honest with my friends.'

Newton admitted that he was heartily ashamed of his part in the Mr A plot and Lord Halsbury asked when the feeling of shame came upon him.

Newton, honestly: 'With the likelihood of exposure'.

Lord Halsbury wanted to know about Monsieur Lemoine and Newton said he had known him for many years. Asked if his proper name was von Koenig he said he didn't know but he used many names in the government work he did. (In an earlier deposition to the police, he had said that Lemoine was Stallmann.) Lemoine had been to Mr A's country, at the invitation of the ADC, to get payment of the second cheque. He was asked about Hobbs: 'He is the adviser of most of the scoundrels in London, isn't he?' Lord Darling made them all laugh when he observed, 'He must have a large clientele.'

He was asked if he had taken the ADC's share of the payout from him at cards and blackmail. He replied: 'I never played cards with the ADC and, regarding the blackmail, I have paid the ADC, very foolishly, considerable sums of money myself, because he has blackmailed me.'

He explained that the ADC was so certain that the second cheque would be paid that he gave him 600,000 francs for his share. When the second cheque was not paid, the ADC sued him for the return of that money, £17,300, but settled for £1,000.

'He knew at the time I had plenty of money and, if he had anything like a fair or legitimate claim against me for any amount of that kind, he would not have settled it for £1,000,' said Newton.

Lord Halsbury insisted on bringing up the past again and asked if he knew ex-Chief Inspector Gough. 'He was the officer who arrested you on the occasion when you got twenty months' hard labour for forgery?' Newton agreed. And then it emerged that Gough had been to see Lemoine in Paris about the Mr A case and, Newton said, he had bumped into him at Lemoine's flat quite by chance. 'Did you tell him that if Robinson was prepared to make over £25,000 of what he got in this case to you, you would refuse to come over and give evidence?' Newton denied this.

Eleanor Cadney – Nelly – the parlour maid, who came with the Chapel Street house when Maud rented it, followed Monty Newton into the witness box and was questioned by Mr Rayner Goddard, KC, for the bank. She said that when the rental began in August 1919, Mr and Mrs Robinson lived in the house. She saw Mrs Bevan in November. She had seen Newton a good many times at the house and, if she remembered rightly, he became a visitor *before* the Victory Ball.

She remembered the ADC visiting the house, once alone and other times with Mr A. One day she remembered particularly was when the ADC visited and Mrs Bevan, Mrs Robinson, Mr Newton and, she thought, Mr Robinson were all there. It was fixed in her mind because Mrs Bevan's teenage daughter was there, too, and when the ADC came she was sent down to the kitchen to have tea and then left by the back door.

She said Robinson lived at the house until about the beginning of December. Mrs Robinson had told her that if anybody asked for him she was to say he was abroad.

Mr Goddard: As things turned out, was that true?

Nelly: No.

Mr Goddard: How do you know?

Nelly: Because he called at Chapel Street during the time he was supposed to be abroad.

Nelly said she thought that during that time Newton came to the house with Mr Robinson and dined with him. When Mr Robinson came to the house he rang the bell and she let him in; he did not call when Mr A was about. She said she remembered Mrs Robinson and Mrs Bevan going to Paris. They came back on 27 December. She remembered Mrs Robinson going to Paris again in January and Mr Robinson came back to the house towards the end of January or early in February. 'During such times as Mr and Mrs Robinson were living together in the house how did they appear to be one with the other?'

'Very friendly.' This was contrary to the story the Robinsons had told.

Cross-examined by Lord Halsbury, she said she did not like being in the house after Mr Robinson left; Mr A was visiting the house and she did not approve of it. Sir John Simon then took over the questioning.

Sir John: When Mrs Robinson and Mrs Bevan returned from their trip abroad were they spending money?'

Nelly: They seemed to have money. Mrs Robinson had very many more clothes when she came back from Paris than when she went away.

Sir John: And Mr Robinson?

Nelly: The same.

She also said there were originally four front door keys to the house. Mr and Mrs Robinson had one each, she and Rebecca Witte, the cook, shared one and there was a spare. When the tenancy ended one of the keys was missing.

Mark Waters, Mr A's solicitor, was the next witness. He told Sir John how the ADC called on him on 29 December 1919 and said he had come from Paris to consult him on behalf of a male friend who had been found in bed with a woman at a Paris hotel by the woman's husband. He asked what he should do. He would not tell him the name of the friend or of the woman but said the man was a very important person.

Mr Waters told him his friend could not avoid a divorce petition and he should do nothing until he was served with one. Then, on 14 January 1920, the ADC called on Mr Waters with Mr A and told him they had settled the matter. 'We have given a cheque for £150,000 and another cheque for the same amount, which is to be held up until such time as it can be met.' I expressed my amazement and, turning to the ADC, I said: 'I told you to do nothing.' He shrugged his shoulders and both he and Mr A gave me to understand it was absolutely essential that there should be no publicity and that they had paid this huge sum in order to avoid a scandal. Mr Waters advised Mr A to stop the second cheque. At that time he still thought it was Mr Robinson who had caught Mrs Robinson with Mr A but the legal gossip machine was working hard and Mr Waters soon heard rumours. He went to see Hobbs on 19 January to complain. 'I said: "This matter had been disgracefully dealt with, and I shall want a good deal of that money back. This is a blackmailing plot." I informed him that Mr A, on my advice, had stopped the second cheque. He told me that Mr and Mrs Robinson were well known to him and there had been no plot and I said that the information I had already gathered tended to show there had been a plot. Hobbs apparently acquiesced quite readily in the stoppage of the second cheque and said he would advise his client to put it behind the fire.'

Lord Halsbury could see how Mr Waters would have the cheque that had been cashed but was curious to know how he came to have the second, which was said to have been destroyed. Mr Waters said he received it from Mr A's London bankers, who had it from the ADC. The ADC had asked to be paid £20,000 for the cheque but, stupidly, he had already put it in the post to Mr A's bank.

Lord Halsbury: Was the ADC trying to make a bit more money for himself?

Mr Waters: So I gathered. He threatened me with a writ and I said: 'I hope it will arrive.'

Lord Darling: Did it?

Mr Waters: No, my lord, not yet.

This revelation is confusing, for Mr Waters did not say when he received the second cheque, which the court was told earlier had been destroyed; and why did the ADC bother to return it when he knew it had been stopped?

The next witness was Charles Midgley, a partner in the firm of Goddard and Smith, estate agents, who had acted for the owner of 28 Chapel Street when the house was let to Mrs Robinson. Asked by Sir John Simon why a letter demanding the second instalment of the rent was sent on 31 December 1919, when it was not due until 9 January, he said the landlady called on him and said: 'I have received certain information about the tenants in my house and I think they are having parties there, not quite proper parties.' She was under the impression that they were gambling parties and she said: 'You will make immediate application for the rent. Get it in with the least possible delay.'

The name of Lemoine came up again when Robinson's solicitor, Hyam Davis, gave evidence. Mr Davis said he learned about the second cheque in April or May 1923. He went to Paris to see Newton to find out if he was the man who had instructed Hobbs to start divorce proceedings and Newton refused to see him unless Lemoine was present. Lord Darling asked: 'Who is this Lemoine?' And Davies answered 'He is Newton's agent.'

* * *

After hearing from some minor witnesses, Sir John began his address to the jury. It took up the whole of the afternoon of the seventh day and half the morning of the eighth. He reminded them that the ADC left Paris on the evening of the discovery which meant Mr A, in his terror, signed and parted with the two cheques within a few hours of being put in his frightful position. 'Was it not perfectly obvious that this scoundrel, the ADC, went to the extreme limit to which villainy could go and used those few hours in inflaming the anxiety and increasing the horror of Mr A, who was thus to be robbed of his money?'

Turning again to the secret questions and the mysterious purchases from the strangely named Longman and Strong'th'arm, Sir John said: 'How did I know? I knew because it is in the statement made by Newton, who knew these things had happened. There was only one conceivable reason how Newton could have known and that was because Mrs Robinson told him. If there was nothing else, that proved to demonstrate that Newton and Mrs Robinson were on the most intimate terms.'

He said it was not disputed that Mrs Robinson knew it was not her husband but Newton who entered her bedroom. 'If she had been honest she would at once have said to Mr A: "My dear Mr A, that man, I assure you, is a scoundrel. We will put the police on him. He has a conviction against him." Instead of that, she treated Newton as her husband – and nobody could have said: "I bid you good day" with greater grace and affability than Newton'. There was laughter in court at this. 'Mrs Robinson had nothing to fear by being honest because she was going to the east to live in splendour with her devoted admirer, Mr A, and was not coming back again. But, instead of that, she left the wretched man under the impression that it was her husband and the moment the ADC had got hold of the cheques she skipped back to London with Mrs Bevan and the ADC, leaving Mr A in Paris.'

Coming to the fate of the money itself, Sir John said that Mr A's cheque was cleared by 6 January and £147,000 was drawn out in two lots, £130,000 on 6 January and £17,000 on 16 January. Of the £130,000, £120,000 was proved to have been paid into the Paris branch of the Anglo-South American bank by Hobbs; £40,000 was then paid out to the ADC, £40,000 to Newton and £40,000 to Hobbs. They wrapped the matter up as well as they could by buying French securities. As to the £10,000 left in ten notes of £1,000, it had been proved that one was cashed by Hobbs over the counter of the Anglo-South American bank and that one note was cashed at Cox's in Paris but it was not known by whom. Thus, after 6 January there was only £8,000 left of what had already been drawn out. If Hobbs was going to produce £25,000 on 17 January and had only £8,000 of £130.000 left, he must get £17,000 more. Consequently, another cheque for £17,000 was drawn on 16 January and so Hobbs had enough.

'If Robinson was told that £25,000 was what he could get, there was no reason why it should be shared among six people unless there were six people in the plot. The thing that finally damns Robinson's case is that this £25,000 went to six people and that is the strongest confirmation that there were six people in the plot.'

He turned to etiquette. 'And the matter of Mrs Bevan's daughter being sent below stairs for tea when the conspirators were meeting; would they ever have believed that a lady in high society, conducting her house properly, would send her best friend's daughter down to the kitchen for tea? The parlour-maid and the cook had given the daughter tea and then let her out by the back door. What was the significance of that? Because Mrs Robinson and her friend, Mrs Bevan – who dared not go into the witness box – did not want her to hear what was going on. That circumstance was the strongest possible confirmation that the horrible plot was being hatched in Chapel Street in December.'

Then it was Lord Halsbury's turn to review the evidence for the jury. 'Consider the position of Mr Robinson,' he said. 'If you find him guilty of being in the conspiracy, he knows perfectly well that he and his wife would be prosecuted and that he would get a severe sentence and yet he went on with his action. He was prepared to take the risk of that because he said: "I am innocent of any conspiracy. I am not frightened of going before a jury." Mrs Robinson was never in the plot. She said she had to ask no man or woman to get anything she wanted out of Mr A and she could have been provided for life. These other people came in and spoilt her game. It might have been an immoral game but it was no plot or blackmailing of Mr A. According to the story, she was to give up the possibility of going out to India with him, with all his vast wealth, for £4,000. Do you think that likely? And, supposing she were in the plot, why should a cynical blackmailer whose coup had succeeded have a nervous breakdown?'

The Judge summed up at great length and then gave the jury five questions to answer to settle the case. They retired at 3.24 p.m., the list of questions in hand, and returned an hour and twelve minutes later with their answers – which caused some surprise, to say the least. The Clerk to the Court asked if they were all agreed and the Foreman replied that they were. Lord Darling asked for their answers.

Lord Darling: Was there a scheme or a conspiracy to catch Mr A with Mrs Robinson with a view to getting money from Mr A?

The Foreman: Yes.

Lord Darling: Was the plaintiff a party to any such scheme or conspiracy?

The Foreman: No.

Lord Darling: Then, was Mrs Robinson a party to any such scheme or conspiracy?

The Foreman: No.

Lord Darling: Was Mr A induced to part with the two cheques through fear or alarm?

The Foreman: Yes.

Lord Darling: Was Mr A's mind so unsettled by the circumstances of the discovery that his action in parting with the cheques was not free and voluntary?

The Foreman: Yes.

Lord Darling had some more questions for the jury about what he called 'the banking part' of the case. So they retired again at 4.55 p.m. and returned an hour and a quarter later to hand the list of questions and their answers to the Judge, who read them out.

Lord Darling: Question one: were the words 'Pay to the order of Mr C Robinson, Appleton and Co' appearing on the back of the cheque for £150,000 dated 30th December 1919, written by some person as agent for Appleton and Co.?

The Foreman: No.

Lord Darling: Question two: had Hobbs and/or Appleton and Co. any intention of transferring their whole rights, if any, in the cheque for £150,000 to the plaintiff?

The Foreman: No.

Lord Darling: Question three: were those rights, whatever they were, in the £150,000 cheque ever transferred by Hobbs and/or Appleton to the plaintiff? [The jury had not been able to answer this one.]

Lord Darling: Question four: did the bank, in paying out the £150,000 obey the mandate under which they received and cleared the cheque?

The Foreman: Yes.

Lord Darling: Question five: did Hobbs, in drawing out the money, purport to act under the same authority under which he paid it in?

The Foreman: Yes.

The Foreman said he did not think the jury would be able to answer the unanswered question so the Judge, acknowledging that they had spent a lot of hours on the case, discharged them. A juror then stood up and asked if they could be exempt from future jury duty after such a long case. Lord Darling thought this a cheeky request and replied, gazing round the crowded Courtroom: 'I don't think so. It has not been one of the dullest cases for you.'[15]

Like the Judge, I am left with some questions: why did Sir Hari give a blank cheque to his ADC? Why he gave two is even more of a mystery. The original reason given in Monty Newton's evidence was that Sir Hari needed time to arrange funds to meet the second cheque but why, if he did not know how much the cheques were to be filled in for? I cannot imagine any rich man, even if he had total trust in a servant, would give him two blank cheques. Had the ADC perhaps, in the anguished hours of Boxing Day, suggested that £300,000 might be demanded by Mr Robinson and then taken the blank cheques to London to get the agreement of the gang before returning to Paris to have the amounts filled in, which was done by a member of Sir Hari's staff?

CHAPTER EIGHT

But Who Won?

Lord Birkenhead, who was Lord Chancellor in 1919, and who was at the Victory Ball in the Royal Albert Hall where this story started, was Secretary of State for India by now, and he was keeping Lord Reading, the Viceroy of India, up-to-date with the progress of the case. He wrote to him on 27th November, in a letter marked 'Secret. Private:'

> The £125,000 case has caused extraordinary scandal as you may imagine in this country and, indeed, in almost the whole of the civilised world. From our point of view the case seems to be in every way deplorable. Carrying out, as I understand them, your wishes, I saw Darling (the trial judge) and informed him that if the interest of justice permitted it, it would be desirable that the name of the person principally concerned should not be mentioned. He said that he would do his best and has done so. But secrecy in such a matter is hardly permanently attainable: far too many people know the facts. The name has already appeared in the American press and I anticipate that its publication in that country will become general.
>
> Much unfavourable comment has been caused in this country by the selection of such a scoundrel as Arthur to be the Raja's ADC. It is not considered very important that he was specially asked for by the Raja himself for it is replied that we do after all assume ourselves a direct selective responsibility by giving assent to such an appointment. I rather think that Colonel Bannerman

of this Office, who was in Kashmir at the time [he was the British Resident Officer] expressed the opinion that Arthur was not particularly suitable; but apparently someone in authority took a different decision. I think one ought to know who was the person actually chargeable with the decision. Questions are almost certain when Parliament meets. The Judge has more than once spoken of him as the greatest scoundrel in the whole case. It seems indeed almost certain that he conceived the whole wicked plan to entrap his master at a time when he was being paid and trusted to protect him. Anticipating as I do that the names cannot be permanently suppressed, I am sure that it is very desirable that there should be prosecution of these criminals. If it can be said against us – as, unfortunately, it can – that this young Indian was betrayed and swindled by English criminals we should, I am sure, make it possible at least to add that the arm of British justice was long enough to place these scoundrels in jail for lengthy periods. I expect without knowing that it will be necessary to take Newton as King's Evidence, which ought to enable the prosecution to get all the other persons involved, including Arthur, who is hiding somewhere in Paris but whose whereabouts, I believe, are known to the French police.[16]

The English police thought the same way. They were so confident that the jury would find that the Robinsons were in the conspiracy that while the case was still going on, Detective Chief Inspector Alfred Helden and Detective Sergeant Percy J. Smith had slipped out of the Court and gone to a suburban police station to apply for warrants for the arrest of the Robinsons, Hobbs and Captain Arthur. 'Had we applied for the warrants at Bow Street the news would have gone round the town in a flash and the birds might have flown,' Percy J. wrote in his memoirs many years later. In fact, two of them had already escaped: Newton by giving evidence against the gang, and the ADC by remaining in Paris, out of reach of Scotland Yard. The policemen were stopped in their tracks when they returned to the court to hear the verdict that, although there *had* been a conspiracy, the Robinsons were not part of it.

That left only Hobbs for them, but in spite of a round-the-clock watch of his house and the court, he was missing, too. Hobbs had realised that he would be arrested the moment the Mr A case finished. The police had, after all, known about his activities for at least twenty-five years, but Hobbs had always cleverly managed to avoid arrest. For the past three years, though, it had been the talk of the criminal classes that he would be arrested sooner or later for his part in the Mr A case. The anxiety of it all was taking its toll; his failing health had reduced him to a shadow of his old, masterful self, said people who knew him. His hair was grey and his face haggard. Fearful of the coming storm, he had resigned his position at Appleton and Co. in 1922 and transferred the bulk of his £250,000 fortune abroad (not bad savings for a man on a solicitor's clerk's wage of £6 a week.) His partners in crime (Hobbs did not have friends, his arrogance and greed turned people against him) advised him to get out of the country and, before the end of the Mr A case, he knew the time had come to run. His plan was audacious. Among Hobbs's many dodgy acquaintances was Willy Clarkson, who owed him a few favours. Willy Clarkson was the most famous wigmaker and theatrical costumier of his time; he was even *perruqier* and *costumier* by appointment to Queen Victoria and dressed her amateur dramatics at Osborne House and Balmoral Castle, even cut her daughters' hair. After Victoria's death stage wigs went out of fashion and his career was on the slide. He got rid of his redundant stock by staging fires in his storerooms and claiming on the insurance, with Hobbs's help.

Clarkson was a master of disguise; he could disguise a man so that his own wife would not recognise him. Now he made up a man as Hobbs and hid him in the cloakroom at the Royal Courts of Justice. A few minutes later Hobbs left the Court and went downstairs, closely followed by a detective. The detective discreetly waited outside while Hobbs went into the cloakroom, swapped hat, coat and walking stick with his double and locked himself in a lavatory while the double slipped out and left the building, again followed by the police. Then Hobbs made a run for it. Unfortunately for him he was recognised at Gravesend, about to board a ship for Rotterdam, and was arrested. He appeared at Bow Street Magistrates' Court the next day, 29 November. His skin was yellowish and there were bags under his eyes, but his grey moustache and goatee beard were neatly combed. He was remanded in custody charged with receiving a cheque for £150,000, which had been stolen abroad.

Lord Darling's court sat again on Tuesday 2nd December when, in view of the rather inconclusive nature of the verdict, both Lord Halsbury and Sir John Simon asked for judgment to be entered on their client's behalf. After much legal argument the Judge made it clear he thought the Bank had won. It was quite true, he said, that the jury had exonerated Mr and Mrs Robinson from any part in the conspiracy to obtain money from Mr A but the Court could not allow a man, however innocent, to claim part of the proceeds of a theft which took the form of a threatened man paying for the concealment of the 'defilement' by him of the plaintiff's wife. So Robinson won and he lost.

* **

At the same time, the police were looking for the ADC who was also accused of receiving the cheque for £150,000 that had been stolen abroad. He was known to be living in Paris and working for a travel agency in the Champs Elysees. To avoid the chance of his slipping away, his photograph and details were sent to all French police stations and frontier posts and a warrant for his extradition obtained. He was arrested in the Champs Elysees on 1 December and his name was revealed. The same day, while in custody, Arthur gave an interview to a *Daily News* reporter saying he intended to waive the extradition formalities and return to England to clear his name. Had he been guilty, he said, he would not have returned to Europe from the US two months earlier. His arrest caused quite a flurry in the travel agent's office. The manager refused to comment but other members of the staff said nobody had any idea he was the ADC they had all heard so much about.

The policemen Helden and Percy J. Smith arrived with the warrant for Captain Arthur's arrest on 2 December, having escaped the appalling weather in London. There was fog and rain and at midday it was still pitch dark; the buses were lit up and the sparrows were still asleep. Dawn still had not broken by 4 pm when the Weather Reform Society issued a resolution urging the

Government 'in view of the fact that the British Empire extends all over the world, the advisability of at once considering whether the Motherland might not be removed to some more suitable environment.' To applause, the President of the Society said: 'With all our idle shipping, it should surely not be impossible to transfer our railways, our industries, Mr Churchill and all that England holds dear, to that great tract of unoccupied land, Australia, for instance. This would mean the settlement of the unemployment question, incidentally, and it seems ridiculous to keep going in all this fog when we might establish a new England in the sunshine.'

The Meteorological Office said that the 'Great Darkness' was caused by a secondary depression over southern England, bringing low clouds; the unusually high temperatures and the absence of wind meant that all of London's smoke was kept under clouds and could not escape.

So Helden and Smith were glad to get to Paris. Arthur had changed his mind and decided to fight the extradition application and engaged a counsel, Maitre Paul Gide. He knew that the grounds that his client was of Irish nationality and it was the British government that was requesting his extradition would not be sufficient, he told the *Petit Journal*; but there was a fifty-year-old treaty with Great Britain governing extradition that might afford some surprises, so he intended to study the question thoroughly.

Maitre Gide added: 'It should be understood that the ADC, like Mr A, is the victim of blackmail. He has already parted with a tidy fortune.' The next day, in an interview with the *Daily News*, he was asked why Captain Arthur did not go to London to give evidence in the Mr A case. He said that, according to Arthur, a few days before the opening of the case he was visited by a man who said he was from Scotland Yard. They met in the lounge of the Ritz Hotel and the supposed police officer informed him that the British Government did not desire his evidence and that Scotland Yard thought it more desirable that he should remain out of England, which he agreed to. Maitre Gide said that Captain Arthur was absolutely willing to go to London to give his account of what really took place but Mr A had agreed with the police and instructed him to stay silent.

Captain Arthur also told M. Gide how, in February, after the Paris affair, he decided to rid his master of the two women, so he went to the British Embassy in Paris and asked for authority to request the help of the French police. This was granted and Arthur saw an official at the Prefecture of Police and told him that the women were in Nice where Sir Hari was on a visit. The official telegraphed orders to the Nice police, and Captain Arthur then went to Nice where he pointed out the two women, who were asked to leave.

Captain Arthur was interviewed by police on 2, 3 and 4 December and on the afternoon of the 4th he appeared before an examining magistrate at the Palais de Justice for an interview that lasted for three hours. His appearance had changed dramatically in the few days since his arrest: he arrived at the court haggard, depressed and looking under-nourished. He was wearing the thick blue overcoat in which he was arrested but his collar, tie and bootlaces had been removed, as was the custom. There was a delay before he entered the room and he asked for a glass of wine. A bottle was brought and he drank two tumblers full 'with avidity' once his guard had removed the handcuffs. M. Gide now opposed extradition on the grounds that the alleged offence, which he denied, was committed in Paris and only a French court was competent to try him. He came out and explained the private proceedings to the waiting reporters.

My client maintained his innocence from beginning to end, and emphatically repeated that he had been faithful to the Rajah both in matters of finance and in those which concerned his dynasty. He said it was untrue that he cashed a cheque for £150,000. According to Captain Arthur, the facts are that the Rajah signed two cheques for £150,000; one that was cashed and the other stopped. Captain Arthur declared that after he and certain other persons had witnessed the destruction of a document, he was shown the second cheque for £150,000. This, of course, in itself, was valueless but the person who brought it to him had a number of photographs and documents. Captain Arthur, who had by then left the Rajah's service but still had access to his former master, promised he would give the man a million francs – about

£20,000 – for the cheque, documents and photographs. He borrowed the money from a Mr X and, in order to show his fidelity, he sent all these documents by registered post to the Rajah's bank in India. But he said that the reply he got for his fidelity was a curt letter from the Rajah's secretary demanding by what authority he had paid out money on the Rajah's behalf. Mr X he described as a big man of affairs and he hoped it would not be necessary to reveal his name.

Newton was keeping up his friendly contacts with the police and told Chief Inspector Helden that Lemoine had written to him saying: 'The case against Arthur hangs in the balance. There have been so many lies told by Arthur's counsel that the authorities are in a quandary as to the true facts.'

Captain Arthur successfully resisted extradition on the grounds that too much time had elapsed since the alleged crime for extradition rules to apply. This was not much comfort to him though, for he remained in La Santé prison awaiting trial in Paris for the same offences, some of which had been committed in France.

The police denied newspaper stories that officers at Scotland Yard had interviewed Maudie and she issued a statement. Sir John Simon had taunted Robinson about what he would do with the money if he won the case and had manoeuvred him into saying he would return it to Mr A. Now Maudie announced that her husband would lodge an appeal against Lord Darling's decision and had made a deed of assignment making over his rights in the £125,000 claim to the Public Trustee to repay Mr A and if Mr A would not accept it to give everything to any hospital or charity nominated by the Public Trustee. 'I have begged him to fight this case up to the last ditch.' In a mood of righteous indignation her statement went on to say: 'Having regard to the nature of the bank's defence, my husband considered that, although from the moment he had full knowledge of the circumstances under which this money was paid, he made up his mind that neither one of us would touch one penny of it.'

One of Maudie's friends told reporters that Maudie intended to publish her story but she had no intention of appearing in a film, as had been rumoured. 'To do so would be disloyal to Mr A and all through Mrs Robinson has remained loyal to Mr A. To write her story is a different matter.' Maudie seems to have thought better of the idea for no story ever appeared and her husband lost his appeal.

Although the ADC's name was disclosed on his arrest, the identity of Mr A was still a secret, an open secret for the whole of Paris knew his name and one paper had been so bold as to publish his initials. Finally, on 3 December, the India Office gave permission for his name to be revealed and the first to announce it was the London radio programme 2LO, which interrupted a music programme for the purpose.

Lord Birkenhead, the Secretary of State for India, later said that had he known the full circumstances of the case he would not have agreed to the Viceroy's request for anonymity for Sir Hari, as that decision led to fevered speculation all over the world. Everyone wanted to know who Mr A was. Some guessed the Shah of Persia, others the Emperor of Japan, and nearly every famous Indian came under suspicion and opposed the secrecy.

With the publication of his name, all the London papers ran background pieces about Sir Hari and in particular his wealth (£12,000,000 according to some, half that according to others) and speculated as to his whereabouts. The *Daily News* of 4 December said it was possible he would come to England shortly 'in view of certain proceedings which are likely to take place', a reference to the arrest of Hobbs. Two days later it was saying that Sir Hari had arrived in France but his exact whereabouts were being kept secret by the India Office. On Sunday 7 December the *News of the World* had him in Monte Carlo and said he would be required in London as a witness in the Hobbs case. It was unlikely he would ever return to Kashmir wrote Mrs Elsie Tinline in the *News of the World*: flouted tradition and outraged religion provided an insuperable barrier to his return. He was regarded as 'contaminated' by a white woman. On the same day *The People* said Sir Hari was already in London and staying *very* quietly at the home of a high official. He had been living quietly at Mentone, left for London on Thursday the 4th, and was being guarded by a Special Branch officer. 'Sir Hari's voyage to Europe was taken with every precaution and the shipping company was asked not to divulge the identity of the traveller.' It went on to say that Sir Hari feared that if he moved about in London he would be recognised at once but the paper thought he worried unnecessarily: 'There are in all thousands of dark and yellow-skinned men of culture in London, most of them between the ages of twenty-eight and thirty. An Indian is, of course, so familiar a sight in the London streets that a second glance is very rarely given him. Were the Rajah to wear a lounge suit and an English hat it is not thought that he would be readily detected by passers-by.' *The People* said Sir Hari's evidence in the Hobbs case was indispensable and his appearance in court unavoidable.

They were all wrong. He was still in Kashmir on 19 December, on crutches and nursing a leg badly broken by tobogganing. Sir John Wood, by then the British Resident in J and K wrote to Lieutenant Colonel S. B. A. Patterson, the political secretary to the government of India in Delhi on 19 December 1924 saying that Sir Hari was in a state of great depression after the Mr A Case and was prepared to go to London to give evidence in Hobbs's trial 'though he evidently shrinks from the prospect.'[17]

Lord Reading wrote to Lord Birkenhead on Christmas Day 1924 in a letter marked 'Private and Personal':

Hari Singh has written a private letter to my Private Secretary expressing his greatest contrition to me for his conduct in the affair and generally doing his utmost – poor fellow! – to prevent my forming a harsh judgment upon him. I am causing a sympathetic reply to be sent to him, from which it will be obvious to him that I am not disposed to lay too much blame upon him for frailties and errors of conduct and judgment committed by him in his early youth. He informs me that the Maharaja of Kashmir – his uncle – has behaved extremely well over it, has refused to accept Hari Singh's resignation as leading member of the Council of Ministers and has given him leave for two or three months to enable him to recover his balance of mind.

I have communicated with you about the ADC, Arthur, and there is little more that is useful to tell you. From my experience the Government of India is very careful in making recommendations of this character; in this particular case Hari

Singh seems to have been captured by Arthur and to have pressed his desire for his company in Europe. The military authorities were not in favour on a judgment based upon his military record but there was nothing substantially against his character, although they certainly regarded him as unsatisfactory and inclined to be wanting in balance. In the end the Political Department of the Government of India appears to have been influenced by Hari Singh's wish and to have backed his request and, unfortunately, prevailed.[18]

CHAPTER NINE

Trouble behind the Scenes

People thought the Judge had been too droll throughout the Mr A Case and Sir John too harsh, which led to some sympathy for the Robinsons. But there are still mysteries about Maudie's behaviour. If she was not in the plot, why did she return to London for the payout? Why did it matter what her husband thought if she was intending to go to Kashmir with the Rajah anyway? If she *were* in the plot, why did she try for a second bite of the cherry by going to meet Sir Hari in Nice? Did she believe this was an opportunity to dump her old life and start again? Was Sir Hari's rejection the reason for her breakdown? Surely her husband had told her Scotland Yard knew of the plot and she should have realised that Sir Hari must have known about it, too, by then. Had she taken leave of her senses?

The verdict of the jury had astonished Lord Birkenhead. He had written to the Viceroy on 4 December, marking his letter 'Secret. Private'.

The great case is now over and it did not end as I had predicted. The verdict of the jury exculpating Mr and Mrs Robinson is generally looked upon as perverse. I am told at the Bar that Simon was too harsh and Darling too jocose for the taste of the jury. I have been compelled to direct publication of the person principally involved, having regard to the facts – (1) that the name had appeared everywhere in the American and in many continental papers and (2) that the impending criminal proceedings would, in any event, have made further concealment impossible.

I am extremely sorry for the young man who, when little more than a boy, was vilely abused by a gang of English swindlers. It is ironical enough that the very vastness of the sum, which he paid to avoid publicity, is the very element in the matter that has produced it. As to the appointment of the ADC, disastrous as it has been in its results it is, of course, as your telegram suggests, fair to consider what was the young man's contemporary dossier at the date of his appointment. Colonel Bannerman's recollection – he was in Kashmir at the time – is that he entered a caveat but only upon the ground that, in his opinion, Arthur was at that time shirking real military service. Some of the papers have been commenting upon the very apparent singularity of the appointment and I shall await anything you have to say upon the subject with interest.[19]

The Viceroy replied with what looks like an expensive telegram dated 11 December 1924:

Private and Personal. I have now examined the available papers relating to Captain Arthur. They do not show what authority recommended Arthur to Hari Singh. Papers show that when it was decided that Hari Singh was to go to Europe. The Political Secretary advised him to take European officer with him, and names of suitable European officers were discussed by Wood, then Political Secretary, with Bannerman, then Resident, Kashmir. Names of officers originally suggested did not include Arthur's; this was in November 1917.

Later, Hari Singh spoke to the Viceroy regarding the visit to Europe and seems himself to have suggested taking Arthur with him. Arthur had been on sick leave in Kashmir and the inference is that Hari Singh became acquainted with him in Kashmir.

Enquiries were made from the Army Department about Arthur. Army authorities did not give satisfactory account of Arthur from a military point of view. Arthur had been invalided from France for shell shock in 1916 and posted to the Royal Garrison Artillery in India. In 1917, he applied to resign commission on account of ill health after his appearance before Medical Boards, who found him suffering from neurasthenia. [A condition allegedly due to exhaustion of the nervous system; a term not used today.] It was decided to send him home for light duties under the War Office. Instead of proceeding to Bombay, however, he went to Kashmir. He appears to have applied for employment under the Kashmir State while in Kashmir. He was discovered there by the Provost Marshall and sent to Rawal Pindi to appear before another Medical Board who found him to be in a highly nervous condition. Army Department eventually thought he had been insubordinate and undependable during his military career but the opinion held in the Political Department at the time, in which the Viceroy concurred, was that, in view of Hari Singh's peculiar temperament, it was desirable that he should take Arthur with him because if thwarted in the matter and given some other officer not of his own choice, he would resent opposition to his wishes and ignore the advice of officer for whom he had no special liking or regard. The War Office was in consequence asked for Arthur's services to accompany Hari Singh.

Papers do not reveal whether any officer or authority originally recommended Arthur to Hari Singh and I am making further enquiries on this point. Bannerman, who was Resident at Kashmir at this time, may be able to give you some information at this point.

Lord Birkenhead clearly did not know of Arthur's two pre-war visits to Kashmir. Behind the scenes, they were looking for someone to blame. A question *was* asked in the House of Commons, as Lord Birkenhead predicted. On 17 December, Sir Nicholas Gratton Doyle asked if the Secretary of State for India would say 'whether the appointment of the *aide de camp* referred to in the recent case in the Law Courts of Robinson *v* Midland Bank Ltd was made by, or with the authority of, the Foreign Office and, if so, upon what recommendation, if any, the Foreign Office relied.' Advance notice of this question prompted much soul-searching within the India Office; memos flew to and fro discussing how to answer it without revealing how incompetent the Government of India had been. A non-committal answer was given along the lines that there were no rules about the employment of European officers by princes, each case was examined on its merits but the

Government of India can only overrule a prince's wishes when they have real cause for concern in his selection of an individual.

Viceroy Lord Reading wrote again the next day, a letter marked 'Private and Personal. For the Secretary of State alone'.

The £125,000 case is a most deplorable affair and of course will be made the most out of here by our critics and opponents. I quite understand that it became necessary to publish Sir Hari Singh's name. The most unfortunate part of the whole wretched business from our point of view is the part that Captain Arthur played and apparently you will not be able to bring this scoundrel to justice. He seems to be safely sheltered in France by some limitations of time under the extradition laws. Hari Singh is naturally most dreadfully worried about the whole affair. I do not think he is likely to go to London. I saw him only six or seven weeks ago when I was in Kashmir and he then told me that he hoped to pay a few months' visit to London early the next year. At that time, I hadn't the faintest notion of the case of which I first learned by your telegram. I don't suppose you have met Hari Singh. He is, as you know, the heir-apparent of the old Maharajah of Kashmir, who is some seventy-five years of age – a great age for India – and Hari Singh will thus succeed to one of the finest States in India. Hari Singh is very fond of sport and is a good shot. When I saw him he was on crutches having broken his leg badly when tobogganing in Kashmir. It is most unfortunate that we had had several very bad affairs in the last few years. There are various minor incidents, which certainly do not enhance the prestige of the Englishman in the East. Scoundrels and swindlers seem, however, to pale into insignificance compared with Arthur and his associates.[20]

The Viceroy wrote again on New Year's Day, another 'Secret and Private' letter:

In my last letter to you I dealt with the Hari Singh case and in relation to the assent of the Government of India to Arthur accompanying him to Europe. There is one feature of this wretched business which still troubles me and I feel should be stated to you. As you will have gathered from our correspondence, the military authorities did not regard Arthur favourably for reasons already explained to you. Nevertheless, Arthur was allowed to proceed. Of course it is easy to write after the event and no one could possibly have anticipated that Arthur would turn out such a scoundrel; yet I am somewhat surprised to find that Hari Singh, who was then very young, had had his way. As a result of my investigation it appears, as I told you in my last letter, that the Political Department's views prevailed. This means that Sir John Wood, who was then Political Secretary, obtained Lord Chelmsford's assent [Lord Chelmsford was Viceroy at the time] to Arthur's departure with Hari Singh. I should not have thought it necessary to proceed further with the matter, but for the fact that Sir John Wood is now the Political Resident in Kashmir and, therefore, is brought into much contact with both the Maharaja and Hari Singh.

Lord Birkenhead thought about his reply for three weeks before writing back on 22 January 1925, a scathing letter marked 'Private'.

I read very carefully what you say in your letters of the 25th December and the 1st January about the Hari Singh case. Personally, I am extremely sorry for this young fellow. Like another, he fell among thieves and worse, and there was no better Samaritan than Sir John Wood's protégée, Captain Arthur. Having paid so much and got so little for it – not even privacy for a squalid amour. I was a little alarmed by a phrase in your letter, which indicated that the hero – or victim – of this conspicuous melodrama might come to Europe within the next year. My earnest advice to you is to keep him away for two or three years. If he were to visit this country in the next twelve months every placard in England would display the simple announcement: 'Mr A arrives' and thereafter the young man would know no privacy from reporters.

I have carefully considered what you say about Sir John Wood. My own view is that he committed a very gross error of judgment. As the moment of Arthur's appointment, India was full, and England was fuller, of gallant and distinguished officers invalided from the war.

The Political Department should have felt a deep responsibility when sanctioning the appointment of a protector to a Prince so young, so inexperienced and so wealthy. To have sanctioned the appointment at such a moment of a man with a bad military record and disapproved of by the military authorities seems to me in itself to have been a scandalous error of judgment. I agree with your observations that it is easy to be wise after the event; but while making full allowance for this reflection, I cannot acquit those responsible for what they did. At such a time of all others, they should have selected for this position an officer of Field rank who had played his part and exhausted his usefulness in the trenches. I agree with what I understand to be your view that Sir John Wood can hardly remain at Kashmir. But I am not, of course, competent to make any suggestions for substituted employment. I must simply leave the matter in your hands.

The Viceroy's next letter was also dated 22 January, so they must have crossed in the post.

You will remember that in my letter of January 1st I gave you further particulars regarding the permission granted to Captain Arthur to accompany Sir Hari Singh to Europe, and I told you I had asked Sir John Wood for further information. I have just received it. Wood was then Secretary of the Political Department – the head official of the Department of the Government of India concerned – and immediately under the Viceroy. The military reports, according to his view, condemned Arthur as a military officer but did not carry any suggestion of moral delinquency. A military officer of high rank described Arthur as a personal friend whom he had known for several years and apart from considerations of health he knew of no objection to Arthur accompanying Sir Hari Singh to Europe. From letters in existence from Wood to Colonel Bannerman [the British Resident in Kashmir in 1919] and also to the Military Secretary to the Commander-in-Chief, it appears that the facts of the case were fully represented to the then Viceroy. The Viceroy gave the decision, as would ordinarily happen, when the case was brought to him. Wood adds that the Viceroy was personally acquainted with Captain Arthur but of this I know nothing save that it is clear from the papers that the final decision was the Viceroy's and also that the facts as known were fully brought before him by Sir John Wood. Wood expresses his keen regret at the result of the unfortunate selection but urges – and I think correctly – that it was hardly practicable on the information available to form a correct and complete appraisement of Arthur's character. This is certainly true, although it may be still said that unless the recommendations from all quarters were first-rate, Arthur should not have been selected. None could have had the faintest notion of the depravity of Arthur as now exposed. From the military point of view he was a very unsatisfactory officer but, even so, the disposition, especially in 1919, was not to visit too harshly upon men who had fought in the war any unfitness to continue in the Service. I have given you the whole story at length because I wanted your knowledge to be co-equal with mine. I am not disposed to take any further action in the matter, especially as Wood's term of office will naturally expire in a comparatively short period. His duty was to present all the facts to the Viceroy and also no doubt to recommend the course to be adopted. But the decision was the Viceroy's and apparently based upon some personal belief in Arthur.

* * *

In the Oriental and India Office Collection of documents I found the original letters about the choice of ADC, which do not confirm Sir Hari as the wilful and difficult young man the India Office described. At the beginning of January 1919 Sir John had written to Colonel Bannerman about his reservations about Sir Hari's choice of travelling companion. Bannerman took this up with Hari and, surprisingly, the young man listened. He wrote to Bannerman on 1 February 1919:

In view of what you said about the trouble Arthur had got into and as you had left Delhi and the matter was urgent I asked Sir Claude Hill to enquire privately from Army headquarters as to whether they considered Captain Arthur a suitable person to go with me to Europe.

The opinion of the military authorities will appear from the following quotation which I got through Sir Claude Hill: 'I don't consider Captain Arthur a suitable person to go with Sir Hari as personal secretary.' Under the above circumstances and according to your apprehension, I think you will agree that I should get someone else.[21]

If he had stuck to this decision we should be without our story; but something happened to change his mind and happened in a most unexpected quarter. A week later Sir Hari, still in Delhi, wrote to Bannerman:

Since writing my last letter to you dated the 1st February referring to Captain Arthur and my proposed visit to Europe, I have seen Sir John Wood and Sir Claude Hill and have been informed by them that the difficulties in the case of Captain Arthur had been placed before His Excellency the Viceroy, who still considers Arthur a suitable officer to go with me to Europe as my Personal Secretary.

So Sir John had done his duty and Hari Singh had been quite willing to abandon Arthur but was persuaded by the Viceroy that he was the man for the job. What influenced the Viceroy? Sir John Wood had said the Viceroy, Lord Chelmsford, was 'personally acquainted' with Arthur. Charles Chenevix-Trench, son of R. H. Chenevix-Trench, a civil servant in the Government of India, noted in his book *Viceroy's Agent* that Captain Arthur was a distant cousin of the Viceroy's wife. This could be true for she was the Hon. Frances Charlotte Guest, the granddaughter of Colonel Mervyn Doyne Vigors, the Vigors family being one of the landed gentry of Ireland, as was the Arthur family. So could this explain Lord Chelmsford's 'personal belief' in the captain?

So no heads rolled. Sir John had been wrongly accused; it was all the Viceroy's fault.

CHAPTER TEN

The Tea-time Conspiracy

The Mr A plot was hatched over the tea-tables of the West End of London. Tea-time in England then was as sacred a ritual as the two-hour lunch was until very recently in France. Such a genteel occasion seems an incongruous rendezvous for a gang of con artists, but there was a reason. Unlike dinner, when the parlour-maid would be constantly popping in and out with dishes, tea-time offered privacy. The maid would set up a little table in the sitting-room, bring in a three-tiered plate-stand loaded with cucumber sandwiches and dainty pastries and withdraw, leaving her mistress to boil water on a spirit burner to make the tea and her guests to warm muffins on a toasting fork in front of the fire.

I had gleaned a fair amount of information about the Mayfair Mob from reports of the Mr A Case but there were tantalising hints of things that did not come out in court: Newton's mention of informers talking to Scotland Yard in January 1920, for instance, and Sir John Simon asking in court about certain people but never following up the enquiry. I wrote to the Metropolitan Police Archives Office to see if they had any records of the Mr A Case. Unfortunately the files were destroyed during the Second World War – apparently 'recycled for the war effort'. I was getting nowhere when, three months after my initial enquiry, Christine Thomas wrote from the Archives Office to say they had just received a copy of the privately published notes and memoirs of Norman Kendal. Kendal, a grandson of Thomas Kendal, founder of the business that developed into the

Manchester store, Kendal and Milne, was appointed legal adviser to Scotland Yard with the rank of Chief Constable in 1919. Christine had noticed 'quite a large section dealing with the case of the blackmailing of an India Rajah' and thought it might help. Help? It was solid gold: a copy of Newton's original statement made to Chance and Chance, the Midland Bank's solicitors. A couple of weeks later she wrote again, this time to say that a colleague had visited Norman Kendal's family and collected a suitcase full of memorabilia relating to his police service including photographs of the two cheques. What serendipity! As Christine wrote: 'Some cases really do want to be found out and information that has been lost for years just surfaces at the same time as an enquiry is received.'

So here is Newton's statement. It is rather fuller – and more amusing – than his examination in court during the Mr A Case.

Some time in November 1919, Mrs Robinson called me up at Half Moon Street, and asked me to go round and have tea with her at Chapel Street, Belgravia, where she was then living with her husband. I had known the husband Charles Ernest Robinson for some years. I had known of him as a man about town who lived on his wits and his wife's immoral earnings and had a speaking acquaintance with him but had never been engaged in any affair with him. I met Mrs Robinson some little time previously to the date above mentioned – I knew she was an adventuress.

I proceeded to Chapel Street in accordance with the appointment made by Mrs Robinson and met her there alone. She told me that she had met Captain Arthur, the aide de camp to Sir Hari Singh, Rajah of Kashmir and a man of enormous wealth. She told me that Arthur complained of the Rajah's meanness, said that he was sick of his job and that he was keen to get money out of the Rajah; that with this object in view he had suggested that the Rajah should be caught in bed with a woman which would result in his parting with a very large sum of money. I gathered that she had already made the acquaintance of the Rajah posing as a Society lady and after explaining the character of the proposal and intimating that it was suggested that she should play the woman's part she went on to say: 'If I am to play the part of the woman I must have another husband, as Charlie' –meaning her husband – 'looks like a butcher and no one would take him for the husband of a leader of Society.' She went on to say that she thought I looked the part and asked me if I would undertake it. I said 'yes' and she arranged for me to meet Arthur at the house the next day for the purpose of obtaining his approval. She told me that the persons who were interested were Mrs Bevan, who was looking after the Rajah's Native Secretary, Robinson, Arthur and herself, so that I should make the fifth and she suggested that the proceeds should be divided equally.

On the following day I met Mrs Robinson and Captain Arthur at the house in Chapel Street. Arthur looked me up and down and said I would do for the 'husband'. We discussed the scheme. It was thought then that the trap would be sprung at Chapel Street. So far as I was concerned the idea was that Mrs Robinson should go to bed with the Rajah, that I, being on watch and having ascertained the fact, should wait about half an hour and then go into the house. Mrs Robinson would leave the door unlocked and I was to walk in and say: 'This is my wife' and 'I am going to see my Solicitors.' We discussed the division of the plunder. Arthur said that the Rajah had £600,000 in cash in a bank in India and added, 'He (meaning the Rajah) will pay whatever I advise him.' There were five of us in the scheme and whatever was obtained was to be divided equally.

At one interview at this time, I am almost sure it was the interview when I first met Arthur, Mrs Robinson said she was going out with the Rajah that night and asked me if I would dine with her husband that night and discuss the details with him. I agreed and that night I met the Plaintiff, C. E. Robinson, at Chapel Street and dined with him. I explained the scheme in full detail. He had heard of it before from his wife but I posted him with the latest developments. Among the details we discussed his wife sleeping with the Rajah, the amount Arthur expected to be able to get, my impersonating the husband and the division of the spoils. It was agreed that it would probably be best to spring the trap in Chapel Street and he agreed that I should watch the house and have a latchkey so that I might get in for the purpose of carrying out my part. He, Robinson, then gave me the latchkey.

For some time afterwards I saw Mrs Robinson, Robinson and Arthur daily. I used to take tea with Mrs Robinson at Chapel Street; sometimes Arthur came in. I used to wait till Robinson came in about 6.30 or 7.00. Mrs Robinson would go out about 7.30 or 8.00, and leave Robinson and myself together. At these interviews the whole matter was discussed from every angle. Mrs R was posing as a Society lady and thought it desirable to preserve her pose with the Rajah. She told me at an early date in the presence of Robinson that the Rajah was very desirous to sleep with her but that she thought it better to keep him off for a time as the longer he waited the keener he would be.

On various occasions when I took tea with Mrs Robinson, Mrs Bevan was there – sometimes with her daughter. I had been told by Mrs Robinson that Mrs Bevan was with her when she first met the Rajah. I believe that the introduction was effected at an Albert Hall entertainment by Arthur, who had taken care that the Rajah should occupy a box adjacent to that occupied by the women. This information I got from Mrs R.

At a fairly early stage Arthur mentioned Hope-Johnstone to me. He said that he was interested in the man, who came from an old Irish family, but was unfortunately a dope fiend and was then in a nursing home – Arthur told me he had put him into the nursing home, that he was then able to get out a little and asked me if he might bring him to see me one afternoon. I agreed and one afternoon (a Sunday, I believe) Arthur brought Hope-Johnstone to tea at my flat in Half Moon Street. Immediately conversation was opened Hope-Johnstone started raving about the scheme. He suggested that the Rajah should be induced to go to bed with a boy and be photographed in that compromising position. He said he could get a boy for the purpose and explained that his brother owned some journal – the 'Academy' or the 'Studio' or some such name in which cameras were largely used and said he could get a camera and proposed to dash into the room and take a photograph of the Rajah in bed with the boy. I regarded this as the raving of a lunatic and said nothing. There was no talk of shares or of anything else relating to the scheme in his presence. I saw Arthur afterwards who told me that he had taken H. J. into the scheme. I said that in that case I would have nothing further to do with it, as the man was a raving lunatic, and dangerous to everybody. Arthur agreed to drop him but said he would continue to pay his fees at the nursing home. [A surprising expression of kindness from Arthur; was H. J. another invalid from the battle of the Somme?]

I only saw Hope-Johnstone once afterwards – shortly before I left for Paris he met me in Piccadilly – he accosted me saying that he knew the business had come off and demanded his share. I told him to go to hell and he followed me along Piccadilly demanding payment of his share and screaming threats.

At one of the discussions about a fortnight after the matter was first broached to me Arthur insisted that a solicitor must be appointed to act for the husband as immediately the trap was sprung he [Arthur] would probably be instructed by the Rajah to consult a solicitor.

Robinson first told me of this one night at dinner and said that Arthur was coming to Chapel Street that night to discuss it. I said: 'Well, I suppose you know a solicitor.' Robinson said, 'Yes, I have a man Davis who acts for me but he wouldn't go into a scheme like that but you know Hobbs and I know Hobbs, why shouldn't we bring him in?' Arthur came later in the evening and this suggestion was put to him and he agreed and it was arranged that we should get into touch with Hobbs.

The next day (Sunday) I rang up Hobbs at his house in Putney. He told me to meet him at Clarkson's, in Wardour Street where he had some business arising out of a fire. He was busy about the fire when I saw him and I just said that there was a business in which he could make big money concerning an Indian Rajah and gave him an outline of the scheme. He wanted to know who was concerned and when I mentioned Robinson's name he said he had known him for years and had acted for him. 'Of course, you mean Charles Bloomfield, I suppose.' He made an appointment for the next day in Bedford Street.

On the following day I went to Bedford Street, accompanied by Robinson, and saw Hobbs, to whom he gave the full details of the proposal. Hobbs insisted that Robinson must leave the house at once, which Robinson agreed to do. Hobbs said that as I intended to watch the house he would send someone to go with me. It would make it look more regular and would provide corroborative evidence. It was arranged that Hobbs should share equally in the amount obtained from the Rajah.

Robinson left Chapel Street immediately afterwards, i.e. he ceased to sleep there. He, however, still visited the house...

At about the time Hobbs came into the scheme there was another interview either at Chapel Street or Half Moon Street at which Robinson, Mrs R, Arthur, Hobbs and myself were present. Mrs R reported that the Rajah was getting very keen and that the time was coming to bring off the coup. She suggested that the Rajah might want to take her back to Curzon Street. She said that she had been to the house and it might have to take place there. Arthur drew a plan showing the position of the various rooms in Curzon Street and gave me a latchkey. He said that the Rajah's bedroom was at the back and it was arranged that if the drawing-room light was left burning for some specified time after she had entered the house with the Rajah and then went out I was to go in and the plan would show me where the bedroom was.

At this time I was seeing everybody daily and on several occasions dined with Robinson at Chapel Street... Arthur would look in on his way to dinner and have a drink. Once he came in on his way to a fancy dress ball at the Albert Hall in a hunting dress suit. He kept out of the way when Mrs R was about, as he did not think it wise to be seen with her. Sometimes he would knock me up at 2 in the morning.

At this time I commenced to watch at Chapel Street and Curzon Street. I did not watch every night but only on nights when I received a hint from Mrs R that something might happen that night. She would say 'We are dining together tonight and perhaps he will want to take me back to Curzon Street' or 'I will try and bring him back to Chapel Street.' The watching extended over a period of 14 days. I think I watched about three times at Chapel Street and about twice at Curzon Street. I remember that one of the occasions on which I watched was the night of the Beckett-Carpentier fight. Owing to the unexpectedly rapid termination of this affair Mrs R was not in to meet the Rajah and so nothing happened. [It lasted for five seconds. Frenchman Georges Carpentier and Joe Beckett were fighting at the Holborn

Stadium on 4 December for the heavyweight championship of Europe. Carpentier knocked Beckett down with his first blow.][20]

Hobbs sent Rose and Gorringe to assist in the watching. With regard to Rose's statement these are the facts. He came to Half Moon Street one night in a taxi having Gorringe with him. Rose knew me perfectly well having been outdoor clerk to Appleton and Co (who in the person of Hobbs had acted for me for many years) and I had frequently been in their office. The taxi arrived at about midnight. I expected it and got up to meet it being at the time ill with lumbago. I expected Rose but not Gorringe – the former was drunk and so I got Gorringe out of the taxi, and he told me that he had come along to look after Rose who was drunk. Rose got out of the taxi and was evidently drunk. We drove to Chapel Street and stayed there in the taxi until about one o'clock, waiting for a light in the drawing room, which would show me that the Rajah was in the house, and its subsequent extinguishment that would indicate in the absence of the Rajah's departure that they had gone to bed. Nothing happened and in due course we left. Rose was talkative and abusive in his cups, shouting 'Where's that f****** nigger? Produce him. I'll show him' etc. etc. I had great difficulty to keep him quiet. When I left the men I gave them money. The next time I saw Hobbs I asked him what he meant by sending a drunken man whom I had to restrain. He said he would send Gorringe alone in future. I believe Gorringe watched with me afterwards but I forget when or where.

The Rajah did in fact at this time sleep with Mrs Robinson on one or more occasions when I was not on watch. One day when I went to Chapel Street to have tea with Mrs R I found her in tears. I asked her what the trouble was and she said there had been a row with her husband. She explained that the Rajah had insisted upon her shaving her private parts and that she had shaved herself with a safety razor. (This she thought rather fun.) Her husband had been in that day and had discovered what she had done and had made a terrible scene and struck her. She said that R did not object to the Rajah going to bed with her but regarded the shaving as an indignity upon him, and was angry and violent. When I calmed her somewhat, she told me that she was 'quite beginning to like the Rajah as a lover' but that he had a funny way of doing it. When I asked what she meant by that, she said that some people called it unnatural, but that she rather liked 'the back way of making love'.

After I had received my money I had two gold matchboxes made, one with a safety razor done in enamel which I gave to Hobbs, the other with a sirloin of beef in enamel [an allusion to Butcher Robinson] which I gave to Arthur. The boxes were made by Longman and Strongi'th'arm.

I now became tired of the watching. As I have explained I was not in good health and it was not very convenient to be called out of my bed on fruitless quests at midnight and it appeared that Mrs R. could not make arrangements with any certainty. Moreover, the Rajah had certain public functions to perform which brought him into prominence and further Arthur told me that the Rajah and Jung used to go out together and pick up street women insomuch that Arthur deemed it desirable to have him shadowed by detectives for his protection. Furthermore I gathered from Hobbs and [sic] Hope-Johnstone was threatening to make himself unpleasant, that I had been watched and that one of H. J.'s friends had tried to see the Rajah. In view of all these circumstances Arthur came to the conclusion that it would be better to carry out the scheme in Paris where the Rajah and Mrs R could stay at the same hotel secure from annoyance or publicity. This was arranged at a meeting at which Robinson was present. We were still meeting every day.

On the 16th December 1919, I applied for and obtained a passport for France. I knew when the others left and in accordance with a pre-arranged plan I left on the 23rd December for Paris, and went to the Westminster Hotel. With regard to the discrepancy between the hotel books I suggest that I probably arrived on the night of the 23rd when one entry was made and the other was made the following morning. Arthur knew I was coming and either on the day of my arrival or the following day (probably the following day) Arthur came in to see me and on I think the following day which was Christmas Day took me to see Mrs R at the St James and Albany. I saw Mrs R and Mrs B in the private sitting-room at their suite at the St James and Albany Hotel. I remember that the table was littered with the remains of brandy and other liqueurs. The bedroom, which would be occupied by Mrs R and the Rajah was pointed out to me and it was arranged that the affair should be carried out on the following morning. I was to come very early between 6 and 7 and Mrs R said she would leave the door open so that I could walk in. I do not recollect the position of the room quite clearly nor do I remember the number, but the room identified to me as 216 was probably the room although it is a little higher than I thought before seeing the room with Mr Cornwell.

On the morning of the 26th December I paid my visit to the St James and Albany Hotel. I entered the hotel by the Rue de Rivoli entrance very early in the morning – between 6 and 7. I went straight up the staircase and on reaching Mrs R's suite opened the door and walked in. I did not speak to the concierge who took no notice of me. I have lived in Paris for some time and I find that a well-dressed Englishman can go anywhere provided he displays sufficient assurance.

There were two beds in the room. One was unoccupied and unused and the Rajah and Mrs R were in the other. The Rajah said nothing but went green. Mrs R screamed 'My husband. My brute of a husband,' and jumping out of bed pretended to beat, pull and scratch me in so realistic a manner that I was obliged to give her a whispered warning to 'steady on or you'll bust my coat.' The Rajah tried to calm her down saying 'Maudie, after all it is your husband' but she continued to cry out 'You brute. Just the sort of thing you would do' etc, etc. I then said 'Now I have the evidence I want' and turning to the Rajah I said 'I bid you good day, Sir.' He said 'Good day' and I went, Mrs R maintaining her reproaches to the end. As far as I am aware the chambermaid did not see me.

There was a second bedroom on the further side of the sitting room and as I left I caught a glimpse of another female figure in a dressing gown coming through the sitting room – no doubt Mrs Bevan coming to see the fun.

I saw Arthur almost as soon as I got back to the Westminster. He came to know how I got on and I told him what had happened. He said, 'I hope you didn't catch them "rogering", I hope he wasn't going through the back door.' I saw Arthur again at five or six o'clock that day. He told me that the women and he were going back to London that night and that it would be well if I went. He said that he had been all day sitting with the Rajah talking things over, that he had told the Rajah that he mustn't come back to London but must remain in Paris as no subpoena could be served in Paris but that he (Arthur) would go to London to settle the case.

That night, Arthur, the two women and I returned to London. The next day I saw Hobbs and Robinson by appointment, probably arranged with Mrs R en-route to London. Arthur was also present and we told Hobbs and Robinson all that took place. We also discussed the amount to be demanded. Arthur said that everything must be left to him and that we would get as much as possible. We agreed and Arthur went back to Paris. The next day or thereabouts at an interview between Hobbs and Robinson Hobbs discussed with R several things that had happened during our absence. Hobbs told me afterwards what took place. He told Robinson that Lewis and Lewis [solicitors] were on the scene, that Scotland Yard had been informed and were making enquiries and that Hope-Johnstone was writing to the Rajah and going to the India Office. Robinson immediately became alarmed and said, 'There's a stink about this. We shall get nothing and we shall all go to jail. I advise that we don't go on. I am out of it and don't want to hear anything more. If I am asked I don't know anything about it – I am here with you for the bankruptcy business and here is my Power of Attorney for this purpose and if the police come you can show them this and say that I came on this business.'

Robinson came to see me immediately he had left Hobbs and confirmed the whole of the above except about the Power of Attorney. Mrs R commented on some occasion when Robinson was showing the white feather: 'My husband is always the same. In all the business we do my husband likes to take a back seat.'

A day or two after this Arthur returned from Paris with his cheques each for £150,000. He came to Half Moon Street with Hobbs and threw the two cheques on the table and explained that one could be cashed immediately and that the other was undated and the Rajah was arranging to have money sent from India to meet it. He was told of Robinson's attitude and the question of sharing out the £150,000 was discussed. No one was inclined to give Robinson anything but I pointed out that the women must be paid something and that we couldn't pay them without paying Robinson something. Ultimately it was arranged that £125,000 should be divided equally between Arthur, Hobbs and me and the remaining £25,000 should be divided into six parts, and shared between us all equally, Robinson and the women being informed that £25,000 was the total amount recovered from the Rajah. Arthur said he must get a solicitor to act for the Rajah and had telegraphed his Solicitors in Ireland for the name of their agents in London. On the next day, or perhaps it was the same day, Hobbs and I had lunch together. Hobbs said that an account must be opened with the cheque in the name of C. E. Robinson and he proposed that the account should be opened at the London Joint City and Midland Bank, Kingsway. I understood that he had an account at that bank and that Appleton and Co's accounts were kept there. He endeavoured to persuade me to go to the bank and open the account but I refused. We took a taxi to Kingsway and during the whole of the journey Hobbs was endeavouring to persuade me to go and open the account. I still refused and we drove up and down Kingsway while Hobbs endeavoured to persuade me to take the cheque and go into the bank and open the account. I persisted in my refusal and eventually at a few minutes before three Hobbs said with a sigh: 'Well, I suppose I must take it in myself.' He stopped the cab at the Post Office in Kingsway and walked over to the bank. I saw the cheque during this conversation. It was endorsed 'Make payable to the order of C. E. Robinson' or in some similar words and was signed 'Appleton and Co.' There was no other signature on the endorsement.

I saw Hobbs again the next day. He said that he had paid the cheque in and was having it specially cleared and that the money would be available in a few days. At this time I gathered in conversation with Hobbs and Arthur that they had told Robinson that there was a chance of getting £20,000 from the Rajah but no more. Hobbs said that Robinson scoffed at it as ridiculous and ultimately the offer was increased to £25,000 and

Robinson expressed his willingness to take his share of that sum. I saw nothing of the women after my return from Paris.

Between the date that the cheque was paid into the bank and the 7th January, I saw Hobbs every day for the purpose of ascertaining the position as regards the cheque that had been paid in and for taking my share as soon as possible. The cheque was cashed a few days after it was paid in (I take it as the 6th January from the bank's solicitors.)

The day or second day afterwards I went to Paris with Hobbs who took with him the notes he had obtained from the bank. Hobbs's idea was to open an account in Paris for himself, Arthur and myself. I was unwilling but as the others agreed, I fell in. We arrived in Paris on the 8th January. This date I take from the hotel book. The negotiations with the Anglo-South American Bank were carried out by Hobbs alone. My share (some £40,000 – the exact amount will be obtained upon inspection of my account with the Westminster Bank in Paris) was paid to me in bondes de defence that Hobbs obtained and with which he either opened a security account with the Anglo-South American in my name or arranged for the bank to hold the bonds in my name. I left the bonds with the Anglo-South American Bank for a short time when I got them and put them into the Westminster Bank at Paris. In about October 1920, I closed the account at the Westminster Bank and transferred it back again to the Anglo-South American Bank. I returned to London on the 12th January. I take this date from the information given to me as to the contents of the book at the Westminster Hotel. The 12th would be about the date. A few days after our return there was a meeting at Bedford Street at which were present Hobbs, Arthur, Robinson, Mrs Robinson and myself, Mrs Bevan being absent. Hobbs produced £21,000 in notes of various denominations, and divided it between the rest of us, having already paid himself £4,000. Mrs Bevan's share was handed to Mr Robinson. I heard that the second cheque had been stopped. I do not recollect very clearly when, but Arthur told me one night when he was drunk and he said that he had stopped it or had induced the Rajah to stop it.

Some months after this Hobbs saw me about the second cheque and suggested that it might be collected in India. He arranged for me to get a passport in the name of Robinson and I filled up a form applying for a passport for India in the name of Charles Frederick Robinson, which Hobbs put through. An account was opened in the name of Robinson at Lloyd's Bank, St James's Street, with £500, which I subsequently withdrew. I do not know if this passport was ever issued, as I have never seen it. I went to India under my own name with my own passport and from the time I left England to my return I never had any other name but my own. I went out to meet the Rajah at the Calcutta races. I got into touch with Arthur but before anything could be done Arthur saw me one day and told me that the Rajah's wife had died and that he had gone back to his house for the mourning which would last two months during which he could not be approached. I thereupon gave up the quest and returned home. I did not go to Kashmir and I did not see the Rajah. The only time I ever saw the Rajah was on the 26th December 1919 at the Hotel St James and Albany in the circumstances above mentioned.[22]

So Maudie and Charlie Robinson might have been cheated out of their full share of the £150,000 but they also cheated the loyal Lyllian Bevan out of her full share and she had to wait months before Maudie gave her the £2,500.

George Granville Hope-Johnstone, the 'dope fiend', was almost certainly Percy J. Smith's informant and Percy was right when he suspected the tipster who told him about the 'swell mobsmen' who fleeced the Indian potentate of £300,000 was acting out of revenge for not being included in the scheme as, according to Monty Newton, Arthur had wanted. As Monty said, Hope-Johnstone came from a grand old Irish family but he had fallen on hard times. He was working as a bookmaker in London when he was bankrupted in 1914 owing £6,500. He blamed his downfall on having to pay £500 in settlement of a claim brought against him by a lady for slander, false imprisonment and money lent. No wonder Judge Darling called him a blackguard.

Once the case was over Monty Newton sold his life story to *The People* newspaper in twelve long episodes. It was the story of a global crook's tour. He had been round the world three times and cheated at cards in Moscow, China, Peru, Germany, Italy, Canada, the United States, Mexico and Australia. He had crossed South America and southern Africa on horseback; always accompanied by a man he called Count Leo. Newton said he changed all the names for his newspaper articles but I am certain Count Leo was Lemoine, who was mentioned in the Mr A Case. Newton normally called him the Baron von Koenig, the title he had used for twenty years. As recounted later in greater detail, Newton and Lemoine were partners in crime for twenty-five years before the Mr A Case came up; although he was in the wings during the drama of the fleecing of Hari Singh, he was not part of the plot.

Was Newton telling the truth? It seems so. His story tallies with passport office records and with hotel registers in Paris. The bank's tracing of the banknotes to the members of the gang matches his account of the share of the spoils, his account of the shaving proves that Maudie confided in him. He did not turn King's Evidence for the money as he made his statement to the bank's solicitors in October 1923, long before they had decided it was imperative for him to give evidence in person and offered him £3,000 to come to London.

CHAPTER ELEVEN

The Truth Comes Out

Here, put together from Newton's writing, depositions (statements to the magistrates which were not produced in court) and files in the National Archives and in the Oriental and Indian Office Collection, is the story of what really happened at Christmas 1919. It shows that what came out in court was a fraction of what actually went on. It also shows how desperate the British Government was to keep the whole business secret, for many files in the National Archives were ordered to be kept closed for eighty or a hundred years instead of the usual thirty.

Monty Newton explained how he had carried off his role in catching Maudie and Sir Hari together with such aplomb. 'I have schooled my emotions rigidly as long as I can remember. I have cultivated self-control in just the same way that a businessman cultivates a good memory for facts and figures. I have learned to play poker with the world. Poker is a game where a man who displays his emotions must lose against players who do not betray their feelings by the slightest twitch of facial muscle or even by the most quickly passed and instantly repressed gleam of interest or excitement,' he wrote in his memoirs.[23]

The Mr A coup? 'It called for much less resource and self-control than has been necessary on many occasions in themselves much less important. But as regards my own emotions and feelings I may as well say at once that I had none. I had in front of me a beastly job which had to be done and I just carried it out according to plan.'

Captain Arthur was just the opposite. He was Newton's first visitor when he checked into the Westminster Hotel in Paris on 23 December 1919. 'Arthur is certainly not a man who has schooled his emotions in the least. He was almost trembling with excitement.' Arthur took Newton over to the St James and Albany Hotel to show him Maud and Lyllian's suite. It was furnished in what he called 'loud hotel luxury'. 'I had an impression of mirrors and a good deal of gilt furniture. Several empty glasses stood on one of the tables and it seemed to me that someone must have been trying to get up a little Dutch courage. Arthur suggested that I should take a dose of the same but I refused the invitation. I hold no pussyfoot ideas but I have always found that on occasions like this, when one has to have all one's wits about one, it is fatal to take artificial stimulants. Getting to work with a clear head is half the battle.'

After viewing the suite Newton took himself off for a brisk walk, along the Rue de Rivoli, across the Place de la Concorde and the length of the Champs Elysees to the Arc de Triomphe, enjoying the bright lights and the Christmas crowds. After that there was an excellent dinner, another stroll and a good night's sleep before his 5 am call. After giving Maudie and Sir Hari *their* wake-up call he returned to his hotel for his *café complet* at his usual time.

Arthur came round to see him a little later in such a state of excitement that he had to take a couple of aspirins before he could pull himself together enough to ask Newton how things had gone. Arthur returned in the afternoon to say he and the women were returning to London that night and Newton should go with them. He had advised the Rajah to stay in Paris while he settled everything in London.

We know Captain Arthur suffered psychologically as a result of the horrors of the battle of the Somme but by the time of the sting his mental health had taken a remarkable turn for the better. He was transformed from a nervy insomniac unable to think straight to a man with immense concentration and nerve, for he was at the very centre of the plot and he came very close to discovery, as we shall see.

Sir Hari moved from the St James and Albany Hotel back to the Brighton immediately after the Maudie debacle and wrote to his bank, Boulton Brothers, from there on 26 December to say he had given Captain Arthur two signed blank cheques which he had instructions to fill in. After his conference in London on 27 December with Newton and Hobbs, Arthur returned to Paris briefly where the cheques were filled in by one of Sir Hari's staff. Writing from Sir Hari's house in Curzon Street to Sir Hari's bank in London on 30 December, he told them that the cheques had been filled in for £150,000 each and asked them to visit Sir Hari in Paris to arrange transfer of funds from India for the second cheque.[24]

Sir Hari received a telegram from Arthur on New Year's Eve: 'Settlement agreed to other difficulties have arisen. Am leaving for Paris tomorrow please send car meet me quarter to six.'[25]

Captain Arthur had overestimated Sir Hari's riches and the cheque had bounced when Hobbs presented it. Sir Hari was short of money in his London account, having bought £240,000 of French government bonds on 19 December. There was now less than £6,000 in his account. The bank requested that Captain Arthur ask Appleton and Co., Hobbs's firm, to whom the cheque was made out, to wait for a couple of days before presenting it and they wrote to Sir Hari on the same day, 30 December, care of Claridges, Paris, where he was by then staying, pointing out with due deference and discretion that:

> We have today received a letter from Captain Arthur enclosing a letter from yourself, with regard to the question of two cheques of £150,000 each. We think perhaps you are under some misapprehension with regard to the funds at your disposal here, as we received instructions from you dated the 19th December to pay for fcs.[francs] 6,000,000 (nominal £240,000 French Government 5% Bonds) which we have undertaken with Messrs Hope Pollack and Co. to do on your behalf. The balance, therefore, at your disposal, will be absorbed.
>
> We have advised Captain Arthur in your interests to request Messrs Appleton and Co. to hold the cheque before presentation, pending arrangements with you which you may wish to make.
>
> After interviewing Captain Arthur we understand that it would be your desire to remit funds from India in a similar way which

you did before, and we therefore enclose you three letters of instructions for your signature, which if you will kindly let us have by return, the matter will have our immediate attention. On receipt of these instructions we will cable to India.

Your Highness will understand that to regularise the position it is necessary for us to have the enclosed instructions signed by yourself, so as to place your account in funds at this end.[26]

Happy as the love-struck young prince was on Christmas Day, Sir Hari had a miserable New Year. On 1 January he wrote to his bank, Messrs Boulton Bros and Co:

With reference to my cheque in favour of Messrs Appleton and Co., for pounds one hundred and fifty thousand on which you have deferred payment in view of my current account with you not being in funds, I shall be glad if you could kindly arrange to meet this cheque immediately on the security of my Bonds which Messrs Hope Pollock and Co. are purchasing for me, as the matter is very urgent.[There was a postscript]: On my return to London I would like to go into the question of my financial affairs here. I hear that Mr. William Boulton is leaving for India about the same time as myself and I shall be glad if he will have time in India to look into the question of my finances there and put them on a sound business footing.[27]

Then he wrote to his friend, Charles Arthur:

My gross yearly income is £90,000 (please note this does not represent the net income.) My expenditure totals about £70,000 on running the estate and my personal and family expenses, leaving me only a net profit of £20,000 a year.

The securities left me by my late father are Trust Securities and I have the use of the income only. The income from the securities is included in the total gross income stated above of £90,000. The original capital, failing my leaving an heir, reverts to the State at my death. This will show you that it is impossible for me to touch any of my capital, except that which I have saved (from my income) since the death of my father.

As mentioned above my savings are about £20,000 a year and I have been in possession ten years. My total savings amount, therefore, to somewhere about £200,000. You know I have spent over £55,000 from these savings on this trip leaving me with a balance of £145,000; therefore, on the fact of these figures you will realise the absolute impossibility of my being able to meet any greater amount than £150,000 and even this payment will necessitate my borrowing from the bankers.

In view of these facts I presume the matter in question will be looked at from a more reasonable point of view and a settlement agreed at accordingly. You know I am only too anxious to make any reparations for the unfortunate occurrence and in this settlement I am doing all that is in my power.[28]

Lieutenant the Hon. Frederick Hayworth Cripps, a partner in Boulton Bros. arrived in Paris the next day to have a heart-to-heart with the prince. The bank wrote to Appleton's on 3 January saying they could now present the cheque that was endorsed 'Pay to the order of Mr C Robinson, Appleton and Co.'[29]

Hobbs took it to the bank in Kingsway on 6 January (after the taxi ride Newton described so hilariously in his statement) with a letter from Appleton's asking for an account to be opened in the name of C. Robinson, plus a sample signature. The letter was not signed by a member of the firm, but bore the name of one Miss Maud Bligh.

Maudie's New Year was no better than her lover's. She had taken against the Chapel Street house and decamped to the grand Adelphi Hotel in Liverpool on New Year's Eve; perhaps it was because she had fallen foul of the servants who came with the house. As the parlour maid, Nelly Cadney, said in court, she remembered opening the door to Newton many times, she remembered that Robinson moved out of the house at the beginning of December, not September as he had said in court, and sometimes he returned to sleep there. She said that when Mrs Robinson and Mrs Bevan returned from Paris they seemed to have money. Mrs Robinson had very many more clothes than when she went away and her husband had more suits. In a deposition she made to magistrates before Hobbs's trial, which followed the Mr A case, she remembered a visitor called Joe Radcliffe who came to stay for a week in October; he slept in the spare room next to the one she and Rebecca Witte, the cook, shared. Mr Robinson was in the house and slept in the dressing room. Mrs Robinson said Mr Radcliffe was her cousin.

> During the whole time Mr Radcliffe was at the house Mrs Robinson stayed in bed till the afternoon. She said she was not well but I saw no trace of illness. Mr Radcliffe used to go and sit in her bedroom most of the day from the time he got up until she got up. In the evenings he sometimes used to take her to dinner. I don't know whether Robinson went, too. I never went to the bedroom except when rung for or with meals or a letter and on these occasions I used to see Radcliffe in the room. On other occasions I saw him going there. Radcliffe was a man of about thirty-five years and appeared to be possessed of means. Radcliffe used to sleep in his bed for some part of each night but I don't know what he did after we went to bed. He could have got into Mrs Robinson's room without going through Robinson's room, the dressing room. Mrs Robinson called Mr Radcliffe Joe. He called her Maudie.

When Mr Robinson visited the house for clean clothes she had to let him in which was odd, because there were four keys: one for each of the Robinsons, and one that she and the cook shared, plus a spare one. When the tenancy ended one of the keys was missing.

Miss Witte showed more curiosity, stating in her deposition: 'From the luggage labels I ascertained that his name was Everard Joseph Radcliffe and his address was Rudding Park, Knaresborough and on looking up Who's Who I found he was the son of Sir Joseph Edward Radcliffe.'[30]

In another farcical touch typical of this story, Nelly Cadney revealed that Mrs Robinson could not get into the house on 27 December when she returned from Paris because she had not taken her front door key and there was nobody in the house. In the excitement she had forgotten she had given the servants the four-day Christmas holiday off. She returned to the house on the 28th and slept there.

* * *

By the middle of January Sir Hari and his entourage were back in London and staying at the Carlton Hotel, which was in Pall Mall. Sir Hari and Arthur visited his solicitor, Mark Waters, on the 14th and shocked him by saying they had settled the matter. On the 16th Waters wrote to Sir Hari saying he had been making enquiries about the people he had been dealing with and 'the result is very disquieting.'

He had, in fact, been to see another solicitor, a Mr Poole, of Lewis and Lewis, who had told him something about a Captain Simmonds. Mr Waters advised Sir Hari to stop the second cheque – and the first if it was not too late. In fact, he was so worried that as soon as this letter was posted, he rushed to the Carlton Hotel and wrote out another one saying exactly the same thing and asking to see Sir Hari the following day to explain further. When Sir Hari heard Mr Waters's story he asked him to arrange to have the Robinsons watched by a private detective; he also arranged to have a former police sergeant on duty in the hotel lobby, to keep away unwanted visitors. Arthur was not present at this meeting but Mr Waters wrote to him saying that the detective, a man named Arrow, was anxious to have complete descriptions of the Robinsons and Mrs Bevan as well as their addresses. Captain Simmonds – Mr Waters did not identify him any further – went to see Mr Waters on 22 January and told him the whole story, saying that Captain Arthur was in the swindle but Waters could not believe anything bad of the charming Irishman.

'I had no suspicion at the time of Captain Arthur nor any suspicions of Mr Hobbs based on what I had been told,' he said. He even told Arthur that he had heard rumours of a conspiracy and asked him to pass this on to Sir Hari.

Here was Arthur at his coolest, for the success of the plot depended on him and he was close to discovery. But he was the spy in the enemy's camp, knowing what Sir Hari and Mr Waters were planning and able to influence their plans to his own advantage. He was betraying both Sir Hari and the Robinsons. He used his charm to get Captain Simmonds to retract his accusation and apologise. He wrote to tell Waters about it:

I had a letter which I enclose you from Simmons yesterday, he came to the Carlton last night to see me; he started to apologise to me for having, through being misled, brought my name into the matter; he then handed me all his documents, suggesting that the Raja would like to make him a present, he required money to get out of London as he was in fear of being assaulted. I returned him his papers telling him they were of no interest to the Raja and as he suggested taking them to Scotland Yard I agreed that it was quite the best thing to do. Will you please send the Raja all the papers you have, c/o Cook and Son, Piccadilly branch will always find us. When I return in March I hope to see you. The Raja wishes me to convey his thanks to you for all your kindness. Yours sincerely, C. Arthur.

Waters wrote back saying that Simmonds seemed to have been doing a bit of blackmail of his own.[31]

Meanwhile, Mr Waters had telephoned Hobbs about the second cheque; he felt it was a nasty weapon in the hands of a blackmailer and wanted to get it back. Hobbs said he would destroy the cheque if Waters would bring Captain Arthur with him to identify it. He also said that Robinson had complained of being shadowed; Mr Arrow was clearly a clumsy operator. On 30 January Mr Waters took Arthur to see Hobbs and both assured him that any shadowing of Robinson did not come from their side. Here was Arthur at his very best. Hobbs produced a cheque, Arthur purported to identify it, going through the motion of comparing its number with a number on a piece of paper he held and said: 'Yes, that is the cheque.' Mr Waters said he saw the cheque passed from hand to hand and saw the signature on it. Arthur handed it back to Hobbs who then tore it into fragments and threw the pieces into the fire. But it was a dummy; Hobbs had locked the real cheque in his safe, with a view to blackmailing Sir Hari again as soon as Mr Waters was out of the way. As insurance, Newton later had the cheque photographed.

Arthur had bluffed and charmed his way out of a very tricky situation and returned to France with Sir Hari the next day, sending a telegram to Waters from Dover to tell him to stop all enquiries as the matter was to be regarded as definitely closed. Arthur had clearly reassured Sir Hari on the train to Dover that the whole thing was better forgotten. He sent a letter from Paris confirming this on 3 February. Captain Arthur had got rid of Waters, now he had to find a way of getting rid of Maudie Robinson. An idea came to him in Paris.

In spite of the expense of Mr Robinson, Sir Hari loitered in Paris as his ship was not due to leave Marseille until 28 March. He splurged on jewels and was in Nice on Valentine's Day, the day Maudie said they planned to meet. The women kept the rendezvous and the evening found both parties at the casino. A member of the entourage, signing himself VJ, probably Mahboob Jung, Lyllian's special friend, wrote to Mark Waters to tell him what happened then:

> They attempted to come up to us but having ladies in our party, I suppose they thought better of it. Leaving the casino we went on to a restaurant for supper and there I received a letter from Mrs Bevan asking me to see her, in the same note was a line to Hari from Mrs Robinson making the same request. This letter I returned with no answer. Later on, a telephone message came asking me to speak over the phone. This was also ignored.
>
> On return to the hotel another phone message awaited us to talk that was similarly refused. The next morning Hari received a note from Mrs Robinson. I enclose the letter, the contents of which I will not repeat again.
>
> The ladies were staying at the Hotel de Paris, Monte Carlo, and had come over to Nice on the 14th. They stayed over at Nice the 14th night and the 15th at the Westminster hoping, I suppose to meet us. On Monday 16th Captain Arthur saw the Chief of Police at Nice and explained that these two ladies were causing annoyance to Hari Singh, and asked if he could assist in any way to prevent their continuing to do so. The Chief of Police promised to look into the matter. I enclose a second letter received by Hari Singh from Mrs Robinson. It was from this letter we learnt of the ladies having been requested to leave.
>
> Hari Singh thought it advisable for you to have this information and I am to request you to kindly favour me with your opinion in the matters. Yours sincerely, V. J. [32]

Poor Maudie, St Valentine, the patron saint of lovers, had not looked kindly on her. Sir Hari either regrets his brief fling with

Maud or realises that he has been the victim of a sting but he still has no idea that Arthur is double-crossing him. Nor has Waters; he wrote back to Jung: 'I think Captain Arthur did the best thing possible in turning on the police and I am glad to note the result.'

Mark Waters also made a deposition to a magistrate four years later, before Hobbs's trial, which was a pretty damning reflection of his gullibility and of Captain Arthur's audacity: I got nothing useful out of Simmonds at any time. I didn't think he had any precise information. He told me that Captain Arthur was in the swindle.'

CHAPTER TWELVE

Arthur's Travels

Charles Arthur did not return to Kashmir after the sting and set about spending £44,000, the equivalent of around a million pounds today, with singularity of purpose. He travelled constantly between London, Paris, Vienna, India, the Far East, and Australia. He was in Calcutta in August or September of 1920 to meet Newton when he arrived to try to collect money from Sir Hari on the second cheque, even though it had been cancelled.

Arthur told Newton that Sir Hari would probably be at the races the next day and it would be as well for him to be glimpsed by Sir Hari, who would presumably be alarmed at his reappearance and Captain Arthur would then talk to Sir Hari about what to do. But when the day dawned Arthur told him Sir Hari's wife had died suddenly and he had returned 'up country for the usual religious rites'. In fact, Sir Hari's wife did not die until 3 December 1920 in Jammu; he sent a telegram to the Viceroy the next day to tell him of his loss. Was Sir Hari really in Calcutta in the summer? Was the story of the wife's untimely death a way for Arthur to get rid of Monty Newton, as he had got rid of Mark Waters and Maudie Robinson? Arthur still had the second cheque, although it had been cancelled, which he had handed to Monty, who inspected it and gave it back. Arthur was so sure that Sir Hari would pay up that he bought Monty Newton's share of the cheque for the knockdown price of £17,000 and Newton returned to London within the week.

Arthur was back in Paris in February 1921, when his wife's writ for the return of conjugal rights was served on him. He ignored this, and as we have seen in chapter 4, in May Monty Newton burst into another hotel room, this time at the Metropole in Folkestone, to find Arthur in bed with a woman not his wife, and provide evidence for a divorce.

Monty did not have a very good memory for dates. In one of his several depositions he said that Lemoine went to India about July 1922 'or it may have been in 1921. I think it would be in 1921' to see what could be done about getting a little more money. He added that Lemoine was the man also called Stallman who had been 'released' by his government to go to India. In one account he said he travelled out with Lemoine, in another he said Lemoine was there 'considerably' before him.

'Lemoine went out to India to lend a hand in getting money on the second cheque. He was going to assist Arthur whose position was difficult. Arthur wanted to get the second cheque met and at the same time he had to appear to assist the Rajah.'

Monty said he stayed for about three weeks this time and travelled back to Europe with Lemoine. Perhaps this is true and Lemoine made a return trip to India, for he was there in October 1921 when Charles Arthur took him to Kashmir – there was talk of him getting a job as adviser to the Rajah. While in Srinagar they carried out a nasty scam on a carpet dealer – the town was an important centre for carpet dealing, particularly antique Persian rugs. Arthur took Lemoine to the shop of Haj Mohamed Jan and Son on 10 October and bought a number of carpets, cashmere shawls and embroideries from Bokhara. He chose the best goods and struck a hard bargain, insisting on a ten per cent discount. Mr Jan agreed only because he had known Arthur for a long time. He did not usually accept cheques on foreign banks, insisting on cash but, again because Arthur had introduced this extremely good customer, he accepted two cheques amounting to £750. Lemoine watched while the carpets were packed according to his precise instructions and the couple left for Bombay and the Taj Mahal hotel, the smartest place in town, right at the Gateway to India where the liners tied up.

This is where, a few weeks later, on 17 November, the Prince of Wales was to arrive on HMS *Renown* – the very warship that Sir Hari was shown over in Portsmouth Harbour during his visit to London – for a four-month visit to India, worried about the reaction of Mahatma Gandhi to his arrival. Gandhi had ordered members of his radical Congress Party to strike on the day of the prince's arrival and to stay indoors as a protest. The thought of being greeted by empty streets was too awful for the usually popular prince. There *were* some crowds and there *were* some disturbances, riots and street fighting, although Gandhi did his best to stop the troubles. After three days in Bombay and Poona, the prince set off on 20 November with his retinue of at least a hundred Europeans and Indians, including Maharajahs and Rajahs. They were transported in three trains: one for the prince, personal staff, servants and luggage, one for the Press and a travelling post office, and one for the landaus and the horses to draw them for his State entries into the cities he was to visit. There were also twenty-five polo ponies lent by the Indian princes. Even the Prince of Wales was impressed. He visited Kashmir where Sir Hari greeted him wearing a diamond replica of the Prince of Wales's feathers in his turban.

Arthur and Lemoine's visit to Kashmir in 1921 means that Sir Hari still did not know that Arthur had been part of the conspiracy or he would not have been allowed into the state. After the couple returned to Bombay with the carpets, Arthur sent Lemoine back to Kashmir on 19 October with a letter to Mahboob. Arthur was still after money from Sir Hari and had concocted a story that Robinson was making threats of some sort and needed to be paid off.

At my particular request, the Baron, the bearer of this, goes right through from Delhi to see you, on a matter of urgent and vital important [sic] to us all, he is absolutely reliable and discreet and will explain everything to you verbally, you can absolutely rely on his discretion and he maybe of very great service.

Needless to say I will do anything I can to be of assistance but if R carries out his intentions there will be a terrible scandal. Therefore in my own interest I am leaving for Europe by the Ching next Saturday to place the whole matter before the India Office.

I sincerely hope all will be well. C. Arthur.

Arthur had the name of his ship wrong; it was the SS *China* and it left Bombay on Sunday 22 October 1921 and arrived at Marseille on 5 November. On the same day Lemoine wrote to Mr Jan from the Taj Mahal hotel about the carpets which he said Arthur had taken back to Europe for him. He complained that Arthur had sent a cable saying that when he unpacked them he found they had got wet on the voyage because they had been packed badly; the colours had run and the carpets had many repairs and patches and were not worth half the money paid so he was cancelling the cheques. The goods would be returned at once by Arthur who was at the Westminster hotel in Paris and would deal with the whole thing 'as I shall not be back in Europe for some time'. Mr Jan replied that antique carpets usually had to be repaired and that the carpets had been packed according to Lemoine's instructions. Arthur wrote another of his strangely spelled letters: 'The Barrow Lemoine refuses to take delivery of the carpets. Kindly let me know the name of your agents there so that I can hand them over to him. I am astonished that you could have treated anyone is such a disgraceful manner.'

The carpets were never returned; poor Mr Jan's bank charged him £70 for the cancelled cheques and officialdom refused to help him. He wrote to the British Resident in Kashmir, who wrote to the French Consul General in Calcutta, who referred him to the British Ambassador in Paris. They decided nothing could be done by the Indian Government over a commercial transaction gone wrong.[33]

Arthur spent Christmas in London, writing from the Windham Club on 27 December to Mahboob saying his wife had an inoperable cancer and she was having radium treatment. He asked how Sir Hari's horses had done. He was back at the Westminster hotel in Paris on 8 January 1922 when he wrote to Mark Waters saying he was coming to London for a few days to see him and that he wanted to return as soon as possible to Austria because of his wife's worsening illness. Who is this wife? Rose Violet was granted a decree nisi on 21 June 1921 and would get her final decree on 16 June 1922 so it was not she.

The story he told Mark Waters when he visited him at his Lincoln's Inn Fields office on 12 January 1922 showed that he was still desperately trying to raise money. He told Waters that

Robinson had again approached the Rajah and demanded payment of the second £150,000 cheque and that Arthur had secured a number of papers including the unpaid cheque. Waters reminded Arthur that they had both seen the cheque destroyed by Hobbs in 1920 and that he had received a letter from Hobbs signed by Robinson saying that the matter was closed between him and the Rajah. Arthur told him the second cheque was at that time in transit between his bank and the Rajah's in London. This must have been when he asked Waters for £20,000 for the documents but, by then, the cheque was in the post.

A couple of days later he wrote to Mahboob telling him of his visit to Waters and saying he was surprised that Mahboob had not written to him:

In November Robinson saw me in Paris and demanded my immediate return East with him, which I refused. And then stipulated that as a condition of my going that I should have possession of all documents. This was eventually arranged on the condition that I paid to him as a guarantee, a million francs, equal for £20,000. I got the papers into my possession on November 28th and the following day I handed them in a sealed envelope to the custody of the Anglo-South American bank, requesting them to forward them to the Bank of Bengal for you. I enclose you their letter. The papers consist of cheque, statement of affairs and letters. When I heard the matter would be taken up in London I instructed the bank to wire for their return to be handed to your agents here.

I don't see what can happen now as we have the papers. I am completely puzzled by the whole affair. I go back to Vienna next Wednesday or Thursday, Will be in London I expect next month. Send me a line there.

Hope you are both going strong.

Yours, C. Arthur.

A fantastical story and he wasn't finished. He had another go at raising money a couple of months later, this time from Monty Newton. He sued him for various sums of money lent between June 1920 and November 1921 amounting to £17,300. Monty

Newton retaliated by listing money he had spent on Arthur: 'Gold matchbox with enamelled design – £37.10s'.(This was the after-sting present, one of the matchboxes mentioned in the secret questions in the Mr A Case, enamelled with the design of a sirloin of beef, an allusion to Butcher Robinson.) 'A gold watch and chain, bought for Arthur at his request – £80. Loans in Paris amounting to £59.10s'.

He added that Arthur had given him twenty thousand French francs (about £400 then) in Paris to give to the husband of a Mrs Schmid, a German woman whom Arthur was taking to India as his wife. (Was this the sick wife he was writing about?) The husband would not let her go unless the money was forthcoming. And there was a cheque for twenty-five thousand francs given to him by Arthur to cash – the proceeds were to be given to Lemoine to pay for his visit to India.

Newton denied that the money Arthur had given him was a loan but was, in fact, what he had paid him for his share of the second cheque and the fact that the cheque was never paid was not Newton's fault. Arthur dared not go into court to tell the truth about the £17,300 and he was content to settle out of court for £1,000.

On 20 May 1922 Waters went to the London branch of the Alliance Bank of Simla and received a packet which contained, among other things, the second cheque for £150,000. Arthur's story was all lies, of course, for Robinson knew nothing of the first £150,000, let alone the second, until July 1923 when Arthur told him and he immediately went to his solicitor. And the solicitor, Hyam Davies, testified in the Mr A Case that he did not hear of the second cheque until April 1924, from either Newton or Lemoine in Paris.

A year later and Captain Arthur made another attempt to get money. He wrote to Sir Hari from the Windham Club on 31 May 1923:

My dear Sir Hari,
I have just got back to this country from South Africa where, you will be sorry to hear, I have lost my wife.
I only heard the other day when I was lunching with the Maharajah of Khaputaba that Mahboob was no longer with you,

which I take it explains why I have never had any replies to my letters to him about the Robinson affair. They probably never had been passed to you.

It is now over a year and a half since my wife paid on your behalf the sum of £20,000 to recover your cheque, the papers and save you with parting with a much larger sum of money, as you then wanted to do. And that amount has not yet been returned to me. So will you please do so and write me here, to the Windham on receipt of this.

I have seen a lot of Col. Winctham the last week and heard all the Kashmir news. I hope to get out for next Winter and see Kashmir again.

Best of luck,

Yours,

C. Arthur

By now Sir Hari would surely have heard about Arthur and Lemoine's swindling of Mr Jan, the carpet man in 1921, because Srinagar is a very small, gossipy place, Arthur was well-known and known to be a friend of the Rajah. An understandably cold letter was sent back, registered and dated 30 July 1923:

Dear Captain Arthur,

Sir Hari Singh has asked me to reply to your letter dated the 31st of May, 1923. I am to say that he has no knowledge of the alleged payment made on his behalf. Perhaps you can furnish me with a copy of his written authority.

I am,

Yours truly,

Chief Secretary[34]

By this time, of course, Arthur had been to Robinson and started the course of action that would lead to the Mr A Case and Mark Waters would have told Sir Hari that he had received the cheque from Charles Arthur. Having thrown the cat among the pigeons in London, Arthur managed to scrape enough money together to continue travelling. His reply to the Chief Secretary was from Borneo and dated 18 March 1924, saying Sir Hari's letter of

30 July 1923 had only just reached him in Java as he had been travelling continuously and would be going on to Sydney.

* * *

At first all went well for Monty Newton and his stock market trading in sugar futures; his £44,000 became £100,000 by the beginning of 1924. He wanted to sell. 'I pictured to myself the glorious future that was being opened out for me,' he said. 'I had in mind a life free from the worries and cares of having to do the best I could for myself,' a self-pitying lament from someone who had spent his life cheating others. His stockbroker, also into sugar, advised against selling.

Charles Arthur had come back into Monty's life in July 1923, telling him of Hobbs's extortionate rate of interest on the £15 he had loaned him. 'Arthur was a fool – and Hobbs was greedy. I could write a whole volume dealing with the follies of Arthur and another volume on the avarice and cupidity of Hobbs,' he wrote. He was in Paris when, a month later, he had an urgent call from Hobbs to visit him in London; there he learned that Robinson was suing Hobbs for the return of £125,000, the balance of the Rajah's £150,000.

'I flew over to London next morning, hoping that if he met me at Croydon [airport] we could spend a couple of hours together and I could catch the afternoon aeroplane back to Paris. But this was not to be. Hobbs was in such a state that my presence in London appeared to be absolutely necessary so I stayed with him, caught the night boat back to Paris to adjust my own affairs and was back again with Hobbs within twenty-four hours.' Newton advised Hobbs to come to a settlement with Robinson. Hobbs finally agreed but expected it to be paid with Newton's money. What's more, he demanded that Newton gave *him* the money and said he would hand it over. Naturally Newton would not agree to this but he went on flying between London and Paris, trying to sort things out – after all, he had known Hobbs for twenty years. Then Hobbs turned against him and swore an affidavit that he knew Newton as Robinson and that Newton had been the one to sign all the documents and cheques. That was the end for Monty and when Robinson finally abandoned his attempt to get money out of Hobbs and decided to sue the Midland Bank instead, Newton agreed to make a statement, which he did on 19 June 1924.

Then disaster struck: sugar prices fell and Monty lost all his money. He asked his bank manager, 'How much have I got left?' The answer was less than £500 out of £100,000. How he wished he had sold at the beginning of the year. And how useful was the £3,000 that the Midland Bank offered him to come to London to give his evidence.

* * *

By November 1924, while the Mr A Case was going on, Charles Arthur was working for the travel agent in the Champs Elysees, Paris, where he was seen every day in the company of a tall, elegant woman, according to the *News of the World*. The paper added that the American newspapers said Arthur had been engaged in bootlegging there without much success.

Even after his arrest on 1 December and while he was on remand in prison, Arthur refused to accept that his friendship with Sir Hari was over. He wrote to him from prison in March 1925, after Detective Inspector Helden and Detective Sergeant Percy J. Smith had failed to get him extradited to England, appealing for help:

Now that the extradition has been refused I am writing to ask you to come to my assistance. Up to now you have only had the opportunity of hearing things to my detriment so you do not realise that in the whole matter I have been just as much a victim as yourself. At the hearing of the bank case I, for grave reasons of State, was prevented from appearing. The fact of my appearing would have disclosed your identity. I never anticipated that an English judge would take advantage of my absence and heap blame upon my shoulders. The Crown also withheld certain facts, which would have materially altered the aspect of the case in my favour. Therefore, in view of the unfair treatment I was subjected to, including my Irish nationality being brought into question, I could not expect fair play at the hands of the English so I decided to protest against the demand for my extradition and to seek the protection of the French courts, where I would be certain of having a fair and unprejudiced hearing, enabling me to clear my name.

He went on to write he could prove that not one penny of the money was used for his own personal use; that he was forced to open a bank account and accept the transfer of money to incriminate himself and under threats to expose the lady he hoped to make his wife 'whom you know' when she obtained her divorce. He believed he had witnessed the destruction of the second cheque and only became aware of its existence the following January when, to his astonishment, it was shown to him. The letter went on:

> So you will realise that I had an impossible task to protect you, whose interest you know I have always had at heart and, at the same time, protect the lady – my intended wife – who has since suffered cruelly. As you yourself will readily admit, had certain relationships not been hidden from me, disaster would never have occurred. You, against your better judgment, allowed yourself to be influenced by others. I therefore request you to help me to clear my name, which you can do by a personal letter to one of my lawyers informing him that you have had, and will have, entire confidence in me.[35]

Sir Hari did not reply to the letter so Charles Arthur came up with a new line of attack: a month after his arrest he sent a woman friend to India – not the one he had mentioned in his letter to Sir Hari, for this one was not married, let alone awaiting a divorce; she was Peggy McCutcheon. Scotland Yard and the India Office knew about her and were alert to certain suspicions about the lady but not very efficient at dealing with her. Lord Birkenhead sent a telegram to the Viceroy on 9 January 1924: 'Secret. Miss McCutcheon is reported to be leaving for India and may have left Marseille in S.S. Naldera on 2nd January. She is connected with Newton and the Hari Singh case. Suggest surveillance. Letter follows.' He sent another telegram on 15th that explains things:

> Margaret McCutcheon is a close friend possibly mistress of Captain Arthur who is involved with Newton in endeavours to obtain payment of second £150,000. She has travelled extensively

in British, French and Belgian colonies, and Americans regard her with suspicion. Scotland Yard desire copy of her passport photograph and suggest careful customs examination of all papers in her possession and if possible her own person.

Is this the tall, elegant woman Captain Arthur had been seen with in Paris just before his arrest or yet another of his harem? Margaret 'Peggy' McCutcheon, 38, was born in Kansas City. In 1923 and 1924 she travelled extensively, visiting Monaco, Italy, Greece, French colonies, Spain, Capetown, London, Addis Ababa, the Belgian Congo, Denmark, and Sweden.

Soon a note of caution crept into the government gossip. Colonel S. B. A. Patterson, Political Secretary in the Indian Government, wrote to Sir John Wood, by now the Resident Officer in Kashmir, that the government had no definite information that Miss McCutcheon was out to blackmail Sir Hari Singh, was connected with Newton, Hobbs and Co or that she had any intention of visiting Kashmir: 'Her movements are being closely watched and you will be supplied with information regarding these and with means for her identification.'

There was another secret telegram from Lord Birkenhead to the Viceroy of India dated 10 March 1925 saying: 'Newton sold his share of second cheque to Arthur and Miss McCutcheon who met A and became his mistress about a year ago and now endeavours to visit Kashmir. She was not implicated in the original case but her present journey can obviously be regarded as endeavour on the part of Arthur to communicate with Kashmir.'

Telegrams are not easy to understand because of the lack of punctuation. If you put a full stop after 'Arthur' and delete the following word, 'and' as well as the 'and' following 'ago' it reads: 'Newton sold his share of the second cheque to Arthur. Miss McCutcheon, who met A and became his mistress about a year ago, now endeavours to visit Kashmir...' it makes more sense, for Newton sold his share of the second cheque to Arthur in 1920, not 1924 as is suggested here.

Peggy McCutcheon and her travelling companion, Mabel Cook, made a fine tour, visiting Rangoon and Sri Lanka before arriving in Delhi, where they were asked to see Col. Patterson, the Political Secretary. On 14 March he jotted down a triumphant memo:

We now appear to have something really definite about Miss McCutcheon and it looks as if she is out to try and get her share of the second cheque. I think it would be best if, on arrival at Delhi, she were asked to come and see me. I could then tell her that friends of Captain Arthur are not welcome in Kashmir, that the Kashmir Darbar have asked that she should be required not to enter that state; and that the Government of India strongly advise her not to do so as if she did enter her position would undoubtedly be extremely uncomfortable. I think that when she sees the game is up she would probably retrace her steps. I may add that I understood that Sir Hari Singh will shortly proceed to the C.P. [central provinces] where he has a block in the Chanda district for tiger shooting.

The women went to see Patterson who reported:

I asked Miss McCutcheon if it was her intention to visit Kashmir. She replied that it was. I informed her that in that case it would save her time, trouble and expense to know that Kashmir Darbar had asked that she be required not to enter the state. She asked me why. I replied because the Darbar understood that she was a friend of Captain Arthur's and that friends of Captain Arthur were not welcome in Kashmir. She then replied that she was not a friend of Captain Arthur and that she had influential connections in England and America who would prove this. I told her that I was conveying to her the message of the Kashmir Darbar, and I strongly urged her to accept their advice. Miss McCutcheon asked whether I was acting on behalf of the Government of India and I said that I was. She said that she had a letter of introduction to the Viceroy. I made no comment.

She asked who was the head of the Government of India to whom she could reply and I said: 'Lord Birkenhead'. On that she replied: 'That fellow. He is no use. No wonder such things happen.' She was gradually losing temper while I was extremely polite. She asked if I knew Captain Arthur and I said I did not.

She said:' If you did, I don't think you would associate me with him and as a southern American no one would certainly associate me with that nigger Hari Singh.' I think she said 'damn nigger' but I am not quite certain on that point. I said I had nothing to do with the matter and was only conveying a message to her from the Kashmir Darbar, which I again strongly advised her to accept. She asked me what the Kashmir Darbar meant. I said: 'The Government of Kashmir' and explained that Kashmir was not part of British India. She said: 'Oh, black men, I suppose.' She asked me what the Kashmir Darbar would do if she entered the State. I said: 'They would act on their own discretion in the matter.' She then gave a long list of names of American ambassadors and senators in various parts of the world, to whom she would apply, and told me that the world would ring if any ill treatment were accorded to her in Kashmir. I replied that I could only repeat the advice that I had given her. She told me that she intended to go to Kashmir. At this point she quite lost her temper. I let her rage a bit and she left the room uttering abuse of 'your rotten government'. She struck me as an extremely second-rate woman. Miss Cook appeared to be of a higher class.

Peggy McCutcheon knew when she was beaten and on 4 April 1925 she left Bombay for Marseille on board the SS *City of Simla*.[36]

CHAPTER THIRTEEN

The Evil Genius of the West End

While Peggy McCutcheon was cavorting round India, William Cooper Hobbs was on trial in London. There were huge queues to get into court. He faced six charges, four of which the Judge threw out. Newton was again the star and spent five hours in the witness box, cross-examined by Hobbs's lawyer. Then he sat in the body of the court, his hands clasped round his knees, his buffed nails catching the court lights. He charmed Mr Justice Avory who said: 'Many hard things have been said about Newton and I don't say they are too hard. It is fair to him to say, however, that he has this one merit, namely that he does not pretend to be what he is not. It is so much easier to deal with a rogue who admits that he is a rogue than it is to deal with a hypocrite who cloaks his sins under an affectation of honesty.'

Hobbs denied everything and insisted that he knew Newton as Robinson and believed he had been acting for the real husband. This was a lie because he had known Charlie Robinson for years. The Judge asked: 'If he really believed that Newton was Robinson, why did he not hand over the cheque for £150,000 and say "here is your money?"'

The jury found Hobbs guilty of unlawfully obtaining the two cheques and conspiring to cheat and defraud Sir Hari Singh and he was sentenced to two years' imprisonment with hard labour.

Next day the newspapers were full of background pieces about Hobbs and his forty-year career of crime; forty years without arrest or charge, remember. They called him 'The Attorney of the

Underworld' and 'The Evil Genius of the West End'. There were stories of his activities: how he sold shares in non-existent oil fields, financed burglaries, cheated a duke's son. It seems likely the papers were briefed by the same person, perhaps Chief Inspector Helden or Detective Sergeant Percy J. Smith, who had both given evidence. Maybe they were even given a typewritten handout to copy, for some of the stories were identical, word for word. Percy J. Smith's books about his career as a policeman contain much of the same material. Percy's resume of Hobbs's life and crimes is irresistible:

Hobbs was sixty when he was convicted and for forty years he had been playing fast and loose with the law. He was not a solicitor but for twenty years he had made a rich living organising the defence of villains. When any big man in the criminal world was in trouble he would call for Hobbs and he briefed top lawyers on their behalf. The moment the police heard that his firm, Appleton and Co., was acting for the defence they were on the lookout for some trick, which would result in the prisoner being acquitted. Yet they could never pin anything on him. It was said that no crime or fraud was too small for him, reared as he was in the 'avaricious atmosphere of a pettifogging lawyer's office where clients could be diddled out of only a few shillings.' 'He retained all his life an ineradicable habit of always trying to swindle people even if it was only for half a crown,' wrote one reporter. He would even cheat his fellow criminals. He was known to be extremely thrifty, not to say mean, and in the end it was his meanness and his greed that was his biggest mistake and led to his downfall.

He was ruthless and powerful and used to boast about the way that racecourse toughs looked after him. 'I am better guarded than the Prime Minister,' he would say. An insurance broker in the city who made enquiries about Hobbs was startled when a stranger walked into his office and suggested that his health would not suffer if he abandoned the enquiries. The insurance broker telephoned a contact in Whitehall who told him he would be running a serious risk if he pursued the enquiries. There was another story about how, in the early 1920s, Hobbs offered to have the Public Prosecutor's office burgled to get hold of the papers in a sensational prosecution to be launched against a notorious criminal.

Hobbs's parents were honest people, living in Battersea; his father was a barge owner with his own wharf. Hobbs's first job was with a firm of accountants in Smithfield where he was a debt collector and, in spite of the fact that he could only have been in his teens, a legal adviser. When the firm discovered that Hobbs had developed an out-of-hours sideline, he was asked to leave. He had become an early 'ambulance chaser'. He rented a one-roomed office in Waterloo, bought an armful of newspapers every morning, and dredged them for news of road accidents – this was in the early days of motoring and many were the unwary pedestrians knocked down by inexperienced drivers. Hobbs would go to the hospital where the victim lay and get his name and address, either from a nurse or a porter. He would then approach the family and say: 'Sue' and offer to act for them. He would make a claim for compensation and maybe an award of £100 would be made. Hobbs would tell his victim that costs and expenses would take all but £10 or £20. He managed to get £300 compensation in one case, charged £250 as costs and demanded his own fee from the remaining £50. He saved every penny he could and after several years he was able to invest in a money-lending business with offices in a street off the Strand. The owner of the business, Alexander Cahill and Co., was a man named Dodds who was not in good health. Hobbs, the junior partner, had such a forceful character that he was able to bully his employer into parting with his share of the business. Hobbs became the employer and put Dodds on a salary and when the man died in 1895, he was penniless. Hobbs was not without a partner for long. Travelling by train into the city every day from his cottage at Wandsworth Common, he struck up a conversation with Charles Frederick Appleton, a solicitor and after a while persuaded Appleton to enter into a partnership with him, renting an office in Wellington Street, off the Strand, and each taking six guineas (£6.60) a week salary. Mr Appleton was a blameless man but weak and lacking in energy and Hobbs appears to have continued the ambulance-chasing business at Appleton's on a no-win, no-fee basis and a fifty-fifty share of the winnings if they were in luck.

He was brilliant an unearthing 'witnesses' of accidents and it was said he used to have rehearsals where all the participants were coached in what they were to say when the insurance company began to investigate. When the time came to share the damages, Hobbs would call the client into the office and divide the money into halves on the table in front of him. 'Now,' he would say, 'here is your half and here is ours.' Then he would go on to say how it had been a most unprofitable job for the firm; heavy costs had been incurred, and the firm would probably be out-of-pocket on the job. So it was only fair for him to claw back some of the client's money. The business flourished and in 1898 they were able to move to a bigger office in Tavistock Street, and later to Portugal House in Portugal Street, all offices within a few steps of the Royal Courts of Justice.

After Appleton died in 1917 the business was sold to another solicitor, Charles Thomas Wilkinson, and Hobbs continued as managing clerk. According to the news reports, he 'financed burglaries, he received stolen property; he also created his own passport office for criminals who needed to get out of the country quickly.'

A large part of Hobbs's fortune came through his dealings with cardsharps. They would rent a smart house in Mayfair from its titled owner and invite young men with 'expectations' to join card games. Illegal gambling dens were a regular feature of London life after the First World War; fifteen or twenty people would be greeted by a liveried butler, served supper by white-gloved servants and then quickly cheated out of more than they could pay. This is where Hobbs, acting as a solicitor's clerk, stepped in. He would go to the rich father or uncle, threaten legal action and get the money. Out of a payment of £3,000, Hobbs would collect £1,000.

This was a trick Hobbs regularly got up to with Monty Newton and it seems likely that before Maudie and Sir Hari left for Paris, Sir Hari had been subjected to some crooked card games at Chapel Street. An article in *The People* of 7 December 1924; written by 'an Englishwoman who knows him' said that Sir Hari was believed to have lost a considerable sum at cards while in Britain.

Hobbs ran his money-lending business from a pokey little office in Bedford Street – there was no smart brass plate on the door. Opposite the office was a bar called the Bodega where he would hold court each evening and there the Australian conmen he dealt with so often would join him – they liked to boast to one another about their exploits.

When Hobbs's partner, Charles Appleton, died on 9 April 1917, Hobbs heard about it by means of a black-edged letter from the widow the following day. What did he do, telephone the grieving widow? Send her a telegram of condolence, as was the custom of the day? Jump into a taxi and call upon her? None of these. He rushed round to Mr Appleton's bank to cash a cheque for £256 6s, signed by the dead man. The signature was all right but the amount had been doctored. It later turned out that some days before his death Mr Appleton had given Hobbs a pay cheque for £6 and six shillings and when he heard of Appleton's death he had altered it. When the bank manager went to Appleton's office after the cheque had been cashed there was a big row when a comparison of cheque and stub showed what Hobbs had done and Mrs Appleton threatened to go to the police, but Hobbs escaped by producing a typewritten letter supposed to have been signed by Appleton saying he was indebted to Hobbs for the sum of £250.

In his will Appleton gave instructions that the business be sold and half the proceeds paid to Hobbs. He said the best price he could get was £300 from solicitor Charles Thomas Wilkinson. Mrs Appleton got £150 and Hobbs carried on as chief clerk.

Hobbs and his family were upwardly mobile. Once he had a splendid house backing on to Barnes Common in south-west London, then another at 18 Larpent Avenue, Putney, where he was living at the time of the Mr A case. Then he went to Upper Richmond Road and on to Richmond Hill. In 1924, he moved to a big house at Ditton Hill, Surbiton, where he lived in some style, surrounded by antiques. He bought a car to take him to his offices in Covent Garden.

Hobbs had learned the knack of compartmentalising his life. There were three parts. At home he was a quiet family man, enjoying a game of bowls on a Saturday afternoon. His wife knew little or nothing of his criminal activities and his colleagues were not encouraged to visit him at home. During the day he was the suave solicitor's clerk with a skill in writing up large bills of expenses for clients. In the evening he took himself off to his money-lending office in Bedford Street where he conducted the criminal side of his life, in the office and in the Bodega opposite, consorting with the highest and lowest in the land – dukes and conmen, rich men and thieves (though the beggar man and poor man were given short shrift).

In his weaker moments Hobbs had admitted that the two judges he dreaded most were Lord Justice Darling and Mr Justice Avory. Although not called by either side as a witness in the Mr A case, Hobbs had made statements to the court presided over by Lord Darling and, when charged with conspiracy in the blackmailing of Sir Hari Singh, he had Mr Justice Avory sitting in judgment on him and still his luck held. He had told friends he expected at least seven years' penal servitude but he got away with two years' hard labour and still he appealed. The appeal failed.

Once out of prison Hobbs sought revenge against the newspapers. He brought twenty-three libel actions; most were settled out of court and only two of the papers defended themselves. In one, Hobbs was awarded a farthing damages and in the other Hobbs's lawyer flounced out of the court after a dispute with the Judge; the jury had been sworn, thirty witnesses were waiting, so it was necessary to take a verdict and the Judge directed the jury to return a verdict in favour of the newspaper.

* * *

Three times Arthur applied for provisional release from the French prison on the grounds of ill-health but his appeals were rejected and he finally came to trial on 6 November 1925. The Judge had in front of him a pile of documents eighteen inches high from which he drew a letter from Violet Rose Arthur, Hobbs's ex-wife, who had so forgotten the past that she had written to testify to the esteem she had for the accused and explaining that she divorced him in order to put an end to his extravagance and safeguard his property and that of her son. His extravagance *had* ended by now, for the court was told that only 1,888 francs (about £18 at the time) remained in his account at the Anglo-South American bank. His junior counsel, Maitre Trobriant, offered an explanation for his criminal activities when he asked for extenuating circumstances to be considered: Arthur's father and two of his aunts had been shut up in lunatic asylums, Arthur was shell-shocked during the Battle of the Somme and had become a drug addict. He read out testimonials to his good character from the colonel under whom he served in the South African campaign when he was seventeen, as well as from his solicitor, and an Irish vet.

The Judge, recalling the facts of the case, said it arose out of what could only be called the greatest blackmail case of the century, both by its amount and by the audacity with which it was perpetrated. It had all the elements of a 'cinematographic film' in which no element was lacking: 'the love interest: Mrs Robinson, the money interest: the Rajah, a veritable prince of the Arabian Nights, the black gang; the whole being connected in various episodes'. Arthur was found guilty on 12 November 1925 and sentenced to thirteen months' imprisonment and a fine of 500 francs (about £5 at the time.) As he had been in prison for eleven months he was released on the 23rd. He immediately applied for a passport, giving his London address as 105 Piccadilly, a splendid block of flats overlooking Green Park. He then applied for an Austrian visa, giving his address as 14, Rue de la Paix, Paris.

Arthur was removed from the army list on 15 January 1926 on the grounds of his conviction, but his luck held and he charmed yet another woman, a rich Irish widow, Sybil Hardy. They were married on 13 April 1926; after which he embarked on another debt-wracked career.

CHAPTER FOURTEEN

Epilogue

When Hobbs was arrested at Gravesend on 28 November 1924 he and his companion had first class tickets for the crossing to Holland and he was carrying £1,250 in various currencies, given to him by Willy Clarkson who had organised his escape from the court at the end of the Mr A Case. Willy was generous, up to a point; after Hobbs's arrest he applied to the magistrates' court for the return of his money. Clarkson was afraid of Hobbs, who had blackmailed him, according to his sister. It was easy to blackmail a homosexual in those days. Clarkson died at the age of 74 of a brain haemorrhage on 13 October 1934. The insurance companies who had been investigating the many fires at his various premises finally sued his estate in March 1937 for the return of some of the money they had paid out to him on what they claimed were fraudulent terms. Ten insurance companies and nearly 600 Lloyd's underwriters, whose names filled six-and-a half pages on the writ, were involved. The insurance companies won their case. Hobbs did not appear in court nor was his name mentioned but the Judge, Mr Justice Goddard, who had been King's Counsel and Sir John Simon's junior during the Mr A Case thirteen years before, no doubt remembered Newton telling Sir John that he had been to see Hobbs on a Sunday in November, at Clarkson's in Wardour Street 'where he was busy with a fire that had taken place there'.

Hobbs was charged on 19 November 1938 with forging Willy Clarkson's will in his own favour and was sentenced at the Old Bailey to five years' penal servitude. His accomplice, a crooked solicitor, got seven years. Hobbs was released on licence in July 1941 and went back to his old haunts around Covent Garden. He had chronic bronchitis, asthma and arthritis and was often in bed for long periods; but his brain was alert and his memory good. He had become something of a hero to the younger generation of crooks and continued to guide them in their escapes from the law. He continued to threaten newspapers, authors and publishers if they even thought of writing about him. He lived until he was eighty.

* * *

Robinson, deprived of his loot from Sir Hari, went back to his favourite criminal game after the Mr A Case; the infallible betting system. This was a trick that required great patience and a generous budget, as it could take two or three months to set up and involved staying in grand hotels and eating in expensive restaurants. This is how it works: a 'steerer' and a partner, usually an elegant woman, would check into a smart hotel and act like gentlefolk while they identified a likely pigeon. They would make friends, go about together, and drink at the bar. There was no rush. Days or weeks later a third member of the team, the 'trimmer', would appear as if by accident and pass himself off as a slight acquaintance of the first two. He's a racing man, knows lots of jockeys and trainers and always has a good tip. He also has an infallible betting system: all you have to do is give the steerer £1,000 to put on a horse at, say, 20-1, some good time before a race, wait until the odds have shortened to 5-1, then hedge the bet by accepting a wager for £2,000. So you stand to win £10,000 if the horse comes in first or £1,000 if it loses. It never failed to catch the gullible and the greedy. In fact, Percy J. Smith recalled a famous King's Counsel who had prosecuted many conmen losing £1,000 in this way. Of course, the money was never placed, there were never any winnings, excuses were made but often the victim would place several bets with his good friends before realising that something was wrong. Usually the victim was too embarrassed to report the scam to the police but Robinson's luck ran out when a Scottish businessman complained to Glasgow police. They called in Percy J. Smith who showed them his photo album filled with pictures of tricksters and he soon identified Robinson and his accomplice, Edward Cavendish.

Their trial in the High Court in Glasgow was another that aroused scandalised interest. The bet was for £2,000, an enormous sum. Robinson and Cavendish were each given a three-year sentence, Robinson's first and he was shocked to hear it.

After his release Charlie Robinson and Maudie went to the US where Charlie continued his criminal career. He was charged with obtaining £50,000 by confidence tricks and sentenced to eight years. Maudie was not charged but she was deported. When he was released in 1945 he returned to Maudie and they went to live at 421, Highbury Place, a rooming house in Islington. She was with him on 23 February 1946 when he collapsed and died of a coronary thrombosis. He was seventy-two and his occupation on the death certificate was given as commission agent. Maudie, at fifty-nine, was alone and stayed at Highbury Place until 1951. Butcher Robinson did not leave a will; he always said he kept the minimum in his bank account so that his creditors could not claim their dues and I think it is likely that he kept anything he had under the bed, although by the time he was seventy-two, having spent several non-earning years in prison, I do not suppose there was much.

In the summer of 1925 Monty, perhaps sick of his notoriety, perhaps aware that his name was too well known for him to continue his card-sharping career, changed his name to Norreys. A smart sub-editor at the *Daily Mail* headed the story *Mr Norreys changes names*. Monty told the paper he had done it for entirely personal reasons, which were of no public interest. C. E. Bechhofer Roberts, who in 1950 wrote the foreword to an edited account of the Mr A Case trial, said that Monty retired abroad and lived happily, if dishonestly until 'a couple of years ago,' which would have made him eighty.

Charles Arthur also changed his name, taking the first name of Macfarlane. By this time his ancestral home, Glanomera House, was in ruins. The estate was being administered by the Land Commission, which decided to collect some long-overdue rents from the tenants. The sheriff and a detachment of the civil guard were sent to collect. They were met by a crowd of villagers who assumed such a threatening attitude that they decided it was wiser to retreat. They returned with a detachment of troops and were met by another angry crowd, this time armed with pitchforks. Some of the tenants agreed to pay a year's rent on account of their arrears and promised further instalments but no sooner had the sheriff left than they decided to make a return visit as difficult as possible: they cut down the biggest trees on the land and dropped them across the lanes and made all the bridges impassable.

Despite being thrown out of the army in 1926, Arthur continued to use the rank of Captain and embarked upon a treasure-hunting career. There were rumours of millions of pounds' worth of treasure stolen by pirates from Peruvian churches by pirates being hidden on Coco Island, which belongs to Costa Rica. Since the beginning of the century there had been so many expeditions, with treasure-hunters dynamiting any cliff or rock which looked a likely hiding place, that the Costa Rican government sent a corps of police with each expedition to keep order.

The new Mrs Arthur owned a motor yacht, *Our Western Queen*, and in the autumn of 1932 they set sail for Costa Rica. As usual with Arthur, nothing was straightforward; they slipped out of Fowey in Cornwall in the middle of the night, owing money. They put into Gibraltar and left quickly, again owing money. They arrived at Puntarenas, Costa Rica, at the end of the year. Unfortunately, on the way Arthur had dumped three of the West Indian crew in the Panama Canal Zone, who had to be repatriated to their homes by the Canal Zone authorities.

The Arthurs returned to England, resolved to make a better-organised attempt at the treasure. With his distant cousin, Dick Studdert, Arthur set up a company called Treasure Recovery Ltd, with himself as controller of operations, Dick as managing director and Mr E. N. Ellers-Hankey as chairman. They set sail for Coco Island in 1934, an expedition which was not successful except socially: the President of the United States, Franklin D. Roosevelt, on a fishing holiday, paid a visit to Coco Island in the SS *Houston*. Hearing that the President was interested in the progress of the treasure hunt, Dick Studdert visited the ship to present his compliments and was given a forty-five-minute audience with the President, at the end of which he was presented with a signed photograph inscribed: 'To Mr R. D. Studdert with my regards, Franklin D. Rooseveldt. At Cocos Island 10th October 1934'. (He used the original spelling of his name.)

Perhaps Captain Arthur went on board with Dick Studdert: just imagine the fury of the Foreign Office if they discovered Arthur had charmed his way into an audience with the US President. Sir John Simon, the lawyer who unmasked the blackmail plot against Sir Hari, was by now Foreign Secretary and was receiving accounts of Arthur's latest misdeeds with some alarm, for they were damaging Britain's prestige in the region.

Then Arthur committed a great *faux pas* by planting the Union flag on the island, to the anger of the Costa Rican government who sent the army to expel them and then sent Arthur a bill for the cost. There was another attempt the following year but the Costa Rican government refused to let the expedition proceed with Arthur on board, so he and his wife set sail for England on 30 May 1935. A year later, the company went bankrupt, leaving a trail of unpaid bills. Their ship and all their equipment were impounded; the crew was stranded on the island and the Foreign Office had to pick up the tab for repatriating them. A minute by W. D. Allen of the Foreign Office, dated 19 May 1936, on learning of the company's bankruptcy said:

> This is perhaps the only outcome to be expected but it is nevertheless a disgraceful affair... The company have been a perpetual nuisance both to the Foreign Office and to His Majesty's representatives in Panama and Costa Rica ... their internal squabbles have been a continual source of embarrassment to His Majesty's representatives and can have done little to enhance British prestige in the Canal Zone and Costa Rica.

Charles Arthur's entry in Burke's Landed Gentry of Ireland says that he died in 1934 but he was certainly alive in May 1935 and the police were making enquiries about him in 1938, suspecting him of fraud in connection with Treasure Recovery Ltd, but the trail has gone cold; his descendants don't know where or when he died.

* * *

Sir Hari Singh succeeded his uncle on 23 September 1925, ten months after the furore of the Mr A Case, married for the fourth time in 1928 and continued to spend money. He built himself a fine new white stucco palace just outside Srinagar, overlooking Dal Lake. In spite of the modern, low lines of the palace, he lived a feudal court life with his fourth wife, Tari Devi, a simple country girl from a remote village in Punjab.

Sir Hari was to represent the Indian princes at a Round Table conference in London in 1931 but he preferred the spring sunshine of the south of France to the drizzle of London, so he took an entire floor of the Martinez Hotel in Cannes and commuted to London when necessary. His only child, Karan, was born there on 9 March. They stayed in Cannes for six weeks; some said it was to keep mother and son away from the politics of the *zenana*, the women's house, where dozens of Maharanis, ladies-in-waiting and maids lived.

Writing in his autobiography, *Heir Apparent*, at the tender age of twenty-three, Karan Singh said his father was formal, stern and severe, with few friends. He described him as neat, meticulous and aloof, with normal conversation in his presence impossible. He felt his father's forbidding exterior was protective armour he had developed through the circumstances of his own life. 'Brought up in the cloak-and-dagger atmosphere of court and family intrigue, he must have been through a traumatic situation before he grew to manhood. And soon thereafter, on his first visit to England, he became the unfortunate victim of a vicious blackmail plot that brought him a great deal of undeserved censure.'

Karan Singh was brought up in what his father thought of as English style, apart from his parents. He lived in a house of his own from the age of three with British guardians and fifteen servants. He saw his mother for an hour each day and his father three times a week. Two companions came to live with him when he was four but the boys weren't allowed Indian food and sweets. The parents were deeply incompatible; she was warm and gregarious and loved children, so the life Sir Hari imposed must have been hard for her to bear. She was deeply religious, while Sir Hari was a virtual agnostic. Surprisingly, Karan Singh grew up normal and talented and pursued a career in politics and literature, serving as Indian ambassador to the United States from 1989 until 1991.

Maharajah Sir Hari Singh proved to be a tyrannical ruler of a state existing under a vicious system of taxation. He lived in a sumptuous style that was in striking contrast to the desperate poverty of his subjects. He owned a squadron of aircraft, one finished in pure silver, a string of racehorses, and dozens of cars. From early in his reign there were protests and revolts against his regime. With the approach of independence for India in 1947 came the question of what should happen to Kashmir, which was not part of British India. Should it become part of India, which was nominally secular but largely Hindu, or should it become part of the new Muslim state of Pakistan? It had borders with both. The second would be the logical choice as the population of Kashmir was 85 per cent Muslim and the state's communications with the rest of the world lay through Pakistan that depended for its agriculture on the waters of the rivers Indus, Jhelum and Chenab, which flowed through Kashmir. The rivers were essential for Kashmir, too, for timber, the major export, was floated downstream to the port of Karachi. The ruler was to decide but was to take into consideration the wishes of his people. But the Maharajah would not decide. He still had not decided by Independence Day, 15 August 1947. Agitations began in September, sometimes started by Muslims, sometimes by Hindus, followed by a major incursion of Pathan tribesmen from the North West Frontier Province, and believed by all to be supported by Pakistan. Sir Hari appealed to India for help and this was given on condition that the state acceded to India. Lord Mountbatten, by now the Governor General of India, told Sir Hari that the policy was that the question of accession should be decided in accordance with the wishes of the people and that his government wished that as soon as law and order was restored and the invaders driven out, there should be a referendum. Civil war followed. The people never had their referendum; they continued to rail against the Maharajah who was forced to abdicate in 1949 and his son, the twenty-two-year-old Karan, was appointed Regent. When Kashmir became a republic in 1952 he was elected Sadr-i-Riyaset, President, and remained so until 1965 when he became Governor. He resigned this post in 1967 and was elected an MP and became in the same year, at the age of thirty-six, the youngest person to become a Cabinet Minister in India.

From 1949, Sir Hari had been spending the six summer months in Srinagar, where his son attended the Presentation Convent School, run by Irish nuns, then there were two months in Jammu and four in Bombay, where he bought a block of flats and occupied the one on the top floor. A lower floor was assigned to Karan. Sir Hari continued to visit Europe and was a member of Winston Churchill's war cabinet and was in London during the blitz. He maintained the interest in racing horses that was sparked on his first fateful visit to Europe and his scarlet and gold colours were a familiar sight at the Bombay racecourse, for he was for many years the leading owner in Bombay. After leaving Kashmir in 1949 he lived permanently in Bombay, bitter, resentful and feeling he had been treated unjustly. He separated from his wife the following year. He was diabetic, had lost weight and was unable to walk but he was still driven to his stables every day. He had a heart attack in 1962 and died at the age of sixty-six.

I met Dr Karan Singh in Srinagar in June 1989, just as the current skirmishes were starting in the never-ending struggle for Kashmir. It was the day after he had reclaimed forty-two items of the fabled family jewels that his father had put into the custody of the state treasury in 1947. He had not seen them since he was a teenager and thought they might have been sold but they were found in 1983, and he put in a claim for them. There were about 500 pieces, valued at around £3,000,000; the original estimate of £100,000,000 was grossly exaggerated, he said. Dr Singh told me he might display some of the jewellery in his museum in Jammu but this has not happened. They remain under lock and key in a bank. A sad end to the story of the last Maharajah of Kashmir.

PART TWO

The Worldwide Adventures of Newton and Lemoine

CHAPTER FIFTEEN

Rascals

The first I heard of the man called Lemoine, he was in Kashmir, India and it was 1921. Kashmir was about as remote as you could get in those days; high up in the Himalayas, getting there involved a voyage to Bombay, two days by train to Rawal Pindi then another two days by car to cover the two hundred miles to Srinagar. I was researching the story of Maud, the Rajah and the Mayfair Mob just told. Monty Newton, the man who pretended to be the wronged husband, said in court that in 1921 he was visiting India where he met Lemoine. Lemoine was hoping to get a job as adviser to the Rajah who surely needed advice, since Monty was planning to get another fourteen million from him.

From the way Monty talked, this sounded like their first meeting but when the blackmail case came to court in 1925 Lemoine – he was never given a first name – though not part of the mob, was backstage. He was mentioned several times in court and on the front page of *The Daily News*, next to the account of the arrest in Paris of Captain Charles Arthur, the ringleader of the blackmail plot, there were some fascinating titbits: the French police were 'hot on the trail of an alleged swindler on a gigantic scale who is of French nationality and who was mentioned in the recent London bank case. An arrest is declared to be imminent and is expected to cause a great sensation.' A few days later the paper's Paris correspondent revealed that the Frenchman for whom a warrant was said to have been issued 'is known as the Baron. His real name is reported to be Lemoine.' Another paper was expecting details of an 'extraordinary game of poker in which three prominent figures in the Mr A Case were concerned, the other participants being professional gamblers. The game was played at a Paris hotel and the huge sum of £30,000 was lost by one player'; thirty thousand pounds would be about a million and a half today. It is true that Captain Arthur complained that he had lost a lot of money in Paris.

There was another interesting little snippet in *The People*, saying that the police wanted to get in touch with a famous card-sharper, well-known in London and European capitals, who was missing from his customary haunts. 'He is known to have become friendly with some of Mr A's acquaintance and early in 1920 he won huge sums from them at cards' Is this another reference to Lemoine?

When Monty Newton was asked about Lemoine at the Mr A Case hearing at the Central Court of Justice in the Strand in 1925 he said he had many names, worked for a foreign government and was, he thought, German. I was intrigued; my journalist's nose told me there was a story here but how to get at it? I could not get the man out of my mind. Then I came across some diplomatic documents from the Government of India,[1] which showed that in April 1911 the Royal Prussian Ministry of Justice was seeking to extradite a German subject named Rudolf Stallmann, alias Baron von Koenig, alias Korff-Koenig, alias Kerner, to face charges of forgery and cheating committed in Berlin and Wiesbaden the previous year. The police told the victims that von Koenig had been known to them for years as a card sharp. Is this Baron von Koenig the swindler the French newspapers were to name in 1925 as Lemoine?

Slowly I traced Lemoine back from the Rajah's palace in Kashmir in 1921 to a German prison cell in 1899, and forward to death in a French military hospital in 1946. I found the titles he collected, from King of Card-Sharps in Germany, to the Most Important Spy Recruiter of France, then to the Enemy Number One of Nazi Germany, finally the Spy of the Century.

This is not the first time he has been written about. Marcel Proust did; Lucien Rebater, a Nazi writer, produced a best-seller about him during the German occupation of France. There are many stories about this man, many exaggerated, many just gossip. I will keep to the facts I have found in police and intelligence reports but I will also use Monty Newton's *My Confessions*, published in 1925, to try to unravel this man's story.

The Baron lived a triple life that even Scotland Yard and the French police did not know about until Monty Newton told them in 1925. In Paris he was a businessman and publisher of *Paris Turf*, a sporting journal, and spoke perfect French. In London he became Joseph Fisher and/or Julius Steinmann and spoke perfect English and in Germany he was Baron von Koenig and master of many German dialects that were, in fact, completely different languages. Then I found his real name: a man called Wittkop testified that he was Rudolf Stallmann. Wittkop was married to his sister, Anna. In fact, Wittkop had employed him in 1891 and 1892.

I played with combinations of his names. He used many: Baron Korff, Kerner, Neumann, Steinmann, Denman, are some I found. I frenchified his first name to Rodolphe, added Lemoine and turned up an astonishing story:

Rodolphe Lemoine was the French secret agent who, in 1931, bought the first secrets of the new German military Enigma coding machine from a traitor in the German cryptology department in Berlin. This information shortened the Second World War by two years, if not four, wrote Sir Harry Hinsley, co-author of the official *British Intelligence in the Second World War*. And this was the same Lemoine who was Monty Newton's partner in crime for decades. In his book, *My Confessions* Newton said that throughout his career he was closely associated with an Austrian count; they were more or less inseparable. Detective Chief Inspector Percy J. Smith of Scotland Yard knew Newton well and said Lemoine was his travelling partner; he also confirmed two of his stories of trickery, the loss of a huge sum of money in Mexico and the gain of a tiny jade goddess in Spain.

So how do I conflate Monty's mate with the secret service man? In his *Confessions* Monty Newton told how he and his best friend, the Austrian count, had conned their way across Europe and up and down South America. In his book he called his friend 'count' but in 'real life', if anything is real in this man's story, Monty called him the Baron. So Monty's best friend is the German Rudolf Stallman, the conman called Baron von Koenig and also the secret agent called Rodolphe Lemoine. In a deposition to the police concerning another case, Monty Newton said that Lemoine's name was Stallmann.

What made him turn his whole life into a lie? To risk everything, to live one step in front of the police throughout his youth and in maturity to live one step in front of the secret services of several countries – for he seems to have worked for the Nazis and Russians as well as France? I think the answer lies in his brain chemistry: monoamine oxidase is an enzyme that controls our impulses. Some people have much lower levels than average which turns them into sensation-seekers and risk-takers. Professional gamblers, criminal psychopaths, even smokers and drinkers, have low levels of MAO. Dr Jose Carrasco, a Spanish psychiatrist, found that bull-fighters have low levels of the enzyme, too, and they are ace risk-takers. Stallman was not a bull-fighter but he was a professional gambler, a heavy drinker who enjoyed a fat cigar and who thrived on the excitement of the danger of discovery. I set out to unravel the story; whether I have found the full story, the true story, I don't suppose we shall ever know. He used many names – I have counted thirteen, plus two 'work' names for when he was spying. Some days he must have woken up and wondered who he was going to be that day. To me, he will always be the enigma behind the Enigma code.

* * *

Lemoine had a partner from early on; you need a partner to function as a card-sharp and conman. Lemoine's was Monty Newton, a Londoner. I have used his book, *My Confessions*, published in 1925, to help me piece together this story but in it they were sanitised and presented as a pair of loveable rogues – just the way the English like their crooks, (remember the Hatton Garden diamond geezers?) These rascals are always getting into scrapes, always having narrow escapes, always in danger of losing everything but somehow beating the system. Their background is one of glamorous hotels, cases of champagne, luxurious railway trains, foreign travel, fast cars and faster women. They are charming enough to be loved by the ladies but naughty enough to charm the money out of the pockets of rich men. In fact, they were ruthless cheats.

The Scotland Yard copper, Percy J Smith we have already met came to know Newton well and called him 'the daddy of all conmen'. In later years he was happy to spend hours listening to tales of his exploits round the world. Monty was tall, distinguished and polished and spoke with a cultured drawl and could be more entertaining than a theatre of actors, he said. Percy J also knew Lemoine as his travelling companion.

Percy J, who rose to become Detective Chief Inspector, really admired conmen. They rarely hit the headlines the way cat-burglars and bank operators do, so their 'work' was unknown to the public; he wrote his memoirs to reveal all. A clever conman would spend months planning a coup, would cross the world like a millionaire on holiday and spend thousands of pounds following a likely victim. He learned to dress well and to comport himself like a gentleman. He pored over the financial and social columns of the newspapers to follow the movements of millionaires and their money, rehearsed chat-up lines for hours until he was word-perfect.

'Each conman had a work name – or three,' wrote Percy J. 'They are essentially clever character actors with an extensive repertoire.' He recalled taking from one conman a suitcase full of 'props:' writing paper with headings of fictitious businesses, documents of every description, all legal and correct-looking, security bonds, membership cards to fake stock and turf exchanges, seals, dies, books of codes, a small printing press, wads of imitation bank notes – a real fifty-pound note wrapped round a pad of thin lavatory paper – a 'Chicago roll'. (This is similar to the contents of Lemoine's suitcase when he was picked up in 1941 by the French secret service.)

Our pair travelled the world together on a non-stop crooks' tour, evading the police for ten years. Percy J. would hear from other police forces of a team of conmen operating in China or Japan and then a month or so later would come word that they were in South America or Florida or Cuba, or any of the beach playgrounds of the rich tourist. But they were a feckless lot for, no sooner had they fleeced one victim than they would be spending his money on first class liner tickets to take them to yet another exotic resort, planning to trap the next one. These luxurious liners meant a relaxing holiday for the rich and famous; for Lemoine and

Newton, they were a place of work. The passengers were warned of the dangers: there were notices in the lounges warning of the likelihood of cheats but that did not often prevent our men from making a killing. 'Their existence is one endless gamble against law and order,' said Percy J Smith. But it was not all jolly japes; these two were seriously nasty people.[2]

The first record I can find of Newton losing that gamble was in September 1907 and it shows he had worked with a partner, Joseph Fisher, at least since 1899. They were an impressive couple when they walked into the shop of W. J. Hallam, a printer, in Dean Street, Soho on 17 September 1907. They looked like gentlemen, immaculately dressed in top hats and tails and with beautifully manicured hands; the skin was as soft as a woman's, the nails filed to an almond shape and buffed with a chamois leather until they shone. But they were no gents; as card-sharpers, smooth, clean hands were essential to convince the victims they were about to cheat that they were men of means. They also, of course, allowed the playing cards to slip swiftly through their fingers.

Monty Newton took the lead because Fisher was drunk. He handed over a sheet of headed writing-paper from Lewis and Lewis, a well-known firm of solicitors, and asked for fifty more sheets to be printed. 'Am I speaking to one of the firm?' asked Mr Hallam, and did not doubt it when Newton replied: 'Yes.' The following evening, Fisher, pretending to be one of the firm's clerks, collected the thirty-five sheets of the paper that were ready and took them back to the Burlington Hotel in Cork Street, Mayfair, where the two were staying. Using a sheet of the paper, Newton forged a letter to his close friend and accomplice, Violet Fraser, purporting to come from her solicitor, Sir George Lewis, one half of the firm of Lewis and Lewis, saying she was due to come into £5,000 (about £550,000) on 1 January 1908. They planned to borrow against this letter.

Violet, a woman separated from her husband, was lying sick in the Hotel Kaiserhof in Wiesbaden, living on morphine, she wrote to Newton. They had played this trick before without any problems but this time they made a mistake and forgot about the last fifteen of the fifty sheets of writing paper. When Mr Hallam noticed the package lying on the shelf in the Dean Street shop the following

Monday morning, 23 September, he telephoned Lewis and Lewis to remind them, only to discover he had been duped.

Scotland Yard was quickly on the case. Detective Inspector W. C. Gough recognised Newton and Fisher from Mr Hallam's description – he had known Newton for more than two years and Fisher for six months and he knew they had been partners in crime for the last ten years in England and Australia. He soon discovered where they were staying and arrested them there on Wednesday evening, 25 September. Detective Inspector Gough couldn't quite place Newton who spoke in a quiet, confident drawl with an unidentifiable accent. Gough thought he and Fisher were American and opposed bail when they appeared at Marlborough Street Magistrates' Court two days later on the grounds that they might abscond. In fact, Monty was a Londoner, the son of a bookmaker but he had already been round the world three times and had acquired an accent that reflected his travels. Detective Inspector Gough told the court that Newton had been arrested at Boston, Massachusetts on a charge of swindling, by a promise of marriage, a widow whom he met on an ocean liner, but the charge was not pursued.[3]

Poker was Monty's game and he travelled the world to earn his living but in spite of his lawless life he had a patriotic side and left London when he was twenty-four to serve in the South African Special Forces, putting down the uprisings of the Matabele tribe in 1893 and again in 1895-6 in that part of southern Africa that was to become Southern Rhodesia and which is now Zimbabwe. The tribal chief had been persuaded by Cecil Rhodes to allow him the mining rights to his territory, which stretched between the mighty rivers Limpopo and Zambezi. Rhodes, had formed the Consolidated Mines Company in South Africa in 1889 and then made a fortune from diamonds and gold. Now he wanted to expand and set about establishing a British colony in Matabeleland; no wonder the tribe rebelled. Rhodes won, of course, and the new colony was named after him.

It was not an easy journey to Matabeleland, deep in the interior of Africa. Newton went by ship to Capetown, then by train as far as Mafeking, where the railway ended. The lucky ones went on by a coach drawn by ten mules, taking ten days to cover the

507 miles to Bulawayo, in the south of what is now Zimbabwe. Newton talked of crossing southern Africa on horseback, so his journey probably took even longer. It was the Wild West-plus in Matabeleland. As well as tribesmen daubed with war-paint and armed with spears and rifles, there were lions, hippopotamus and elephants, giant ants and crocodile-infested rivers to contend with. It made a man of Newton, who was awarded a medal for bravery.

Soldiers and miners would relax in a mud hut, called a bottle store, or in a bar in one of the settlements that were springing up. Some pockets were lined with gold, some were empty. There was smuggling, thieving and drunkenness, brawling and card-playing. It was probably in one of these saloons that Monty met Joseph Fisher, a mining engineer. They decided to winkle some of that gold out of the miners' pockets and became a card-sharping team.

By 1899 Monty and Fisher had moved on to Western Australia where gold had been found in the desert. They did not join that gold rush; they had heard what conditions were like in the desert. There was no water, miners were living in filthy, overcrowded, corrugated iron huts where typhoid fever, spread by lice, had killed hundreds. They moved on to Sydney, the booming capital of New South Wales, where the settlers already had a reputation for enjoying a punt. Monty and Fisher would settle in a hotel bar and strike up a conversation with a couple of prosperous-looking gents and, by means of innocent-seeming questions, work out whether they had any money and whether they could afford to lose it by playing cards. Walter Chick, a member of the London Stock Exchange, was one of their victims in Sydney in 1899 and said they were 'card sharps of a very low class'. All the same, they managed to cheat a young friend of his of between three and four hundred pounds, around £32,500 today.[4]

Monty's patriotic urge to serve his country returned when the Boer War broke out that year and he went back to southern Africa where his bravery won him two medals, a commission and the rank of captain in the South Africa Irregular Forces – the Scouts.[5] The Scouts were daredevil officers who went out alone on horseback, accompanied only by one African. Their job was to find the enemy's position by following their tracks: the remains of a camp fire, a broken twig or disturbed earth. Colonel Robert

Baden-Powell of the 13th Hussars was a master at scouting. In fact, after the war he started the Boy Scouts movement and dressed his young followers in a uniform based on the one he had designed for the South African Constabulary. There was a wide-brimmed cowboy hat, short-sleeved shirt, cord breeches and puttees, all in a drab colour to blend with the dry grasses of the bush. A pistol on the hip and a bandolier of bullets across the shoulder completed the soldiers' outfits.

Baden-Powell enjoyed hunting lions, wild pigs, ostriches, antelope and wildebeest but hunting 'niggers' as he called them (in his book, *The Matabele Campaign*) he really enjoyed. He would track the tribesmen to a hideout cave and then shoot blindly through the entrance. 'Man-hunting afforded us plenty of excitement and novel experiences,' he wrote.

The Boer War ended in May 1902 and the pair returned to Europe. By now they were more sophisticated and aspired to something grander than rough pioneers' bars and colonial hotels and November 1902 found them living at the Metropole Hotel in Brighton. They were not as good as they should have been at their game and were thrown out when a guest complained they had cheated him at cards. No wonder the dour, old-fashioned Detective-Inspector Gough was bewildered when they appeared in court charged with forgery. He told the magistrate about some letters he found in Newton's room: there was one showing that Violet Fraser, Newton and others were engaged in playing cards with some people whose ability to pay if they lost was discussed. Another was from Wiesbaden, in Germany and was addressed: 'Dear Baron'.

'I don't know whether Newton is the baron or not,' said the prosecuting lawyer, plaintively. He was not; the Baron was what Newton called his partner. Detective-Inspector Percy Smith said that Lemoine was Monty Newton's partner in crime and had taken the title of Baron von Koenig. I had assumed early in my investigation that Joseph Fisher *was* Joseph Fisher, a mining engineer aged thirty-five. Suddenly it was clear: Joseph Fisher was Lemoine *and* von Koenig. And if Joseph Fisher was Baron von Koenig, he was also Rudolf Stallman. And Joseph Fisher was described on the charge sheet as a mining engineer; he had probably picked up some knowledge while in Africa. Newton said he took the lead in the visit to Hallam's shop because Fisher was drunk; I have seen Lemoine described as an alcoholic and large amounts of fine wine and champagne run through this story like a stream, so that is something else that convinced me that Fisher was Stallman.

Stallman was the son of a jewellery wholesaler in Berlin. Not content with a prosperous middle-class life he took to crime early and was only eighteen when he was sent to prison for a week in 1889 for a swindle. After working for his brother-in-law, a wine merchant, in 1891 and 1892, his globe-trotting began. He told police of travelling in South America, taking part in a revolution in Chile, then working as a mining engineer in the goldfields of southern Africa in 1903. Detective Inspector Gough from Scotland Yard said Fisher and Monty had been working together since 1897. Monty Newton was most likely in South Africa at that time and perhaps that was where they met. We can't be sure; policemen pick up gossip, criminals make up stories. What we know is that the pair were card-sharping in Sydney in 1899 and were doing the same in Brighton in 1902. Between 1902 and their arrest for forgery in September 1907 they led a life of luxurious travel. They liked to spend the winters in warm climes – Australia, the Far East, Egypt – and the spring in the south of France. They would move to Wiesbaden in Germany when the weather became warmer – this was at a time when the south of France was deemed too hot in the summer.

Wiesbaden became a favourite of theirs and Monty photographed the large mansion they rented; it had three floors and an impressive pillared porch.[6] The town was a fashionable spa with twenty-six hot springs that were said to cure almost anything. In 1907 a new *Kurhaus* had just been finished in elegant classical style and the town was at the peak of its fame as a fashionable health resort; they called it the Nice of the north. The rich, leisured and ailing came to take the waters and crowded the large hotels along its tree-lined avenues. A spa town made the perfect cover for the cardsharp and conman because it was so easy to strike up an acquaintance while splashing in the warm spring-water pool or sitting at one of the open-air cafes in the English-style park behind the Kurhaus.

Newton pleaded guilty to forgery and conspiracy to defraud and he was shocked to receive twenty months' hard labour. It was his only conviction in a criminal career that lasted twenty-five years. Fisher fared better because Monty, loyal to his partner, told Detective-Inspector Gough that he had no part in the original conspiracy and was only brought in towards the end. Fisher got a month's sentence and, as he had already been in prison on remand for two months, was released immediately, on 29 November 1907.

Right: Sir Hari Singh at the time of his first marriage, just sixteen and straight out of school, Mayo College.

Below: Mayo College at Ajmer in the north-west of India was founded in 1875 by Lord Mayo, an Irish peer who had been Viceroy of India. His idea was to create an Eton college of India where Maharajahs could have their sons educated. It's still regarded as the best boarding school in India.

Bottom: Nishat Bag, the terraced gardens on the bank of the Dal Lake in Srinagar, with its fountains and cascades, was where Sir Hari celebrated his first wedding with a garden party for thousands of guests.

Above: The Jhelum river winds through Srinagar, the summer capital of Kashmir and the view has not changed much since this photograph was taken in 1912: rickety houses several stories high still wobble over the water.

Below: The Dal Lake once thronged with holiday-makers exploring in their shikaras, the easiest way to get around. Political problems between India and Pakistan have cut down the number of holiday-makers. (Courtesy of Vinamra Agrawal)

Right: By the time of the Victory Ball Sir Hari was piling on the weight and looked more like forty-four than twenty-four.

Below: Maudie Robinson, far left, wore a precarious headdress at the ball to advertise her Grasshopper ointment. (*Daily Sketch*, 13 November 1919. Courtesy British Library)

● *Mrs. Robinson and Sir Hari Singh:*
" They met at a dance and struck up
a passionate friendship."

Sir Hari, and Maudie with her modern cropped hair. She was not a conventional beauty but she had many admirers. (*Reynolds Illustrated News*, 23 April 1950. Courtesy British Library)

Above left: Monty Newton, cosmopolitan card sharp who pretended to be the wronged husband. (*The People*, 14 December 1924. Courtesy British Library)

Above right: Charlie Robinson, Maudie's real husband, denied living off her immoral earnings. Note the snappy gaiters.

No. B204561 London 19
Messrs Boulton Brothers & Co.
39, Old Broad Street, London, E.C.
Pay Messrs Appleton & Co: or Order
Pounds One hundred & fifty thousand only —
£150000/-/-
Hari Singh

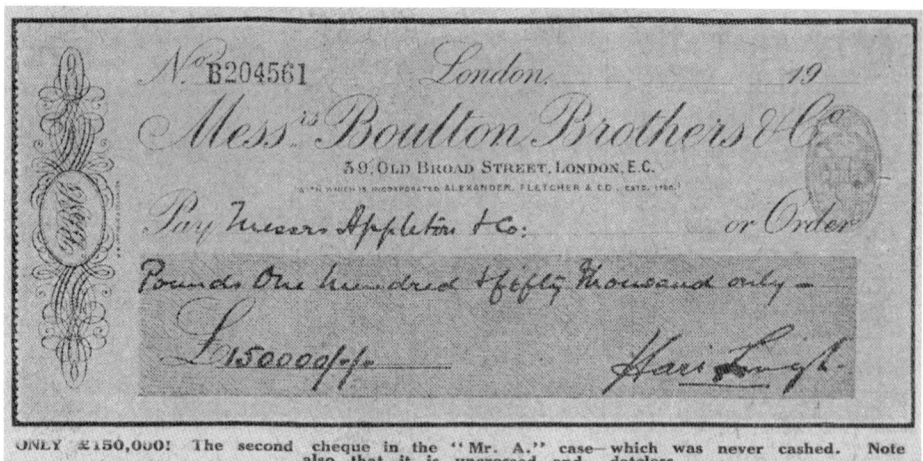

ONLY £150,000! The second cheque in the "Mr. A." case—which was never cashed. Note also that it is uncrossed and dateless.

The £150,000 cheque that Sir Hari Singh signed. It would be worth fourteen million pounds today and there was another for the same amount. (Courtesy Metropolitan Police Service)

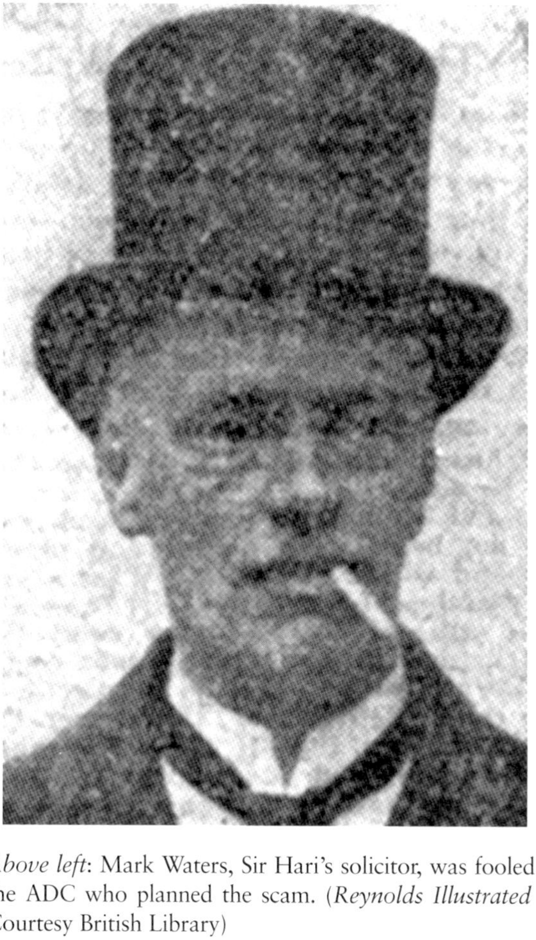

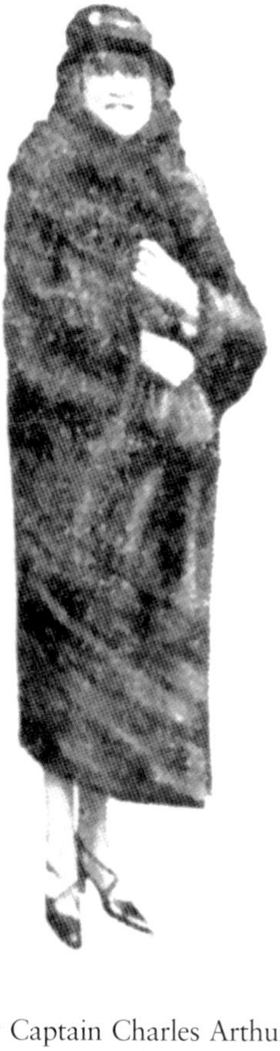

Above left: Mark Waters, Sir Hari's solicitor, was fooled by Captain Charles Arthur, the ADC who planned the scam. (*Reynolds Illustrated News*, 21 December 1925. Courtesy British Library)

Above right: Maudie appeared in court wearing a superb mink coat and a long rope of pearls. (*The People*, 3 May 1925. Courtesy British Library)

Above left: Sir John Simon, spoke for the Midland Bank in the Mr A Case and master-minded Monty Newton's surprise appearance.

Above middle: William Cooper Hobbs was the Mr Big of the London underworld who swindled many innocent card players and help many crooks escape the law. (*London Evening News*, 10 March 1925. Courtesy British Library)

Above right: Sir Hari loved diamonds and sapphires and splashed out on jewels during his stay in Paris with Maudie. (*Daily News*, 4 December 1924. Courtesy British Library)

Captain Arthur went on the run during the Mr A Case but was finally found and arrested in Paris. (*Daily News*, 5 December 1924. Courtesy British Library)

The English garden at the spa in Wiesbaden, where Newton and Lemoine fleeced a young German farmer. (Courtesy of the Library of Congress)

Newton and Lemoine liked to spend their summers in this grand holiday home at Wiesbaden where they found many gullible rich men to cheat. (*The People*, 12 April 1925. Courtesy British Library)

Above: Queen Victoria visited the Baden-Baden spa in the Black Forest and it is just as fashionable today as when it was a favourite hunting ground for Newton and Lemoine: Barack Obama and Victoria Beckham have sipped its curative waters. (Courtesy of the Library of Congress)

Below: Sinaia, in the Bucegi Natural park in Romania, was a luxurious summer playground for the rich and famous but Newton and Lemoine found its high prices too much for them. (Courtesy of the Library of Congress)

The young Monty Newton was twice decorated for bravery during the Boer war. (*The People*, 19 April 1925. Courtesy the British Library)

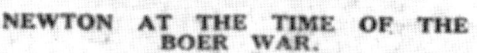

NEWTON AT THE TIME OF THE BOER WAR.

Cecil Rhodes, the son of a vicar in Bishops Stortford, was sent to South Africa to improve his health and became a diamond dealer at eighteen and formed the de Beers diamond company in 1888. Monty Newton and his partner probably met in one of the mining towns he established.

The Dom hotel in Cologne was a favourite haunt of the two men, until Lemoine was arrested there by the Gestapo on 9 March 1938; he promised to help them and was released.

Newton and Lemoine chased one of their victims, Count Gravich, across Europe to the luxurious hotel Bristol in Vienna. (Courtesy of Thomas Ledl)

Above: The glamorous casino at Monte Carlo that Monty Newton wished had never been invented because when he gambled there he always left with his pockets empty. (Courtesy of the Library of Congress)

Right: The newspapers lapped up stories of Newton and Lemoine's casino cons.

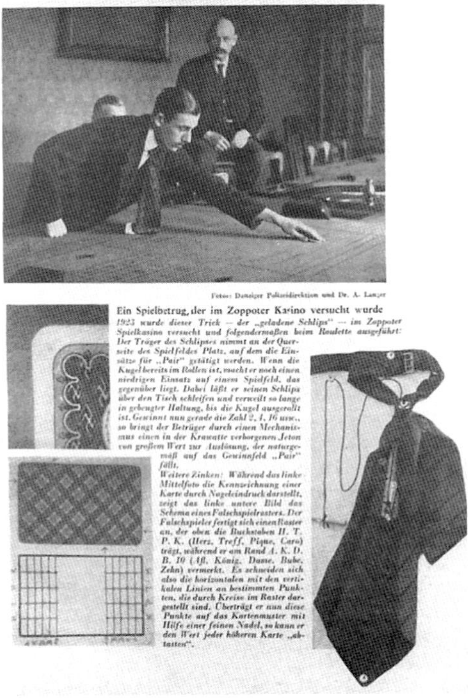

Foto: Danziger Polizeidirektion und Dr. A. Lanyer

Ein Spielbetrug, der im Zoppoter Kasino versucht wurde

1923 wurde dieser Trick – der „geladene Schlips" – im Zoppoter Spielkasino versucht und folgendermaßen beim Roulette ausgeführt: Der Träger des Schlipses nimmt an der Querseite des Spielfeldes Platz, auf dem die Einsätze für „Pair" getätigt werden. Wenn die Kugel bereits im Rollen ist, macht er noch einen niedrigen Einsatz auf einem Spielfeld, das gegenüber liegt. Dabei läßt er seinen Schlips über den Tisch schleifen und verweilt so lange in gebeugter Haltung, bis die Kugel ausgerollt ist. Gewinnt nun gerade die Zahl 2, 1, 16 usw., so bringt der Betrüger durch einen Mechanismus einen in der Krawatte verborgenen Jeton von großem Wert zur Auslösung, der naturgemäß auf das Gewinnfeld „Pair" fällt.

Weitere Zinken: Während das linke Mittelfoto die Kennzeichnung einer Karte durch Nageleindruck darstellt, zeigt das links untere Bild das Schema eines Falschspielrasters. Der Falschspieler fertigt sich einen Raster an, der oben die Buchstaben H. T. P. K. (Herz, Treff, Pique, Caro) trägt, während er am Rand A. K. D. B. 10 (Aß, König, Dame, Bube, Zehn) vermerkt. Es schneiden sich also die horizontalen mit den vertikalen Linien an bestimmten Punkten, die durch Kreise im Raster dargestellt sind. Überträgt er nun diese Punkte auf das Kartenmuster mit Hülfe einer feinen Nadel, so kann er den Wert jeder höheren Karte „abtasten".

Police found this photograph of Stallman/von Konig, as he was then, when they arrested him in 1902. It was taken in London.

Marie Renee Lemoine was nineteen when she married the man she knew as Baron von Konig on 3 November 1905. The 'Baron' was thirty-four and already losing his hair. (*Caras-y-caretas*, Buenos-Aires, 11 November 1905)

Icy eyes and a shaven head gave the Baron an ominous air for this passport photograph taken in the 1930s.

An Enigma encoding machine was about the size of a typewriter. (Courtesy of the Central Intelligence Agency)

The bombe, a machine invented by Alan Turing and Gordon Welchman at Bletchley Park to work out the daily Enigma settings.

Paul Paillole, Lemoine's handler at the Deuxieme Bureau, was suspected of disloyalty although the United States later decorated him.

The French built this camp at Pithiviers at the beginning of World War II to house the German prisoners of war they expected; when France fell to Germany it became a transit camp for French Jews while collaborators and SNCF, the French national railway system, organised their removal to death camps at Auschwitz-Birkenau. Now SNCF is helping to finance the restoration of Pithiviers railway station to turn it into a museum telling the story of the deportations. (Bundesarchiv, Bild 183-L18974 / CC-BY-SA 3.0)

Marseille's old port in 1943. This is where Lemoine hid out. (Bundesarchiv, Bild 101I-027-1474-34 / Vennemann, Wolfgang / CC-BY-SA 3.0)

Reinhardt Heydrich, tall, slim and blond, was a linguist, pilot, violinist, loved children and liked to escort pretty women. Then he became head of the Gestapo, architect of the Haulocaust, and the hardest man in Germany. Hitler called him the man with the iron heart. (Bundesarchiv, Bild 146-1969-054-16 / Hoffmann, Heinrich / CC-BY-SA)

There were eighteen plots against Hitler during his twelve years in power. Admiral Wilhelm Canaris, although head of the Abwehr, the German army secret service, was part of one. He was tried and executed in April 1945, a few weeks before the end of the war. (Bundesarchiv, Bild 146-1979-013-43 / CC-BY-SA 3.0)

CHAPTER SIXTEEN

On the Run

One fine day Monty found himself in Baden Baden, another of the spa towns they were so fond of. It's a pretty town in the hills of the Black Forest, much favoured by crooks and with a popular racecourse. He was unlucky at the races but went on to beat an Austrian Count in a game of dice. Monty thought he was going to be unlucky again when the Count left him; he thought he'd been rumbled and his victim had gone for the police but he returned and invited Monty to dinner. When the Count asked for a month's grace to pay his debt Monty was sure he'd never see the money. Still, it was better than being reported to the police. But the next minute the Count changed his mind and offered his new Mercedes tourer for the debt.

Monty was thrilled and quickly engaged a chauffeur who drove him to Cologne. He took a room at the splendid Dom hotel, right opposite the cathedral. As he was entering the restaurant for dinner, somebody tapped him on the shoulder. It was an old friend, Colonel X he called him, an attaché at the embassy of one of the Balkan states. 'By jove! I've got a business for you,' he said and told him that one of the richest and biggest gamblers of the Balkans – and yet another titled gent – was staying at the Hotel Imperial in Karlsbad. 'If you can get hold of him you are sure to get twenty thousand pounds.' (About £2,200,000 now)

Monty longed to meet the Count and next morning left for Karlsbad in the car and went straight to the Hotel Imperial. And what a disappointment! Count Theodore Gravich had left for

Vienna that very morning. How to find him? Monty charmed the receptionist who told him the Count had asked for his mail to be forwarded to the Hotel Bristol. Now, it's one thing to become acquainted with someone in a spa town, a different thing altogether in a big city. So Monty sent for the Baron.

It took him three days to reach Karlsbad and off they set for Vienna and the Hotel Bristol; it is a very large and very grand – these days five-star – hotel. But there was another disappointment: Count Gravich had left that very morning for one of his properties in Romania. What to do? Having come so far, they decided it was too late to turn back and they determined to carry on the chase. It was not easy, though. Before the Great War Romania was one of the few countries in Europe that you needed a passport to enter. Monty and the valets who travelled with them always carried theirs but the Baron was not, as Monty delicately put it, 'on speaking terms' with his Government. Monty wrote to Colonel X, who had set them on this impossible trail, and asked if he could pull strings to get the Baron into Romania. They set off across Hungary, not even pausing at the magnificent spa in Budapest for a quick game of cards, before crossing the great plain, the *Bussta*. Monty remarked that crossing Hungary by train was very comfortable but doing it by car was 'not a pleasant experience for the automobilist'. This was before autobahns, of course, and they often were stuck in muddy country lanes and had to go in search of oxen to pull them out. There were tyres to be replaced, problems with the engine, impossible conversations with peasants concerning distances, the state of the roads and so on.

Finally they reached the Romanian border and were confronted by a pack of hostile police and soldiers but when the Baron gave his name, they found Colonel X had done them proud. The Chief of Police, in his best gold-braided uniform, greeted them in the royal reception room and took them to the officers' mess for an excellent lunch. Everybody was very kind and finally they were able to raise the subject of Count Gravich. The officers remembered him; he had passed through the frontier three days before. Would they ever catch up with the man! He had told the border officers that he was going to Sinaia; it's a very pretty town, known as the Pearl of the Carpathians, where King Carol had his summer residence. It's now a ski resort, popular with British holidaymakers. Off they went to Sinaia but the Count had three days' start on them. He spent only one night in Sinaia before leaving for his country castle. They were not put off; indeed, they were more determined than ever to get their man. The castle was quite near Bucharest, the capital, so they drove there and staged an old trick: the Baron pretended to be ill, Monty knocked at the gate of the castle and asked for brandy for him. The Count himself came out and insisted on taking Count Leo in and putting him to bed to be looked after properly.

'The plan worked like clockwork,' Monty said. While the Baron reclined on a pile of pillows, Monty chatted with the Count who insisted that they stay with him for a few days. How could they refuse the man they had marked out as their pigeon and chased across Europe? By dinner that evening the two men were like old school friends. There was quite a house party: two Romanian army officers, a banker from Bucharest, a fat man called Abramovitch and his beautiful young wife who hailed from Circassia. Circassia is in the northern Caucasus and its resort of Sochi, on the north-eastern shore of the Black Sea, was the site of the Winter Olympics in 2014. Since the Middle Ages it has been famed for the beauty of its spirited and elegant women and Mrs Abramovitch was no exception: she was known as La Belle Zarina.

The Baron had recovered by the next morning and they all went off for a picnic in one of the hunting-boxes in the mountains. The Baron and Monty felt confident that they had created a friendly, trusting atmosphere. Back at the castle the Count suggested a game of roulette after dinner and the servants carried in a full-size Monte Carlo roulette wheel. Monty's heart sank; he knew from experience that he couldn't win a game where he didn't have an unfair advantage. Sure enough, they lost £500. Next day the house party decided to go to Sinaia. There was a convoy of three cars: one for the Count and co, Monty took the Baron and the two army officers in his and there was one for the servants. So once more they were chasing the Count along the byways of central Europe.

The Baron and Monty had been swept rather unwillingly into this party and they were worried; they had only £300 (£32,500) between them, not enough for the high life of Sinaia with its casino and smart restaurants, So Monty made an excuse and cleared off to cheaper Bucharest, leaving the Baron behind to keep an eye on things, with strict instructions to keep away from the casino and to say he didn't much like gambling.

They all met up two days later in Bucharest. The Baron reported that the Count had won about 150,000 French francs (about two million pounds now) and was more in love with Zarina each day. This alarmed them: if her husband noticed and there was a big row, their prospects of a game, let alone a win, would be ruined. Sitting in his room in pyjamas and enjoying a last pipe, Monty was wishing he'd never met Colonel X, nor the Count, nor come to Romania, when Gravich came to his room with a strange proposition: he wanted to go back to Hungary next day but he didn't want his other guests to know that he wanted to go. So he wanted it to appear that he was going only because Monty and Leo had asked him to accompany them on the trip. They thought it was very mysterious and never discovered the reason, but they agreed to help him out so next day at lunch Monty said he and Leo had to go to Budapest and invited the Count to join them. He refused at first but, as they insisted, he accepted the invitation.

The Count, Monty and Leo had an interesting trip. Gravich was strangely nervous and the chauffeur couldn't go fast enough for him and he asked Monty to let him drive the precious car for a while.

'We had just passed a tumble-down inn when the Count decided to find out if my automobile was good at jumping over cows' said Monty. The result was disastrous. The cow didn't seem to mind but the car suffered and the chauffeur's verdict was that it would take him a couple of hours to repair the damage. There was nothing for them to do but return to the little inn they had just passed, Monty took a few holiday snaps with his new camera of the creeper-covered hovel.

'When we entered it never entered my head that there, in that dingy little room, we were at last to accomplish what we had set out to do but when I saw a greasy pack of cards lying on one of the tables, I said to myself: "It's now or never,"' Monty wrote.

He ordered a bottle of the local wine and suggested passing the time with a few games of *écarté* and the Count agreed. The Baron went to tell the driver not to rush his work and the game began. After an hour and a half the Count owed Monty £22,000 (getting on for two and a half million pounds) which was what he had hoped for at the start of the trip, so he was quite satisfied – but the Count's gambling blood was up and he insisted on playing for higher and higher stakes. Monty could have won each one, of course, but he thought it better to win and lose alternately until his opponent lost his nerve. By the time the chauffeur returned to say the car was ready, the Count owed Monty £82,000 (almost nine million pounds), more than enough, but he proposed playing ten more games for £10,000 each. Monty made sure of winning the next two and then lost the next eight. He shook the Count warmly by the hand and said how pleased he was that the man had won back the greater part of his losses.

They continued their journey to Budapest and Monty told the Count there was no hurry about paying because he intended to stay three days in Budapest. To his dismay, the Count asked him to wait for a week. All he could do was swallow hard and smile pleasantly and say: 'Of course, my dear fellow.' But they didn't have the money to stay that long. They had to raise capital. Thinking quickly, Monty went to the smartest jeweller in Budapest and asked to see some strings of pearls. He chose a small one, offered £2,000 (£220,000) and arranged to return next day to pay. At lunch he told the Count he wanted to buy some pearls for a 'dear little lady friend in London' and asked if he could vouch for the jeweller. Of course he could; it was his family jeweller so Monty asked him to go with him to the shop next day. Once there he said to Gravich: 'As I am unknown here the jeweller might perhaps not like my cheque and it might be easier for you to have the pearls put on your bill and deduct the £2,000 from the money you owe me.' Jeweller and Count were perfectly happy with the arrangement and Monty walked off with a £2,000 string of pearls that had cost him nothing.

There was a problem, though. They had a string of pearls worth £2,000 but they were still without cash. Simple: the Baron took the train to Vienna and pawned the pearls for about £600, (£65,000).

They spent two more days in Budapest before returning to London, parting on the best of terms from their friends. Eight days later Monty had a letter from his bank saying that £20,000 (two million) had been paid into his account by the Count. He posted a cheque for £6,000 to Colonel X who had tipped him off about the Count. He redeemed the pearls, had them sent to London where he sold them for £1,000, a loss of £1,000 of their hard-earned money.

This story shows the extraordinary lengths – and the distances – they were willing to go to fleece a victim; it also shows how cunning they were and their remarkable ability to think on their feet.[7]

The Berlin police had known all about Newton and von Koenig for ten years; they were known all over Europe as 'international crooks'. Stallman was eighteen, in fact, when he was first in trouble with the law. Since then they had tracked his movements round the capitals of Europe, the spa towns and the casinos. He was Louis Guillaume Rudolf, the only son of Louis von Stallmann, a prosperous jeweller who was in business with his brother at No 98 Orianenstrasse, in Berlin. Rudolf had a sister, Anna. He left school at sixteen and took a job in an import-export business. He didn't like being tied to a desk so he went back to school to study languages; he had a gift and was soon fluent in English, French, Italian and Spanish as well as the dozens of languages still spoken in the various states of Germany. His father died when Rudolf was only seventeen and the boy went wild. He was good-looking, 1.75 metres tall, with blond hair and a moustache which curled dramatically across his cheeks; pale blue myopic eyes were his outstanding feature and he always used a monocle. He was short of money, not yet having received his inheritance, and turned to crime to keep up his standard of living – from a well-heeled family he was used to living well. After a run-in with the police his family stepped in and packed him off to Chile in 1890, at the time a popular place to exile black sheep, where young Rudolf made some like-minded friends that he kept in touch with. He returned to Berlin after a year and his brother-in-law, a wine merchant named Wittkop, gave him a job that lasted until 1892.

He was twenty-four when he turned up in Paris on 22 September 1895 with a young woman and a little boy of five or six. Paris was an exciting place in the years between the Franco-Prussian war and the First World War. Later they called it *La Belle Époque* – the good old days. Georges-Eugene Haussmann had ripped out the unhealthy medieval streets of the old city and replaced them with the wide boulevards and gardens that make Paris what it is today. M. Eiffel had built his (temporary) tower as the entrance to the 1889 World's Fair, which show-cased the great technical advances being made: trains and motor cars were shrinking distances. There was the wireless and the telephone to keep everyone in touch. The first Metro line was to open in 1900, with its elaborate *art nouveau* entrances by Hector Guimard. There was renewed interest in ballet and opera. Suddenly, everyone wanted to be in Paris. Even painters such as Pablo Picasso, Henri Matisse, and Henri Rousseau left the clear Mediterranean light to starve in their attics in Montmartre where Henri de Toulouse-Lautrec took to the low-life and painted the dancers at the Folies Bergère and the Moulin Rouge.

Rudolf rented a furnished flat at 45 Rue de Prony, not far from the Parc Monceau. Although he did not seem to have a proper job, he lived well and received many foreign visitors. Generously, he often gave money to a friend called Mansmann. The little group seemed settled enough but then, two weeks after moving in, they left hurriedly, saying there was a family emergency. The neighbours didn't believe this for a moment; they thought he and Mansmann were spies, in the pay of the Germans, especially as their departure coincided with the arrest of a spy called Schwarz. The police had their suspicions, too. Paris was feverish with spy stories at this time, only nine months after the infamous conviction of Captain Alfred Dreyfus

What happened to Rudolf's flat mate and the little boy when he moved out and went to Spa in Belgium is unknown. It's a pretty town in a wooded valley in the Ardennes, a health spa famous for its spring waters. It also has the oldest casino in the world and Stallman loved casinos; they were perfect for cheating at the card tables and for picking up tidbits of diplomatic and military intelligence. He picked up a young girl, too, and travelled with her to Munich. He couldn't pay his hotel bill, spent a month in prison for that and, a little later got another three days for using a false name. He had a lucky escape early the next year, 1896, when he was mixed up with a man called Rieger who was arrested for using false documents. Rieger was convicted but Rudolf escaped the law. He had made friends with a German from Hamburg called, among other names, Jacob Michel. With two accomplices they made a daring daylight theft of jewellery from a house in Ostend. After that he went to South America for a couple of years, travels described by Monty Newton.

Rudolf was back in Nice in January 1898. He liked the warm winter weather there and spent a lot of time on the Cote d'Azur and at Monte Carlo, where he passed his afternoons dressed up to the nines at the casino. By this time he had reached the bottom: pimping. He had arrived in Nice with a young German girl, Elsa von Selten. She was twenty-three and a painter but had clearly hit hard times because she was working as a prostitute from a house in rue de l'Hôtel des Postes. She shared her earnings with Stallman who passed himself off as her husband and was living at the hotel d'Angleterre. The pair had attracted the attention of the police and when an Englishman on holiday at the hotel woke up in room 49 at the hotel d'Angleterre on 4 February and found that someone had entered his room during the night and cleaned him out, they suspected Stallman; Stallman and Elsa got out of town quickly.

He did not reappear in Nice until the middle of December, in time for the winter season. He was with a man from Fontainebleau named W. B. Beaune who appeared to have plenty of money. They stayed in adjoining rooms at the Grand hotel and Stallmann got a temporary admission card to the casino at Monte Carlo that lasted from 15 December to 15 January. By then they had moved to the Riviera Palace hotel but they were thrown out on 3 February after the management received an anonymous letter, posted in Nice, accusing them of cheating. They said they were going to the Hotel Metropole at Monte Carlo but the police could not find them there.

A Baron Ludwig, or Otto von Steinitz, arrived in Nice at the same time as Stallmann. He was a professional gambler and supplemented his income by taking the earnings of a prostitute called Elisa who pretended to be his wife. Steinitz and Stallman later proved to be partners in crime – or espionage.

Stallmann came to London next and worked in a financial house, Harper and Co., in Newgate Street, near St Paul's, where Steinitz also had a job. Stallmann took the name of Baron von Koenig;

he said he advertised it in the newspapers and nobody objected. It was useful, he said, to be known as a baron because you could always get a reservation on a train; and he didn't want his family name to be associated with his gambling career. He was back in Nice in April and arrested for a robbery committed in Munster on the night of 7 September the year before, 1898. This was the first time the French police heard the name von Koenig, according to Eric Maillard, the stepson of Lemoine's yet-to-be-born son, Randal, who has dug into the family's history. I have drawn deeply on his research, with gratitude.[8] After that, he went to Australia with Monty Newton. They were first in Perth then Sydney where they took hundreds of pounds from fellow guests in a hotel, who described them as low-class card-sharps.

The Paris police received an anonymous letter from a Londoner who complained that he was being watched by a German agent known as Rudolf Stallmann and/or Baron von Koenig and who knew a lot of high-ranking German army officers. He had since returned to France, and had given a forwarding address at 33, rue Rue Vilin. From then on he was watched by police; it was quite a job because he never stayed anywhere for more than a couple of nights.

The railways police recorded his movements: he was in Biarritz in September, using a temporary admission card to the casino. He spent a week at the beginning of October 1900 in a furnished flat at 10 rue de Faubourg Poissonnière in Paris. In July 1901 he was at the Grand Hotel des Alpes at Mussen; 5-7 August, he was staying near to the casino at Aix les Bains. On August 11 he arrived in Switzerland and went to Interlaken the next day. On 26 August the French police issued an expulsion order against him but they couldn't keep up with his travels to serve it. In fact, he was in Berne that day. He was back in Aix les Bains by 5 September. By the 7th he was in Paris, on the 13th in Interlaken and then it was back to Paris and the Continental hotel. When he checked out he left a forwarding address in London: Steinitz's address in Pimlico. At the end of the month he spent two days in Geneva where he was seen at the casino with professional gamblers and suspected spies. Then it was back to Steinitz's place, 69 Gloucester Street, in Pimlico. In November he was living in a lodging house in Paris where he got to know a bankrupt wine merchant, Victor Bouchel, who was now making a living at casinos and gambling clubs. Bouchel introduced him to a couple who agreed to accept his and von Steinitz's mail at their flat at 33, rue Vilin, until they began to suspect the two Germans might be spies.

By the beginning of March 1901 the Sûreté Générale was wondering if Stallmann and von Koenig were the same man and they asked the police to keep a discreet watch on Steinitz and von Koenig. By July they had concluded they were part of an international gang of card sharps who regularly pawned stolen goods. They checked von Koenig's bank account: 3,289 French francs. By January the next year (1902) it had grown to 6,000 f. (about £85,000) and he was living the high life at the Hotel Bristol at Beaulieu, near Marseille. He had a month's admission card for the Casino at Monte Carlo where he lost a lot of money, but the watchful police said they could see no sign of spying. The hotel's grand lobby was the place where people gathered at tea-time and von Koenig was there, immaculately dressed as usual, sounding out the fellow guests, working out who had money to lose at cards. He was mixing with a very louche crowd who were well-known to the police.

One day he heard that the son of John Lawson Johnston, who had made millions by inventing Bovril in his Edinburgh butcher's shop, was staying at the hotel. He booked a room next to his and planned to invite the young fellow to a game of cards. But he was unlucky, the man said he was tired and went to bed. The police were also tired, tired of this German crook upsetting their rich casino clientele. They decided to ban him from the country. An expulsion order issued against Stallmann on 26 August 1901 was not served until the police caught up with him on 20 February 1902 at the Hotel Bristol. He was arrested and imprisoned in Nice. There he insisted that his name was *von* Koenig and not just Koenig and that he was born in Hanover on 14 April 1871; his parents were Louis and Ulda Paech. He said he had an interest in four gold mines in South Africa. After six days he was released and given twenty-four hours to leave the country and a commissioner of police called Hiriart was given the job of watching him and told never to let him out of his sight. So they went straight from the prison to the

Restaurant de la Regence where he complained that he didn't know why he had been expelled because he had already arranged to give the French government German intelligence; he knew a German artillery captain plus a young lieutenant who would be able to corrupt him – the traditional honey trap. He didn't want money, just the cancellation of the expulsion order. Nothing much came of this and, as ordered, he left the country and carried on with his whirlwind Grand Tour of the casinos of the world.[9]

CHAPTER SEVENTEEN

Making tracks in Mexico

There was a boom in railway building at the turn of the twentieth century. Henry Flagler had opened up Florida in the 1890s; President Diaz of Mexico was keen to do the same in his country for the railways changed everything: they brought trade, tourism and prosperity to poor and isolated places.

The Baron and Monty were sharing a flat in Mayfair; business was slack so they were excited when an American friend 'in the business' came to see them. From time to time this man would introduce them to likely pigeons. This evening he brought news that an old acquaintance of his was in London and there might be possibilities for the pair. His friend had told him that a famous American railway magnate was planning a railroad through Mexico and was taking out six bankers – English, French and Dutch – to show them the works and get them to invest. Monty was invited to dinner at the Savoy hotel and was seated next to the railway man and by the time they reached the coffee and the brandy he had convinced him that he was looking for somewhere to invest his considerable capital. He was invited to join the party that was leaving next morning and, hopefully, invest some money. Monty doesn't name the magnate but in August 1902 Arthur E. Stilwell, president of the Kansas City, Mexico and Orient Railways Company, was in London to raise money from English and Dutch financiers to expand his railways. By 29 September they were in Kansas City, studying plans for a new railway terminus.

'But I have an Austrian nobleman staying with me,' said Monty.

'Bring him, too,' said Mr L as Monty called the magnate. As an Austrian nobleman and an English gent can't travel without their servants, they were invited, too.

Monty thought he was on to the biggest thing of his life and wasn't at all put off by the short notice. It was one o'clock in the morning when he got home. He roused the Baron and their valets and told them to pack and be ready for the 10 am boat train from Waterloo. He and the Baron sat up all night discussing the prospects. Thanks to the conmen's bush telegraph, they knew there was a big game of baccarat going on at the Turf Club in Mexico City, so they decided to pull off their big coup there and only do their travelling companions for a few thousand pounds on the way out, just so they didn't feel they were being idle. They had forgotten all about the railway; this invitation offered them a free trip to a grand win.

There was only one problem: neither of them was good enough at baccarat to be able to cheat at a public game in a club. 'We decided to call in an old friend, an Italian called Dominici, whose speciality was to 'beat' public baccarat games. Dominici was in Paris and they wrote asking him to leave by the next steamer for Mexico and wait for them in the city. Then they set off for Southampton. There were ten in the party: Mr and Mrs L, a Dutch banker, a French businessman, three shareholders and one American. There were four staterooms reserved for the party on the steamer, each for two guests. The valets, clearly happy to work like slaves for a free trip, bagged the best one for their masters and they lived the high life on the voyage to New York. They didn't have to put their hands in their pockets, apart from spending a few hundred dollars on flowers for Mrs L. They set about 'wiring' their travelling companions, discovering by innocent questions how much a man is good for at gambling and what game he plays.

Disaster! Three of the party were teetotal and had never played cards in their lives, one read scientific books all day and went to bed at ten, one confided, after a second whisky and soda, that he is a very quiet man at home, never goes to the club to play bridge but, once away from home, he didn't mind what he did – but it was for very small stakes. The American businessman was happy to play poker but he had a rule never to lose more than ten dollars at one sitting. Monty gave up and made friends with a beautiful young widow. He proposed marriage, got his wicked way etc but he 'lost' her once they got to New York. They stayed for three nights at the Waldorf Astoria and met lots of rich men but the conditions were never right for a game so they left without making a single dollar.

'This is all wrong,' said Monty. 'We must get busy.'

'And at once,' said the Baron, 'or we shall be broke.'

They boarded the train for the journey to Mexico. They had the private carriage of the railway magnate, which was put at the back of the train where there were fantastic views from the observation platform. The sleeping compartments had beautiful marble bathrooms and, once again, the valets had nabbed the best one for their bosses to share. Good food, too but, horrors, only water to drink. So when they stopped in Chicago for twenty-four hours, awaiting the next locomotive to pull them, they laid in a stock of wines and spirits and their compartment – which converted to a sitting-room during the day – became the bar when they set off again.

They were desperate for a gamble when the coach was uncoupled again and they had to wait at a small town station before it could be hitched to the back of yet another train for the next leg of the journey. They were in a 'dry' state. Various townspeople dropped in to see the financier-railwayman and to sample the bar. One was introduced to Monty with the words 'I want you to meet Mr Johns, our richest citizen.'

Monty was giddy with excitement. The man had a real mug's face, he thought, and when he opened his wallet to take out a business card it was stuffed with thousand-dollar bills. Monty stepped on the Baron's big toe to alert him. Mr Johns was invited to their compartment and after three whisky and sodas he became quite jolly. Monty was desperate by now: how to pluck this pigeon? Cards were out of the question at a social occasion like this and to discover dice in the corner of one's own compartment would not be nice, so he suggested a stroll into the town to find a cigar shop.

They were crossing the square in front of the station when the Baron pointed out a small red object on the ground. To their astonishment, it was a die!

'Keep it as a souvenir,' the Baron said to Mr John who pocketed it. When they found the cigar shop, everyone offered to pay for them. The Baron 'remembered' the die and suggested throwing it to decide who would pay. They did so and the Baron paid. One thing led to another; they each put up five dollars 'for fun' and the winner took all. Johns lost, tried double or quits and by the time he had lost $4,500 – at least that was the enormous figure that Monty Newton later claimed – it was time to run for the train.

'Thank goodness,' said Monty. 'Now we've got a bit of working capital.'

The next stop was at Kansas City for two days. They were put up at the local gentlemen's club. They lunched and dined well but they had to listen to dreary after-dinner speeches about the great future of the new railway. That was not why they had come to America so they looked round for a more profitable pastime. Monty escaped to the smoking-room where he saw four men he'd met at dinner the night before playing an American game called 'seven up'. Watching carefully, he realised it was similar to *écarté* and saw that 'with a little help' he could beat the game.

'That looks easy enough. I think I can play it,' he said to the men.

'I'll play you for a bottle of champagne,' said one of the men – yet another rich banker.

'Why not a case?' said Monty.

The Baron arrived and joined in, betting the banker, on Monty's hand, for dinner for the three of them. Naturally, he won and after the lavish dinner the three went on to play poker. 'It was like pulling teeth,' complained Monty, as the banker didn't want to bet more than twenty dollars a time but by 5 am Monty was five thousand dollars richer, (about £122,000). They went on to play acepots. Monty dealt himself good cards but not good enough and half an hour later his winnings were a hundred and sixty dollars instead of the six or seven thousand he'd planned on.

After two days they went on to Mexico and were greeted majestically at the border with a military band, fairy lights and their national flags. They didn't have an Austrian one for the Baron so they hoisted a German flag instead. A government minister greeted them on President Diaz's behalf and whisked them off to a banquet at the town hall. There were about two hundred guests, the food was good, the champagne flowed and the room was very hot. Monty noticed that the Baron was not holding back on the champagne. He became rather excited, told the minister all about his friend, the Emperor Franz Joseph of Austria, then stood up, delivered a long speech in Spanish inviting everybody present to come to Austria and spend a few months at his place, or his friend the Emperor's castle.

Monty thought the speech a great success and everybody was pleased. Fortunately, no one took up the invitation. Then it was on to Mexico City, pausing at Chichuahua and Zacatecas where they saw the future railway – a lot of Mexicans pushing wheelbarrows loaded with rocks. The railway magnate seemed a bit surprised they weren't more interested; they would have preferred a game of poker. At the city there was another welcome party and they were driven off in state coaches, built in 1800, to the Presidential palace. The Baron was the only Spanish-speaking member of the party so he chatted happily with the great man.

They were getting to the serious business now. Next day they met Dominici who, on the ship over, had made friends with a well-known Mexican who had already introduced him to the Turf Club where the big game of baccarat was going on. As guests of the President they had been made temporary members of the club but the fly in the ointment was that temporary members were not allowed to play in the baccarat room. They lunched and dined at the club where one evening they bumped into – what a surprise – an Italian gentleman whom they had once met at a dinner in the Italian embassy in Vienna, Signor Dominici!

They were not too down-hearted about not being able to play baccarat, as they played poker every afternoon and evening, which was bringing in about four thousand dollars a day. The Baron was sure they could make maybe two hundred thousand dollars in two or three weeks, (around £4,800,000 today).Dominici was bored, though; he didn't play poker and nagged them to arrange a private baccarat game. Now, in the poker group was a very rich young Mexican named Alvarez, the brother of a government minister. Even though he had lost four thousand dollars at poker, Alvarez insisted on joining the baccarat game. They played until six o'clock in the morning and Alvarez lost two hundred thousand dollars but he still wanted to play again next day.

They had done good business but they were uneasy. Discussing the evening later in their hotel room Monty said there was something in the way Alvarez behaved that he didn't like.

'Alvarez has spotted something,' said the Baron. 'But all we can do is wait and see.'

Alvarez didn't show up the next day and they thought they noticed a chilly atmosphere at lunch. In spite of that, they played poker and went back to their hotel two thousand dollars the richer.

Next day Dominici rushed in with news. He had met an Italian friend who kept a small gaming house in Mexico who told him that ten years before, Alvarez, before he had money, was a card sharp himself, working with a Frenchman they all knew well. So it seemed that in spite of not complaining of anything amiss in their game of baccarat, Alvarez, with a professional's intuition, felt he had been trimmed.

What to do? Alvarez had vanished. Dominici wrote to him asking for his winnings as he was about to return to Italy. A secretary replied that he had gone to the country but would be back in three days to attend to the matter.

The Baron and Monty, anxious not to show they were friends with Dominici and as Alvarez didn't owe them anything, decided to return to New York by sea, via Havana. They advised Dominici to return overland once he had collected his winnings. They thanked the railway magnate for his hospitality and told him they would let him know about the million and a half dollars' worth of shares they had applied for. Before leaving, the Baron asked the Austrian ambassador for advice about the railway. The man thought it was risky and there was a good chance of losing money so they had an excuse for dropping out of the deal.

Dominici joined them in New York and told them his story. He waited for three days in the hotel, his trunks packed so that he could make a quick getaway once he had received the two hundred thousand dollars, but nothing came. On the fourth day, loitering in the lobby, he saw a police officer in uniform come in and ask for him. It was all up. He rushed to his room, said 'I'm off!' to his valet and gave the man a hundred dollars to say Signor Dominici was out but would be back by midday. Leaving his luggage behind, he left by the back door, took a cab to the station and was on the first train out of Mexico.

'No use crying over spilt milk,' said Monty philosophically and ordered a bottle of champagne to celebrate Dominici's lucky escape. The Baron and Monty decided to stay on in New York in the hope of better luck but Monty had to leave the restaurant in a hurry that night because the woman he'd promised to marry on the liner coming over spotted him and called the police.

Dining at Del Monico's restaurant a couple of days later, they met an old friend who had just come from Mexico. He told them the Alvarez business was the talk of the town. Monty said his heart stopped beating. Were they discovered? Then their friend told them what had happened.

Alvarez had put his suspicions to the committee of the Turf Club who decided there was no proof the game was unfair and, as it had taken place in the club, the money must be paid and Alvarez must not show his face until this was done. His bank needed a couple of days to sell some securities for him, which explained his visit to 'the country'.

'But what about the policeman who came for Dominici?' said Monty.

'Policeman? That was no police officer. It was a uniformed bank messenger bringing the money. You know how they like to dress up in Mexico.'[10]

CHAPTER EIGHTEEN

A Castle in Spain

After a successful business trip to Rome, the Baron and Monty decided to move on to Spain. They drove to Naples where they loaded the car on to a steamer and set sail for Gibraltar, planning to drive from south to north, to San Sebastian. It was spring and the drive to Seville was lovely, through scented groves of almond and orange trees. One afternoon, sitting in the patio of the Hotel de Paris, they found a Spanish friend, Cayetano, also in the 'profession', who told them of a duke with an estate nearby who would be good for a million pesetas if only they could get to meet him. He had tried everything; he said the duke was once one of the biggest gamblers in Spain but every time he played in private he lost, so now he gambled only in his club, in well-known casinos or with intimate friends. The duke had even made a little museum with all kinds of instruments used for fixing games and he knew more about cardsharping than many of the men who made a living at it. So that ruled out the team's chance of fixing a game. Also, the man had been introduced by a Scotland Yard detective to a famous cardsharp who had shown him every possible card trick that could be played on him. On top of that, the duchess guarded her man and would never allow any untitled stranger to approach. No title, no chance.

When he heard that the duke has a fabulous collection of Chinese curios in his castle on the road between Seville and Cordoba, Monty gave himself a title. He ordered visiting cards and writing-paper stamped with his coat of arms; he had a uniform made for the Baron's valet, who would become his chauffeur and the Baron was to be his secretary. The Baron went back to London to collect a beautiful Chinese curio from the flat they shared. Monty had bought it from a Chinese soldier who had stolen it from the summer palace in Peking; a London dealer had offered £500 (around £59,000) for it but Monty was not in need of money at the time and held on to it. Then the Baron went to the castle with a note from his 'master' asking if he might see his famous collection. They were invited to tea and Monty showed him his own jade god. The duke wanted to buy it but Monty wouldn't part with it.

They saw the duke again next day and he took them to see some things from Roman remains recently uncovered nearby. There were four ivory dice. Monty had seen Roman dice before, in Pompeii, perfect cubes, but these were slightly different: one side was square and the other oblong. Monty persuaded – bribed – the mayor to sell him two and presented them to the duke as souvenirs. Then he suggested they play with them but to play for money with two thousand-year-old dice would be sacrilege so he suggested playing for his Chinese god, which the duke had already offered fifty thousand pesetas for.

'If you win, the god is yours. If you lose you can still have the god but you must pay me fifty thousand pesetas for it,' was Monty's deal.

The duke thought this was not fair on Monty but Monty knew better; he had realised the dice were not perfect cubes... The duke lost something close to thirty-five thousand pounds. Thirty-five thousand pounds for a little green god that had cost him £50 was not bad, thought Monty.

* * *

The Baron and Monty spent a fruitless late summer month at Lake Lucerne and the nights were drawing in. They decided on a change of climate and scenery and set sail for Buenos Aires, hoping for a long and lucrative trip. Before the ship was out of the Thames, however, they spotted a rival gang of three conmen. When sober they were rough characters, and in their cups they were very unpleasant customers. But they provided some entertainment. One said he owned a sheep station in Australia; if the acreage were correct it would be half the size of that continent. He added that the biggest river in Australia ran through it, fed from the Himalayas. His partner said he was wrong because everyone knows the Himalayas are in South America. The voyage was successful, workwise, for the Baron and Monty but they saw that the rival team was so bad at business that they would soon be found out, so they dumped them in Buenos Aires and went up-river to Asunciòn, capital of Paraguay.

The five-day trip was beautiful, the banks of the river only a stone's throw from the steamer; the forest was virgin and they shot more than fifty *fecare*, the South American alligator, from the deck. Asunciòn was a disappointment, dilapidated and dusty and no more than a village, half-hidden in the luxuriant tropical vegetation. It seems a strange choice; perhaps they were in such a rush to get away from their rivals they didn't do their usual homework. The hotel, a little way out of town, was definitely not up to their standards. It was a one-storied mud and brick building with floors of beaten earth. Before going to bed they had to spend half an hour getting rid of 'visitors' – bull frogs, bats, centipedes, enormous spiders and other 'nasty-looking animals'.

There was an 'annexe' for socialising and gambling, a corrugated iron shed with a few tables and chairs, a saggy sofa and an old billiards table, not a promising setting for a big win. They found half a dozen men ready to play poker but were startled when they removed their jackets on sitting down and produced from their pockets enormous revolvers which they placed on the table.

'When in Rome, do as the Romans do,' thought the Baron and went to his room for his own two pistols which he placed on the table. The men were all astonished and asked what he was going to do with them.

'Just return the compliments if there is any dispute.'

They were amused and said they put their guns on the table because it was uncomfortable to sit with them in their pockets. But it was just as well to be armed as there had been five murders at night in the last two months, three on the road from the hotel to the town and two in the hotel itself. After that, as well as looking for insects, they looked under their beds just in case there was a gent who had wandered into the wrong room. They made a killing of sorts, though. When Monty asked for a liqueur after dinner, the proprietor, an old Frenchman, brought a bottle of Chartreuse which Monty, a bit of a connoisseur, recognised as the real, original stuff, poured from the bottle that the monks used before they made their own style of bottle. The hotelier explained that his father had brought a case with him when he emigrated to Paraguay and this was the first bottle he had opened. Monty snapped up the twelve bottles for a pound each and said he would gladly have paid five times that if it had been asked for.

On their last night they won big. When they cashed their cheques at the bank next morning they had to get a man to carry the money to their hotel in a pannier, the double straw basket that donkeys carry their load in. The bank was short of large notes and instead of thousand-dollar bills they made a bundle of two thousand fifty-cent notes, which circulated like a single thousand-dollar note and became very dirty, ragged and smelly.

There was no relaxation on the steamer back to Buenos Aires; they met a South American diplomat and helped him pass the time with three-handed bridge, which cost him £250 (£27,000).

Then it was on to Monte Video, Uruguay, for ten days, after which they took a ferry across the river de la Plata and made for Buenos Aires. They decided to take the train to Santiago de Chile but the track didn't cross the Andes – highest mountain, Aconcagua, 20,900 feet. They didn't mind roughing it, spent the night in a camp in the foothills and next day hired a couple of horses. These two were more like Butch Cassidy and the Sundance Kid than the couple of lounge lizards we knew in Europe. It was a treacherous journey over uninhabited passes, hungry Andean condors hovering above them. Intrepid horsemen do it now as an example of extreme tourism – it takes five or six days. The Baron and Newton rode as far as Los Andes de Chile then took the train to Santiago, then, as now by all accounts, a lawless metropolis. But Santiago did not smile on them and they were short of money – this was something that happened often; they had lost money at the card tables and spent money on high living at the dinner tables. When they decided to go north up the coast to Peru they had £250 between them but when they reached Lima they followed their usual habit and booked the best rooms in the best hotel.

'Something has got to be got,' said Monty. Monty knew of a notorious gambling den run by a Chinese named Lulu, usually known as John. Dice was his game and they knew he threw from a dice box that had been fixed.

'Not the sort of thing you would choose to go into, specially as the Chinese are devilish clever,' thought Monty but they were desperate and they liked a challenge so they decided to take a chance.

The Baron left their hotel and booked into a cheap boarding house, leaving his valet with Monty. He was to make the acquaintance of Lulu, sometimes winning, sometimes losing. After a week, which he spent with a lovely girl at his hotel, Monty went to the gambling den in full evening dress, a sensation, for most of the men in the room didn't even have a collar; the girl from the hotel was with him, also expensively dressed.

Monty had their little capital wrapped round the usual wad of lavatory paper, to make it look like a fat roll of notes, pretended to be drunk, lost at cards, made a scene, bought champagne for Lulu. He 'accidentally' dropped a £50 note on the floor. The Baron, who was at the bar, pretending not to know Monty, put his foot on it. Monty moved on, the Baron picked up the note and Lulu insisted on taking half of it. The Baron paid grudgingly but at this point put in his finest work. He had given the impression early that he'd left Austria for his own good and his family was paying him to stay away. Just the sort of man Lulu needed. He suggested the Baron moved into Monty's hotel and made friends with him.

'I'll soon find out where he's staying,' said Lulu, 'for I told one of my men to follow him.' Monty had no idea he'd been followed. 'If you can persuade him to come here again you can have a third of all he loses.'

'What if he wins?'

'You needn't worry about him winning.'

The Baron soon 'made the acquaintance' of Monty and reported to Lulu that the man liked games of chance and would gamble heavily; he favoured a South African game played with two dice, called Lucky Boer. This was just a question of which player would throw the higher number. The Baron went to an ivory turner and had him make two ordinary dice and two more which would normally throw high numbers. These dice were more successful than Lulu's. Monty won. Lulu could hardly believe his eyes but assumed that Monty was just having a lucky run, so he upped the stakes and suggested playing for £500 (£56,000) a throw, thinking that his luck must turn soon.

'I'm quite willing,' said Monty, 'but when I play for such high stakes, I like to see the money on the table.' Monty won, of course, and grabbed the 20,000 Peruvian pesos, about £2,000 at the time, or around £220,000 now, from the table. 'Give me back that money,' said Lulu, diving for his gun. 'He moved as fast as a snake strikes,' said Monty later. But Monty was just a lightning move ahead of him. When he visited Lulu in hospital a couple of days later – the Chinese had particularly asked to see him – the hole in his arm was healing nicely. Butch and Sundance thought it sensible to leave Lima and made for Panama and a passage home.

The Baron made another trip to South America in 1904 or 1905. On the voyage to Buenos Aires he met a woman and her daughter; her husband, a respected police doctor in Paris, had just died and they were returning to her parents' home in Buenos Aires. The daughter, Marie Renée Lemoine Escalada, soon caught the baron's eye; she was nineteen, fresh and pretty, missing the steadying presence of her father, impressed by the sophisticated older man – he was thirty-four but looked older because his fair hair was very thin by now. Renée, as she was known, was an heiress. Her father was a modestly paid police doctor in Paris but her mother's father was said to possess a massive fortune of several million Marks. After a whirlwind courtship (another woman who had been discarded sued for breach of promise) they were married in Buenos Aires on 3 November 1905. The bride's grandfather settled 400,000 Marks on Renee; her uncle, a Roman Catholic archbishop, officiated but not until the Baron, a protestant, had agreed to have their children brought up as Catholics. He took his wife's name, Lemoine, and her brother, Henri's, passport; so he returned unrecognised to the land that had expelled him a few years before. Renée was bewitched by her husband and readily took to the glamorous life of the casino and the false name he had given her, Baroness Scalda. From the moment they married they were rarely apart; fortunately, Newton was quite happy for the criminal duo to become the criminal trio. The demure bride from Paris gave a touch of respectability to the man who liked to present himself as a mining engineer and successful businessman. Her letters home give a glimpse of the life she was enjoying; only a glimpse, for she never mentioned her husband's activities. It was not always glamorous, though. Their honeymoon trip found them caught in an earthquake at Valparaiso, Chile, on 17 August 1906. They had arrived after spending two days crossing the Andes on horseback and she was dead tired and went to bed. She was wakened in the night by the shaking of the earthquake. 'I saw the wardrobe with the big mirror coming towards me, the stairs moving up and down. I heard a great clamour, calls for help, things clattering, things falling.' She lay fully dressed on her bed waiting for the second shock, and fell asleep until the next morning.[11]

In May 1907 the Baron again offered to work for the French secret service; he wanted to be useful to France because of his love for his wife. The Ministry of Defence looked at his material and said it was useless. This didn't deter the Baron and the following year he renewed his friendship with Jules Sebille, head of security services in Lyon, whom he had met when he was expelled. By this time he was head of the Tiger Brigades, the new flying squads created by Prime Minister George Clemenceau and called after his nickname, the Tiger. Lemoine again offered his services as a spy. From that moment on he worked with Sebille, who credited him with breaking up a German spy network. According to Eric Maillard, it was Sebille who sent Lemoine to Spain in 1914 where his wife and quickly growing family gave him respectable cover.

Before that, though, in October 1908 the trio set off on a world tour. Renée sent a travelogue home: on 21 July they set sail from Cherbourg on the SS *Crown Prince Willhelm* for New York; then they crossed Canada to Vancouver, which they reached on 14 August.

All was not going well for the gamblers and they were short of money yet again. Renée's mother sent them two cheques so they went on to South America, then back to San Francisco, en route to Japan and China. They were in Canton in December and arrived on the island of Java at the beginning of January, intending to stay until 15 February. Java, at that time part of the Dutch East

Indies, now Indonesia, was the colony that made the Netherlands rich with its huge production of spices, rubber, tea, coffee and oil. Renée loved it; she wrote to her mother from Hotel des Indes in Jakarta, starting the letter in English, '*Mother Dear:* My health is very good so far. I don't eat much because of the heat and also so as not to get fat. I would like to be a bit thinner.' She didn't want to get sun-tanned hands but wearing gloves was intolerable in the heat and she complained that her body hair was particularly 'exuberant' and she had to pluck each morning. 'I think my tweezers are the most useful things in my luggage; if I lose them I will die.'

She wrote that Jakarta was so beautiful it would take a whole book to describe it. Monty Newton, writing seventeen years later, thought the same: 'If I had to place paradise somewhere in the world, it should be in Java. I have been three times round the world but I have never made a more delightful trip in more exquisitely beautiful country than on the occasion I motored from Batavia [Jakarta now] via Bandong and Samarang to Rembang.'

'You don't know where to look,' wrote Renée. 'There are nude men with big chignons, tattooed Arabs, women with ear-rings as big as slices of melon, golden horns on their heads. And naked women dancing in the street. And a sun and a sun. Big kisses from your Renée.'

She wrote again in February, complaining that she wasn't getting any mail from home and it was difficult to communicate because of all the zig zags their travels entailed, but they were clearly having fun in the top echelons of society. 'We know everybody; all the diplomatic corps dine with us. We are at all the concerts, all the parties. We take drives in the car, I am covered with baskets of orchids, jasmines, hydrangeas. And the splendid vegetation!'

The climate was irresistible and after three days they felt like locals. They got up early and went out exploring in the car from six until nine, before it was too hot. From nine until midday there was a queue of visitors on their little verandah. After lunch they slept until five o'clock, which was when life began again.

After five weeks in Jakarta they set off to explore the island, visiting little towns in the interior, famous temples, volcanoes. She was amazed at the orchids, some as big as the sun, others as small as flies, she wrote. There were flying squirrels, snakes of all shapes and sizes, plants that ate insects. 'There are big monkeys that look like men and a lot of men who are monkeys.'

'She was thinking of me when she wrote that,' Rudolf added in a PS to his mother-in-law.

They were in love and having a lovely time but Renée's letters don't say where the money is coming from for this lavish life and she doesn't mention her husband's work. Monty Newton describing an earlier visit to Java with the Baron, gave a clue; he said he arrived with £50 and left with £20,000, which had contributed to his enjoyment no end. The trio decided to extend their stay in this wonderful country until the middle of April, then, who knows? Renée wrote. Perhaps they would go directly to Europe and to London, perhaps they would return the way they had come, visiting Japan in spring for '*la saison chic pour des étrangers*' – cherry blossom time – and then return to London via North America, arriving in July. And on 18 July 1909 Rudolf wrote to the French Ministry of the Interior asking for the suspension of the expulsion order against him that had been in place for six years, citing his French family and the services he had previously rendered the French intelligence service. The reply wasn't hopeful because of his previous activities as Stallman, so the autumn found them in Wiesbaden again, a favourite spot for the con artist.

Strolling round the spa, sitting in smart bars, he got to know a twenty-three-year old farmer, Rudolf Kiepert. He took his time to pluck this pigeon; they met several times but never played cards. One evening Kiepert was sitting in the Tannus bar with some friends where they were throwing dice for drinks. The Baron asked if he might join the party and soon after someone suggested playing baccarat and they bought a pack of cards at the bar. Poor Kiepert lost seventeen thousand Marks to the Baron; although rather drunk at the time, he noticed that von Koenig punted very little so he must have won when he held the bank and had an opportunity of manipulating the cards. Von Koenig offered Kiepert his revenge next night, after a good dinner. Unwilling at first, Kiepert allowed himself to be persuaded and this time he lost five thousand Marks. Von Koenig left town the next day after collecting twenty-two thousand Marks (something like £120,000 today) in cash from Kiepert. Sensing that something was wrong, Kiepert went to the police who told him that Baron von Koenig, AKA Rudolf Stallman, had been known to them for years as a card sharp.

On 27 October 1909 Rudolf got his heart's desire: Jules Sebille gave orders to the Paris police to allow him to spend a month in Paris; this was then extended to three months, until 25 January 1910. So they moved to Paris, to a flat rented by Renée's mother, Lastenia Lemoine, for a thousand Francs a month. They bought impressive antique furniture and took on an Egyptian chauffeur for the new car. There were lots of visitors, which intrigued the police who were keeping an eye on the couple. They were soon on the move again, to the Cote d'Azur for the winter season. But in February he was recognised by the police who knew him as Rudolf Stallman-Baron von Koenig, the crook they had expelled in 1902. Jules Sebille, whom the Baron had been working for since 1908, intervened: the man could stay in France as long as he kept away from casinos and gambling clubs.

He kept away from casinos in France all right but Sebille couldn't keep him away from Germany, and on 1 June 1910 he was on the way to Berlin. He was introduced on the train to twenty-year-old Lieutenant George von Dippe by an acquaintance he knew as von Hennrichs. When the train reached Berlin the three men were getting on so well they decided to have lunch together at the Baron's hotel, the newly-built Furstenhof on Leipzig Platz. The décor was gilt and flashy, the service swift and discreet. Von Dippe, who came from a well-off family, said the number of bottles of champagne drunk was 'extraordinarily abundant'. After lunch they went up to the Baron's suite for coffee and brandy. Again, the Baron used a carefully casual approach: he offered to explain the game of bridge to von Dippe and called for two packs of cards. He dealt a pack and laid out the hands on the table, leaving von Dippe to consider them while he started a game of *rouge et noir* with von Hennrichs, who held the bank. They played for moderate stakes and did not put the cash down on the table but kept a book of wins and losses. Presently von Koenig called von Dippe over to help him; the stakes then increased dramatically and von Koenig told von Dippe that if he joined in the game he must share the losses. They played together, winning when the stakes were small, losing when they played for the whole amount in the bank, which sometimes amounted to thirty thousand Marks. When the banker, von Hennrichs, was eighty thousand Marks to the good von Koenig jumped up and cried that this was too high for him. He grabbed the cards and tore them up. They discussed how to settle up and von Hennrichs produced some blank bank draft forms from his pocket and von Koenig and von Dippe each signed a bill for forty thousand Marks.

Von Dippe afterwards heard talk about von Koenig and came to the conclusion that he had been swindled and went to the police. His bill of exchange for von Hennrichs had, in the meantime, been endorsed to von Koenig and the words 'payable at the German Bank, Berlin' added. Von Koenig in turn re-endorsed it to his best friend, Newton, who was using his middle name, Noel, this time. Newton saw von Dippe about payment of the bill who told him to go to the bank in Berlin. Von Dippe telephoned his solicitor in Berlin and when Newton turned up to cash the draft, the police were there and took it from him.

Lemoine, Stallman, von Koenig; what was the true name of Monty's friend? The German police were mystified. Then a man named Wittkop testified that he was married to Anna, Stallman's sister. He recognised his writing and said that the signature on the draft signed 'R. von Koenig' was in Stallmann's hand. And who was Stallman? He was Louis Guillaume Rudolf, the only son of Louis von Stahlmann, a prosperous jeweller, who was in business with his brother in Orianenstrasse, in Berlin.

CHAPTER NINETEEN

The Police Catch up with the Baron

A few weeks later the whole world was excited by a spy story – a young German officer was in trouble in England. Lieutenant Sigmund Helm, of the 21st Nassau Battalion, was arrested at Portsmouth on 5 September while sketching the fortifications at Portsmouth. He had been seen, on three days, in white suit and Panama hat lying on his tummy in the grass overlooking the disused, tumbledown fort in Portsmouth harbour, sketching. When it was announced that he would appear at Fareham Police Court on 16 September, the building was besieged by the spy-crazy public and the chairman of the magistrates had to issue entrance tickets; no photography was allowed and someone who dared to try had the plate confiscated. The charge was of making sketches and plans of the fortress on 3, 4 and 5 September intending to communicate them to Germany contrary to the Official Secrets Act. This was quite pointless as he could have bought a picture postcard of the same scene at any seafront kiosk; even a German newspaper, the National Zeitung said it was a tit-for-tat affair, in revenge for the arrest of two Englishmen, Lieutenant Vivien Brandon of the Royal Navy and Royal Marines captain Bernard Trench at Boskum island, one of the German Friesian islands. They were being held in Leipzig, accused of espionage, and pleaded guilty.

In fact, Helm's arrest was pure coincidence, according to the diary of Major Vernon Kell, in charge of the Secret Intelligence Bureau's domestic department at the time, which became MI5. Brandon and Trench were spying out Germany's northern defences.

(Erskine Childers's novel, *The Riddle of the Sands*, published in 1903, and often called the first modern spy story, describes a similar escapade. It gives an engrossing account of the atmosphere of the time.)

Lieutenant Helm's charge was reduced to a misdemeanour and when he came up for trial at Winchester Assizes on 15 November 1910 he pleaded guilty; the prosecution by now regarded him as a sweet young man and asked for leniency as long as he said sorry and he wouldn't do it again. He said sorry and was bound over in the sum of £250. Brandon and Trench were sentenced to four years' detention each but released in 1913.

Lieutenant Helm was a keen young officer who had come to England to perfect his English; a brother officer had met an Englishwoman, Hannah Wodehouse, when she was in Berlin the year before and suggested he went to see her. She had moved from her London lodgings to Fareham and Helm paid her a visit, not knowing Fareham was close to Portsmouth. Young Helm, a compulsive diarist, note-taker and sketcher, carried a notebook with him all the time. They squabbled when Hannah criticised one of his sketches and she went to the army barracks nearby and reported his 'suspicious' behaviour.

I wonder if he was quite so innocent, though, because I found that an artist's sketchbook or easel is a very good cover used by spies who want to hang around a place watching without arousing suspicion. Later, one of Lemoine's accomplices did such a thing; and Sir Robert Baden-Powell, founder of the Boy Scouts movement, acted as a spy for Britain in Dalmatia, disguised as an English eccentric, carrying a sketch book and paints as well as a butterfly net. He hid the plans for the fortifications of the region in the wings of the butterflies he sketched.[12]

At around the same time and probably aware that the police were on his tail, the Baron adopted a new name, Julius Steinmann, and returned to London with Monty, where they teamed up with yet another title-holder, Count Gisbert Wolff-Metternich, a relative of the German ambassador to London. The twenty-five-year-old Gisbert was clearly the problem child of his grand family: at fifteen he was placed in a psychiatric hospital after attempting to commit suicide. A few years later the family exiled him to a ranch in Chile.

He returned to Berlin in May 1909 with nothing but the thirty Marks a month which his father gave him to pay for the rent of a room. He clearly fell in with the wrong company. One afternoon, in a London hotel, Steinmann/Lemoine, Monty Newton and Wolff-Metternich cheated another young German officer, Lieutenant Fritz Beckhaus, of more than three hundred pounds in a crooked card game. Beckhaus was said to have been in London on private affairs plus 'a bit of military work'. Another spy story, perhaps?

Lieutenant Beckhaus told the German police that he thought he had been cheated and Count Wolff-Metternich was arrested in Vienna two days before Christmas on suspicion of belonging to a ring of international card sharps that included Stallman and Newton. He was extradited to Berlin. A warrant for the arrest of Rudolf Stallmann was issued at Bow Street Magistrates' Court on 12 November 1910 but the Baron had already made a getaway and was on his way to South Africa.

Wolff-Metternich's trial in December 1911 was an international sensation, with newspapers giving various colourful versions and unable to resist sanctimonious comments about the off-duty activities of young army officers. A picture emerged of the broke Wolff-Metternich's intention to marry a rich woman. In November 1909 he became friends with a Frau Wolff Wertheim and her divorced daughter, Dolly Landsberger. He was a daily visitor to their house and seemed confident he would marry Dolly; it didn't happen and in September 1910 he married Claire Walentin, a Viennese actress. Marital bliss ended a couple of months later with Wolff-Metternich's arrest and extradition to Berlin. His wife cut an artery in her wrist, was admitted to a psychiatric hospital and became a patient of Sigmund Freud. By the time Wolff-Metternich came to trial in July 1911 thirty-three complaints of fraud had been investigated; he was convicted of three charges and sentenced to nine months. He had already been in custody for six months so he was soon free. His wife's health improved and she divorced him in 1915.

CHAPTER TWENTY

The Chase – and the End
of an Era

When Lieutenant Beckhaus described Julius Steinmann, the man who had cheated him in London, the German police recognised him as the man they still knew as Stallmann. When he heard this through his grapevine of informers he was on the first boat out of Tilbury to South Africa. But the police had their own grapevine and applied to the South African court for an extradition order for him to face the charges that von Dippe and Kiepert had made, so he moved on to India where he lived safely for six months and very likely found professional company; Edward VII died on 6 May the year before and George V had succeeded him. The new king was to come to Delhi in November for his coronation Durbar; preparations were being made and excitement was mounting. The cream of the British Empire would be gathered there, making Delhi a bounteous hunting ground for con artists and card sharps.

It was not to be for Baron von Koenig. On 11 April 1911 the Consul General for Germany in Calcutta asked for his arrest and extradition to Germany to face charges of cheating Kiepert and von Dippe. The police caught up with him five days later as he tried to escape aboard the SS *Caspian*, which was lying outside Diamond Harbour, Calcutta. He appeared in court under the name of Rudolf Stallman. He denied everything and said the German police were only interested in him because of his acquaintance with the young German officer, Lieutenant Helm, who was arrested in England the year before. What does this show? Was it that he knew Helm and accepted he was a spy?

The extradition hearings went on for weeks and the Baron was kept in prison. We can only imagine what an Indian prison was like a century ago and it drove the Baron to try to kill himself; most unexpected for the daredevil conman we know. The Indian government made a complete mess of the extradition proceedings and the Baron was released on 21 August 1911. He made for Indonesia, a long-time favourite spot, and was back in London by the end of November when the German Embassy informed the police he had been seen. There was already a warrant out for his arrest but it was not until 1 April the following year that extradition proceedings began.

During the drawn-out proceedings at Bow Street Magistrates' Court his barrister, Henry Curtis Bennett, said he had been known by the name of von Koenig for more twenty years and for ten years he had had bank accounts in England and in France in that name. But he denied he had used the name for fraudulent purposes. In 1905 he was married in the name of von Koenig to a Miss Lemoine, who had an annual income of £2,000 (about £230,000 today) and his income from investments alone was £3,000. His father and uncle were formerly in partnership as wholesale jewellers in Berlin and when the uncle died he left his considerable fortune to his nephew and niece. Stallmann said his income came from a number of companies, patents and mines and a newspaper called *Paris Turf* that he had started at the beginning of 1909. Within the last two months he had sold part of his property for £15,000 (£1,680,000).

This time no one could save Lemoine/von Koenig/Stallmann and he was extradited on 16 July 1912 and came to trial in Berlin on 16 March the following year. He was forty-two and told the court he had packed a lot into those years: been a volunteer in the Chilean revolution, ridden across the South American continent and made money speculating in mines in South Africa. Although a passionate gambler, he never resorted to cheating as he had always had ample means of his own. He blamed everything on his double, a man called Rudolf von Koenig, a gambler and adventurer. What chutzpah!

He was sentenced on 10 April to nine months in prison and, as he had been in custody for eight months, he was released a month later. It was not much for the German police to show for their two-and-a-half-year chase. A couple of months later their first child, Randal, was born on 30 July 1913. German prisons allowed conjugal visits.

* * *

Until Monty published his confessions in 1925 he was unknown, except to the police. He does not mention dates in his account of his twenty-five-year criminal career during which he had only one conviction, the one in 1907 for forgery. Lemoine had been in court several times, in Germany, Austria, India and London under different names and for other offences so I have used the dates of those appearances to try to put their story into some kind of chronological order. He was released from prison in May 1913 and made for Monte Carlo for some spring sunshine; he left behind his wife who was seven months pregnant. 1913 is the only date that Monty Newton ever mentions. It was a year, he said, when illegal card clubs were springing up in Mayfair. When he returned one night after a disastrous attempt to cheat the sophisticated players at one of these clubs he found a telegram from a lawyer in Nice saying the Baron had been arrested and wanted him to come at once. The Baron was on a solo trip to Monte Carlo to play one of his many infallible systems; they invariably failed.

'I wish Monte Carlo didn't exist,' complained Newton. 'I always arrive with my pockets full and leave with them empty. If you can stay outside the gaming rooms Dame Fortune is a lady very easily wooed and she has smiled on me on a number of occasions. But at the tables, no, no, no.' But he couldn't abandon his friend so he told his valet to pack for a fortnight and they left for the Riviera the next morning. Monty normally hated rushing through Paris but this time he took a taxi straight from the Gare du Nord to the Gare du Lyon and waited for the first train out. The train seemed to crawl and when they arrived at Nice Monty sent the valet on to the hotel with their luggage while he went direct to the lawyer. The situation was incomprehensible: the Baron had bribed a prison warder to take his letter to the lawyer, telling him to ask Monty to come at once. All enquiries made by the lawyer were met with polite refusals; the police would not say why the Baron was arrested, they would not allow him visitors, they would not even discuss the matter. He was being held *incommunicado*. For twenty-four hours Monty and the lawyer tried everything and everyone they knew to get to see him but without success. So imagine Monty's surprise when he went to see the lawyer the following afternoon to find the Baron sitting comfortably in an armchair, smoking a pipe.

The explanation was quite simple. His gaming system had gone wrong again. He had noticed a German officer at the casino who was playing for very high stakes but who would occasionally play a small game with a friend and the Baron thought this man might prove a suitable victim for his card tricks so he decided to become one of those friends. He cultivated him, no doubt with stories of his own visits to the luxurious spa towns and casinos of Germany, and they went about together a lot. Arriving at the German's hotel for lunch one day, he found the man had been arrested, suspected of being a spy. The Baron, who had been seen with the man every day, speaking German, was nabbed, as a precaution until the police were satisfied he was not involved. Then they released him without explanation or apology. Monty was so relieved at his release that he managed not to rub in the fallibility of the infallible system but swept his friend off to a fine restaurant to hear about his time in prison.

Monty Newton ended his memoirs in 1913 and what then?

> Later I was in a certain country on the continent where strange circumstances threw me in contact with people who thought my abilities could be used in quite a different way; I do not know if I realised their expectations but I do know the people I worked for trusted me and liked me; and those I worked against paid me the compliment of considering me a dangerous enemy.
>
> Politics were largely concerned in the work and I took a part in some rather extraordinary adventures but there is much of what I did and saw and heard that I should not feel at liberty to divulge.

Was Monty a spy? His partner was acquainted with Lieutenant Helm and his arrest for spying in England in 1910. The French had suspected the Baron was a spy in 1902. Had he recruited Monty to the game?

Spy or not, Monty did his patriotic duty when the war broke out. He changed his name to Gerald Norman Montgomery Newton to hide his conviction and lied about his age to join the British Army, saying he was born on Christmas Day 1877. I thought this was a joke, Monty showing he was rather closely related to God and above the laws of man but when I went through the ledgers at the Family Records Office in London I found that he really was born on 25 December but in 1871. He was named Montague, after his father, with the Christmassy addition of Noel as a middle name. His father also had a seasonal touch, his middle name being Gabriel. His mother was Fanny Maria.

Monty was appointed lieutenant in the Army Service Corps on 8 November 1914 when his previous military service in the South African forces was given as fourteen months in the British South Africa Police, service in the Rhodesia Imperial Yeomanry and in the South African Irregular Forces. He was awarded the Queen's medal with three bars as well as the King's medal. His record in the British Army was not as distinguished and he was court-martialled in September 1916 for disobeying an order. He was told to take a draft of soldiers from Catterick camp to Aldershot on 2 August but did not do so, although he made a written report at Catterick that he had. What happened to his men is not recorded – did they go AWOL? Were they left unnoticed at Catterick? Was this part of his war effort on behalf of whoever he had been spying for? Monty was ordered to be 'severely reprimanded' and his seniority was reduced. Three weeks later he was given six weeks' sick leave and finally relinquished his commission at the end of February 1917 because of ill-health – he was suffering from lumbago and haemorrhoids and his honorary rank of lieutenant was cancelled.[13]

Back in London he continued to wear uniform, promoting himself to captain, and resumed his career as a card sharp in the gambling dens of London. He took up with an old friend, William Cooper Hobbs, the managing clerk of a firm of solicitors. Hobbs as we know was more than the humble solicitor's clerk that he pretended; he was the Mr Big of the London underworld. He was not a qualified solicitor but whenever a top man in the criminal world was in trouble, he called on Hobbs, who would brief a star lawyer on his behalf. He loaned money, financed burglaries, received stolen goods and created his own 'passport office' for criminals who needed to get out of the country quickly. He was well known to the police who estimated he was worth a quarter of a million pounds – that would be over ten million today – but they had never been able to pin anything on him.

A large part of his fortune was made dealing with card sharps like Monty Newton and the Baron. Illegal gambling dens were a feature of London life. Monty and Hobbs helped to bankrupt Austin Smith, grandson of Sir Frank Smith, Ontario's first millionaire and one-time president of the Dominion Bank. The young man was visiting London, got in with the wrong crowd, went through his own £175,000 fortune and was introduced to Hobbs, who loaned him the money to pay the gambling debts he owed Monty; this happened over and over and soon he was bankrupt. Hobbs claimed substantial amounts from the estates of the late Sir Frank and young Frank's grandfather, the late Hugh Ryan, and Newton also claimed the equivalent today of some £100,000 to cover his own losses.

They would have to wait a couple of years until the case was heard and so, in 1919, Newton was looking for another big deal… Sir Hari Singh came along in the nick of time and Monty was to earn more than three million pounds for one night's work.

PART THREE

The Spymaster who Bought the Enigma Codes, the Traitor who Sold Them and his Brother – Hitler's Favourite General

CHAPTER TWENTY-ONE

The Baron's War

The baron's war record is not as easily chronicled as Monty Newton's. In August 1920 *La Correspondencia Militar*, a right-wing Madrid newspaper founded to promote the interests of the army officer class, reprinted a five-thousand-word article about him which *La Tribuna*, another Madrid paper, published. The stories are fantastical: lurid tales of murder, betrayal, gangsterism. No dates are given but there is just enough in one of the accounts to make me think that the general outline might be right. This was the story of his

> ... first large-scale fraud in Berlin; he was gambling in one of the aristocratic salons of the German capital with an army officer from whom he won around twenty-five thousand marks in less than an hour. Suspecting the means used by his opponent, the officer reported him to the authorities and he was tried and sentenced to six years in prison. The fake Baron von Koenig conveniently made himself scarce and took refuge in Paris. At the German consulate in Barcelona in 1912 there was a 'wanted' portrait of Baron von Koenig, Friedrich Stallmann on the wall; he was wanted by the authorities as the perpetrator of the fraud we have described and for contempt of court.

This sounds like the cheating of the unfortunate Lieutenant von Dippe, but that happened in a hotel in Berlin in June 1910 and the man lost forty thousand Marks. Or could it have been the young farmer, Rudolf Kiepert? He lost twenty-two thousand Marks in a bar in Wiesbaden in 1909 in a game that went on all night. I know that the baron wasn't arrested so he couldn't have been sentenced to six years. In fact, he was on the run – across Europe, South Africa and India – and the German police were in close pursuit, trying to get him extradited to face these two charges of cheating so there very likely *was* a 'wanted' picture of him in the Barcelona consulate.

In 1914 he arrived in Fuenterrabia in the north, just across the border from France, with his wife Baroness Renée Scalda and their rapidly growing family. After Randal another son, Guy Raoul Rolf, was born in Paris on 19 July 1914 and a daughter, Rhoda, was born at Fuenterrabia on 22 August 1915: a sudden rush to have a family after ten years of marriage. All the children had the surname of von Koenig Lemoine. There is a record of Randal's baptism in Fuenterrabia on 2 September 1915 when Rhoda was twelve days old, so very likely all three were baptised at the same time. Did Lemoine decide that he would rather work from home now that he had a family rather than darting hither and yon round the world? The doting Papa became the director of the casinos at Fuenterrabia and San Sebastian in 1915, he told French police in 1945; San Sebastian was smart, the town the royal court decamped to in the summer when Madrid was too hot.

All of Germany was too hot for Stallman after his conviction; Jules Sebille thought neutral Spain would eventually side with Germany and it would be useful to have a contact like Stallman in situ. He was right: according to French researcher Olivier Baccu, Stallmann helped to dismantle German intelligence networks on the Atlantic coast and in Barcelona.

Barcelona was controlled by big business and business was booming, doing well on exports to France and Britain, but the workers were paid little, treated badly and were in revolt. In fact, since 1883 there had been industrial unrest and there was a growing anarchist movement throughout Catalonia. A terror campaign of bombings began in the early 1900s, there was a general strike in 1917, then a lock-out by the factory owners which led to violence and shootings on both sides. The police had lost control, not surprising as there was only one policeman for every five thousand of the population, and the city administration set up a para-military group in 1919; it worked alongside the police but was financed mainly by the employers' association, the *Federación Patronal*. They were good employers, the members of the gang were paid a lot more than most. Members of the group drank in workers' bars, eavesdropping to pick up plans, they infiltrated trades unions. One group – the only one allowed to carry weapons – provoked unrest among the workers so that the employers had an excuse to retaliate.

Manuel Bravo Portillo was head of the Special Services Brigade until *Solidaridad Obrera*, the workers' anarchist newspaper, exposed him on 9 June 1918 as Germany's top spy in Spain, passing on information on ships and cargoes leaving Barcelona for France and England that German U-boats then ambushed and torpedoed. Submarines were often seen off the north-east coast of Spain, regularly anchoring in quiet coves to refuel and their captains being entertained by local officials before going off to seek their targets. One submarine anchored in one such cove had probably come to rescue Portillo but they did not succeed in getting him away. The city fathers were flummoxed by the news of the police chief's arrest; he had to be charged and was held in prison on remand while the law worked out what to do with this powerful official. Stallmann kindly visited him in prison and, according to his statements to French police when they arrested him in 1945, turned him and persuaded him to hand over all his information; in return the charges against Portillo were dropped but he was banned from holding any post in the city administration. Miro I Trepat, a right-wing Catholic extremist, found a way round that and set him up as a 'security contractor' with his own private army, the *banda negra*, the black gang.

For a reliable picture of Barcelona at the time I have relied on the work of Florian Grafl, a German historian.[1] Times were hard in Barcelona, food prices were high and wages were low. Anarchist newspaper *Solidaridad Obrera*, having trouble paying the bills, was not above taking money from fascist Germany; there is a letter from the German embassy in Madrid listing their contributions towards the paper's printing costs. The editor also allegedly said he himself was paid to organise strikes to disrupt the valuable export trade to northern Europe. He felt the ends justified the means.[2]

Renée was not her usual happy self in Spain. Perhaps she found domesticity dull after her peripatetic life with Rudolf and Monty;

relations with her husband were strained and she decided to go it alone – she was a rich young woman, remember. The scales had really fallen from her eyes. Years later she wrote to Randal: 'In ten years of marriage I never for a single moment concerned myself with material things. Rudolf was a husband who took charge of everything, explained nothing, just expected me to follow him. I had a protected life. I knew as much about the hazards of life as a rat in the field. I didn't have any practical abilities. I didn't have a clue that as a young, pretty and very French young lady I represented perfect beard for the Catalan property owners' ('beard' meaning someone used to conceal a person's true identity).

There was a transport strike, factory strikes and no electricity. She found a flat. Two maids, Margarete and Elvira, brought her three children from Fuenterrabia and all three were ill, with whooping cough she thought. She described trying to heat their sick rooms with 'stinking petrol heaters'. When the spring came she moved to a house on the coast at Caldetas. They called it the Deauville of Catalonia but she found it boring and pretentious but with a beautiful sandy beach for the children, 'We didn't need anything more.'

On top of everything, there came the Spanish flu epidemic. Renée wrote to Randal about it describing the horrors of the thousands of deaths; she took three glasses of cognac a day with ten drops of iodine as a prophylactic. She really hated what Barcelona had become: 'It had been turned into an international capital city by the war; it was full of lost foreigners, spies, deserters and black market salesmen. Anything could be bought. Barcelona had lost its soul.'

She wrote well and Randal published her travel diary in 1940, *La Maison des Sept Destins*. Randal inherited her talent and became a humorist and writer of children's stories. He died childless in 2003 aged ninety. Eric Maillard, whose mother married Randal after his father's death, inherited Renée's letters, to which we owe the account of the couple's travels.

The black gang was rough; if they wanted to eliminate a trades unionist, they would dress up as policemen, arrest him and take him off to a quiet place and shoot him. Pablo Sabater, secretary of the dyers' union, was murdered like this; Luis Fernandez Garcia was convicted of his murder but it was clear that Portillo was behind it and he was shot dead in revenge.

I think it is most likely that Stallman was an unofficial double agent, working for France and making Germany believe he was working for them – he still had his German passport, after all. When they found out, the Germans had their revenge with the press campaign against him in *La Tribuna* and Spain could do nothing but issue an expulsion order against him in June 1920. The French lifted their expulsion order on him on 9 July 1920 in return for his 'splendid and free service rendered to the French Interior and War Ministries from 1907-1920'. He had already left for Paris in January 1920 to help Monty Newton get hold of the second £150,000 the Mayfair Mob had taken from Rajah Sir Hari Singh over the Christmas holiday. The police had heard of the blackmail on their grapevine and 'were on the trail of a swindler who was mentioned in the blackmail case' – Lemoine/von Koenig/Stallmann, of course – and were briefing newspapers about a poker game played between 'professional gamblers and three people involved in the court case.' The game was played in a Paris hotel and the huge sum of £30,000 (£1,250.000 now) was lost by one player, very likely Captain Charles Arthur, the instigator of the plot, who complained he had been cheated at cards in Paris; a £30,000 loss out of his blackmail winnings of £45,000 is very bad luck. That was enough for Lemoine to be going on with and it is the last record I can find of him card-sharping.

Rud von Koenig, as he signed himself, was killed off when he left Spain in 1920, went back to Paris and resumed his partnership with Monty Newton. He now became Rodolphe Lemoine and, according to the French National Archives (Ref: F/7/16006), joined the Deuxième Bureau, the French secret intelligence service and acquired yet another title, not too far from Koenig, which means king in German; he took the code name Rex, also meaning king, The enthusiastic amateur was now officially on the staff. Marital problems were resolved and the family, wife, three children and mother-in-law settled into a house at 16, rue Victor Hugo. Family life seemed calm: Renée, who had given up her French nationality when she married, reclaimed it, her husband and children became naturalised French on 6 January 1926 and Rud changed his name officially to Lemoine on 2 October 1927.[3]

* * *

Monty Newton believed Captain Arthur had taken the second cheque back to India and sent Lemoine there in 1921 to meet him and to try to get it cashed. So the spying cannot have been very demanding at the time – unless France had some interest in the sub-continent.

'Lemoine went out to India to lend a hand in getting money on the second cheque,' Monty said in court when one of his accomplices, William Cooper Hobbs, was charged in connection with the blackmail of Sir Hari Singh. 'He was going to assist Captain Arthur whose position was difficult; Arthur wanted to get the second cheque met and at the same time he had to appear to assist the Rajah.' Newton had turned King's Evidence in the blackmailing case and so he was never charged.

Sir Henry Curtis Bennett KC was defending Hobbs; the life of an advocate cannot always be easy – he knew perfectly well that his client was a crook. When barrister Norman Kendal was appointed legal adviser to Scotland Yard in 1918 Curtis pointed out Hobbs and told Kendal he would not have done his job properly until Hobbs was in the dock. Now he was in the dock and Curtis had the job of *defending* him.

There was another reminder of what a small world it is for criminals and lawyers: Sir Henry asked Newton if Captain Arthur was still ADC to the Rajah. Newton replied that he was not. 'Lemoine was to be brought on the scene, possibly as adviser to the Rajah.' Asked whether Lemoine used the name of Stallman, Newton said: 'Sir Henry, you defended him here,' Sir Henry, to laughter from the court, said: 'I accept the imputation, Mr Newton. It was many years ago.'

'The brief was accepted,' said Newton.

Sir Henry replied: 'The brief was accepted, oh yes, and the fee.' More laughter. This was, of course, a reference to Sir Henry's defence of Rudolf Stallman against extradition proceedings in London in 1912 to face charges of cheating the two young Germans in 1909 and 1910.

***

In 1924 Lemoine was visited in his Paris flat by Chief-Inspector W.C.Gough, who had arrested him and Newton in London on the forgery charge in 1907. Lemoine was acting as a go-between because the police were negotiating to get Newton to make a statement about the blackmail of Mr A. Monty Newton happened to be at the flat and Gough obviously knew him quite well and seemed on reasonable terms but he didn't recognise Lemoine. In the seventeen years since the forgery case the high-living had piled the fat on to Lemoine; he was no longer a sleek young man, his head was shaved and he wore wire-rimmed spectacles. He was an imposing figure but still possessed of great charm.

To recap: he was in Paris in 1920, in Kashmir in 1921, entertained Chief Inspector Gough in Paris in 1924; then there is a blank in his life story which lasts until 1931. The man was an enigma even to those he was spying for; according to Captain Paul Paillole who became head of the Deuxième Bureau counter-intelligence section in 1936, he took French nationality in 1900 and had caught the 'spying bug' in Spain. In fact, as the French national archives show, he didn't take French nationality till 1927 and he had the 'spying bug' long before that, for the French deported him in 1902 – when he was still Rudolf Stallmann – officially for card-sharping, unofficially they suspecting him of spying. Even Paillole did not know the man had been working unpaid for French intelligence services since 1908.

Lemoine had a small office in Paris at 27 Rue de Madrid where he traded with the new world: he had a concession in a gold mine in French Guiana, given by the French government 'for services rendered,' as cover for his espionage work. Paillole didn't know how much the government paid him but he was a *bon viveur* who enjoyed his champagne and Cognac. Money was never a problem because he was given *carte blanche* to make money from the gold mine. When Paillole took over as chief he was told by his predecessor that Lemoine was a strange person and spying was to him what alcohol is to a drunkard. In fact, alcohol was as important to him as spying. Paillole described him as *l'homme a tout faire*, a 'Mr Fixit,' admired, feared and in demand by all the secret services in the world. He was an astonishing man who knew how to compromise a minister or recruit a general. He could force a strong box, produce a Yugoslav passport in twenty-four hours or get you a reservation on a *Wagon Lit* when Thomas Cook couldn't. In short, he was one of their most important agents. Lemoine himself claimed he had corrupted thousands of people to become spies.

Writing later, Paillole felt that when they were introduced Lemoine was rather patronising to him but their second meeting was more impressive. It was at an office party on Christmas Eve 1935 at the Quai d'Orsay, the French Foreign Office. A diplomat called Bodo in the Austrian Embassy confided that he feared there was a Nazi conspiracy in his country. French security thought Bodo might be useful to them as a spy but they needed to check him out before making an approach. Lemoine did it over the holiday and by 2 January he had given Bodo the all-clear. Lemoine bribed the telephone company to install a phone for him, which was well above his pay grade. He also recruited another spy. He knew the Bureau wanted to know about the Japanese air force; Bodo told him that the air attaché at the embassy, an officer named Koser, shared his worries about Hitler's threat to Austria. Lemoine invited the two of them to an expensive lunch at Drouant, the fashionable art deco restaurant near the Opera. And he got lucky: Koser's wife was a translator at the Japanese embassy. Within a week Lemoine had permission to recruit her and Frau Koser became their spy in the Japanese embassy. In 1939 it was her information that led to the arrest of two of their diplomats in Marseille; they had obtained the plans of a new aero engine being worked on in Germany and were arrested as they tried to deliver them to a Japanese ship in the harbour.[5]

CHAPTER TWENTY-TWO

The New Recruit

By 1931 Lemoine was a most trusted and senior agent of the Deuxième Bureau. He was given the job of buying the secrets of the German military Enigma coding machine from a traitor in the cipher office of the German Armed Forces' cryptology headquarters in Berlin. This was something they had been working on for years so the prospect of a breakthrough was exciting.

Hans Thilo Schmidt was forty-three and his parents were from upper-middle class families – his father was a professor and his mother a baroness from a Prussian family. They were not rich but they were well connected and respected in Berlin high society. Hans was twenty-eight when his wife's parents set them up in a house with some land in the countryside at Ketschendorf, near Berlin. An unlikely recruit for spying you would think, but the depression of the 1930s had brought him financial disaster. Hans was saved by his older brother, Rudolf, a high-flyer in the army. Rudolf had been head of the *Chiffrierstelle*, the German cipher office, between 1925 and 1928 and introduced Hans to his successor, a Major Oschmann, who took him on as his confidential assistant. The pay was not enough to keep the Schmidts and their two children in the style they were used to. He had debts, too, accumulated because of his womanising ways.

The ciphers and codes that the department created were kept in a safe in the Major's office and Hans had the key...

He thought about this situation for a few months, then in June 1931 he became a 'walk-in', a person who comes in out of the blue to offer state secrets to another country. He went to the French Embassy in Berlin to say he had some important documents to sell and to ask how he should he go about it. He thought about their advice for three weeks, then wrote to the Deuxième Bureau on 1 July at 75 rue de L'Université. This was a secret annexe of the Ministry of War used by military intelligence. He wrote:

I confirm what I said on 8 June 1931 to your representative [at] the Pariser Platz [the address of the French Embassy in Berlin] who gave me your address. I am negotiating the sale of documents of the greatest importance. To convince you that my offer is serious, I enclose some references. Your specialists will know what they are worth. Will you reply before 1 October to the following address: Hans Thilo Schmidt, 2 Kaufhasgasse – Basel – Switzerland. Failing a reply by this date I will have to look elsewhere. If you are happy to meet me could we make it a Sunday and preferably in Belgium or Holland, near the German frontier.

As a postscript he mentioned two documents he could supply: the users' manuals and the code books of a new machine which the German army had been using since 1 June 1930.[6]

Captain Gustave Bertrand, the thirty-four-year-old head of the Deuxième Bureau's code section, was intrigued by the offer. In spite of all his efforts, he hadn't received any information about the German army's new mechanical coding machine. The French army's cypher section – reputedly one of the best in the world – found the messages they had intercepted impenetrable. Lemoine was called in. He said he was willing to take any risk with this job and he and Bertrand were able to persuade the boss, Colonel Laurant, head of the military Special Services, to give him *carte blanche*. First a thorough investigation was made into Schmidt: debts mounting, parents recently deceased, brother a high-ranking officer in the army. The brother sounded interesting...

***

On Halloween, 31 October 1931, a tall man in his sixties and his wife checked into the Grand Hotel at Verviers on the German-Belgian border; it was Rodolphe Lemoine. He took the best suite.

Next morning, he gave a letter to the receptionist and settled down on a sofa in the lobby, eager to catch a glimpse of the man who was offering to betray his country. At half past ten a rather shabby-looking fellow arrived. He was of medium height and wrapped up in a dark overcoat, with a black hat pulled down over his face. He was tired and cold – the train had been two hours late and his black leather satchel was heavy.

The receptionist gave him the key to the room which had been reserved for him and an envelope on which was written in French: 'to be handed to M. Hans Thilo Schmidt on arrival'. Schmidt didn't notice the watcher in the lobby, pretending to read; he took the lift to his room and opened the envelope. The note inside was in German: 'You are expected at 12 o'clock in room 31 on the first floor.' This gave him time to have a rest and freshen up, as well as to have a look through the documents in his satchel.

He knocked at room 31 promptly at midday and a distinguished looking white-haired woman opened the door and invited him to make himself comfortable in an armchair before disappearing into a neighbouring room; Lemoine usually travelled with his wife who was fourteen or fifteen years younger than him. She would have been forty-six in 1931, so prematurely aged; Lemoine was described as sixty-ish, which would have been right. The room was warm and soft music was playing; there was a trolley well stocked with bottles of whisky, port and sherry, beautiful crystal tumblers and wine glasses and several boxes of the cigars that Lemoine loved.

When Lemoine came in a couple of minutes later, he could see that Schmidt was nervous; no wonder, for Lemoine was quite intimidating. Well over six feet tall, with a shaved head, he had bulked up and was now enormous. But he possessed great charm and soon put his visitor at his ease, asking kindly and in very good German about his guest's wife and two children. Clutching a large glass of whisky Schmidt told him the sad truth: his brother was head of the Cipher office from 1925 till 1928 while he, although a qualified chemist was – like six million other Germans – out of work for two years and couldn't live on the seventy-five Marks a month dole. His brother had found him his job at the Cipher office. 'It is far from brilliant,' he said. 'The pay is five hundred Marks a month for working night and day.' It went some way towards paying off his debts but now, for the sake of economy, he was living alone in a furnished room in Lorenzstrasse, Berlin, while his wife and children were with her parents in Bavaria. His host replied that if their collaboration worked out they would soon all be together again.

Lemoine poured more whisky and let Schmidt talk. It was unusual for someone in such a high-level security job to risk so much and he had to be certain that this man really knew what he was getting into and also, of course, whether it was a trap. After Schmidt's third whisky Lemoine felt confident that the man was genuine; he had deliberately turned his back on his family, their traditions, their reputation, their lifestyle, their reputation, his country. Whatever his motives, Lemoine knew Schmidt could be bought and asked him to return to the hotel the following week with the best documents he could get from the safe. He gave a final warning and told Schmidt what a huge risk he was taking in crossing the border with the documents.

'That's my problem, dear sir. May I hope for another whisky?'[7]

When they next met, on Sunday 8 November 1931, Captain Gustave Bertrand, the young head of the Deuxième Bureau's section D, the decryption department, was with him and there was a bodyguard, Baron Alexandre Schenke, in the lobby. Although Bertrand was head of the cypher department, he was not a cryptologist. The Deuxième Bureau was being extremely cautious. They had arrived the night before; Lemoine took his usual sumptuous suite on the first floor and Bertrand and the photographer were in communicating rooms on a higher floor. They spent the evening setting up the camera and the portable lights for the next day. They were ready for work at 9 o'clock in the morning but the telephone didn't ring till ten: Lemoine apologised for being late and asked Bertrand to come to his room. He hurried down, eager to get to work – and found the party had already begun in room 31. The radio was playing and the room was full of cigar smoke. Schmidt was standing there, looking happy, glass of whisky in hand. He was wearing a cheap suit and when he bowed and clicked his heels, Bertrand saw that those heels were worn down. All the same, his confidence and ease showed a certain class and his blue eyes shone with intelligence. While Bertrand, trying to hide his excitement, had a quick look at the documents marked *Geheim*, secret, Schmidt helped himself to more whisky and quietly asked Lemoine how much he could expect.

'In a minute,' Lemoine put him off – and teased him. 'Shame you haven't brought the daily keys for this month. You promised. You should have brought much more. I could have paid you more if you had.'

'Usually those papers are at my fingertips,' he said but his boss had sent them to be bound and he hadn't dared to ask for the file when it came back.

Bertrand was alarmed: did this mean that Schmidt was backing out? Was he going to stop here? Would he be happy to take a lot of money for this one piece of information and then return to his settled, bourgeois life? It would be a terrible loss for the Bureau.

Lemoine could see that Bertrand was worried but he remained calm and when Bertrand took him to one side and quietly suggested they offer five thousand marks to Schmidt, he said: 'Let me offer double that. I'd like to promise him at least as much again if he carries on helping us. He's too far in now, he can't do anything else.'

Lemoine traded in codes but he was not an expert in reading them. It was a lot of money, about twenty thousand pounds today, but he sensed that this transaction was important. Bertrand was astonished when he saw what Schmidt had brought: two manuals with operating instructions, codes and daily key settings for the new top-secret coding machine.

Bintz, the photographer, and Bertrand went without lunch that day: Schmidt needed the documents back by three o'clock because he had to take the train back to Berlin and replace them in the safe before they were missed. Alone with Schmidt, Lemoine went through the details with him and gave him his work name: H.E. – pronounced Ashay in French. When Bertrand returned to room 31 at three, the party was still going on. There was a heap of cigar ends in the ash tray and Schmidt was now drinking cognac; they must have had lunch in the suite. They were in a very jolly mood and he could see that Lemoine had succeeded. Bertrand marvelled at the man's powers of persuasion, his resistance to fatigue and his capacity for alcohol; he had been 'entertaining' Schmidt for more than five hours. The job was clearly done and he asked Schmidt if he was satisfied with the arrangements.

'Jawohl, mein Herren. Bestes dank!' he replied and with another click of the heels he was gone, back to Germany where he joined the NSDAP, the Nazi party, on 1 December 1931.[8]

Bertrand was more than satisfied; he knew the new recruit would take them right to the heart of the mysterious machine. But when he showed his prize pictures to the cryptography experts at the Deuxième Bureau, they were not as thrilled as he; the manuals explained how to put a message into code but they did not explain how to read an encrypted message. British code experts had a look at the manuals and agreed that they would not help them break the codes. In fact, the British and the French believed the machine was impenetrable.

Bertrand got permission in early December take the photos to Lieutenant Gwido Langer, head of the Polish General Staff's Cypher Bureau. For more than two years they had been trying to decipher the German codes but they, too, thought them insoluble. He saw that this new information was important and useful but it was not enough to read the messages; he asked for more. Nine days later, Schmidt gave Bertrand a list of settings in use, which he passed on to the Poles. Still they got nowhere.

In January 1929 Lieutenant Maksymilian Ciezki, the head of the Polish Cipher Bureau's German section, had set up a cryptology course at the maths department at Poznan university, hoping it would lead somewhere. It was a tough course, using pure mathematics. Its three brightest students, Marian Rejewski, Henryk Zygalski and Jerzy Rozycki, who was only nineteen, were invited to work part-time at the Polish army cypher bureau while they continued their studies. Rejewski graduated on 1 March 1929 at the age of twenty-three and went on working part-time for the bureau as well as teaching maths at Poznan University. In October or November 1932 Ciezski asked Rejewski to do some extra work secretly; he was not to tell his two friends. He knew that to break the code he would have to build a coding machine of his own and when Ciezski gave him the settings Hans Schmidt had sold to the French a year before – it was all so secret that Ciezski didn't tell him where the information came from – it was the break he needed. After a few weeks of intensive study he was able to work out the electrical wiring inside the wheels and the discs of the machine. He had a machine of his own made, it was the size of a portable typewriter. Zygalski and Rozycki were called in to help and, yes! by the end of the year they could read the German messages. Rejewski had built his own Enigma machine, a name first settled on by the German firm of Scherbius & Ritter way back in 1923.

The story of what happened next is not part of this narrative and it is told brilliantly by Hugh Sebag-Montefiore in *Enigma, the Battle for the Code*. My story is not of the code-breakers but of the man who bought those codes: Rodolphe Lemoine. Suffice to say that his purchase of the manuals meant that the Poles broke the Enigma code in December 1932, five years before Alan Turing, code-breaking genius of Bletchley Park, had even started studying cryptology.[9] The Poles could read the Germans' secret military messages long before the Second World War but they did not tell the French or the English until July 1939. What stopped them from finishing the job was in part a lack of resources. Those resources would be collected together and brilliantly organised at Bletchley Park and its codebreaking outstations. The Poles did not inform the Allies of their success, perhaps wanting something in return, which caused ill feeling.

* * *

At the same time that Lemoine was recruiting Schmidt for the French secret service, the Russians were trying to recruit Lemoine to spy for their intelligence service, OGPU. We need to go back a little: Giovanni de Ry, a Swiss dealer, had been a friend and accomplice of Lemoine's since the 1920s. De Ry specialised in buying and selling Italian codes. One day in August 1928 he walked into the Soviet embassy in Paris and asked to see either the military attaché or the first secretary. Under the cover of being one of those was the OGPU resident, Vladimir Voynovich. De Ry told Voynovich that he had Italian diplomatic codes in his big yellow briefcase. He wanted two hundred thousand French francs for them. He also offered future codes, because the Italians changed theirs every year. De Ry, an adventurer, cheat and experienced code-dealer, was tricked surprisingly easily by the Russian, who took the codes into a back room to examine them. His wife, also an OGPU agent, was there and quickly photographed them before Voynovich returned them to de Ry saying they were forgeries, and threatening to call the police. Voynovich was given a special commendation for getting those secrets for nothing.

In October the following year, Grigori Besedovsky, the *chargé d'affaires* at the Soviet's Paris embassy, defected, escaping dramatically over the Embassy wall followed by security men in hot pursuit, and then settled down to write his memoirs. He told the story of how the walk-in with the Italian codes had been told to walk out again, without his name even being taken. There must have been trembles when the memoir was shown to Stalin as the *chargé d'affaires* had denounced him as 'the embodiment of the most senseless type of oriental despotism'. When Stalin read how the OGPU resident in the Paris embassy had thrown away the chance of a never-ending supply of Italian codes, he pencilled in the margin the order: 're-open'.[10]

Dmitri Bystrolyotov was Russia's greatest 'illegal' spy recruiter: that is, he worked underground, using false names, creating phoney businesses and family histories as cover, and with no support from the Russian embassy. He was on his own. He was given the task of discovering the identity of the nameless man, finding him and recruiting him as a supplier of Italian codes.

Ian Fleming could have modelled James Bond on Dmitri. He had film-star good looks – a bit like Errol Flynn – with soft brown eyes and sensuous lips under a neat moustache. He carried a gun and could shoot to kill through the pocket of his jacket. He had wrecked a few jackets perfecting his aim. His usual method was gentler. Dmitri Bystrolyotov was a 'Romeo spy' who specialised in seducing vulnerable women working in embassies and encouraging them to change sides and inform for Russia. He was given six months to find this nameless man; where to start? He went to Paris and interviewed the embassy staff. All they could remember was that he was short and stocky, had a golden tan and a red nose so they called him after that in Russian, Nosik. Dmitri decided to base himself in Geneva, home of the League of Nations, full of diplomats, full of spies from all over Europe as well as Japan and the United States, anxious to winkle the diplomats' secrets from them.

Codes were the thing; they were needed to read the secret mails going to and fro between foreign embassies and their mother country. The man's golden tan suggested that Dmitri had chosen the right place to look, he had noticed that many people in Geneva had a similar glow from skiing in the sunny Alps. The red nose could be sunburn so he guessed that Nosik was either Swiss or a foreigner living in Switzerland.

Trawling the bars and cafes of the lake-side town he found 'prim and boring', Dmitri found two bars popular with foreigners where Nosik was likely to hang out: the smart International Bar and the simpler Brasserie Universal. He called in the help of a Dutch Soviet agent, Henri Christian Pieck, code name Cooper. Cooper liked to paint in his spare time and Dmitri was also a talented artist; they bought sketch pads and pencils and Dmitri sat outside the International Bar and Cooper sat outside the Universal and they sketched everyone who came in who matched the description. They didn't arouse suspicion hanging around for hours on end because many artists were drawn to Geneva: the walls of both bars were hung with sketches of picturesque corners done by previous customers. The two men met on the first evening to compare sketches and Dmitri's hunch was right: he had sketched Nosik in the International Bar and Cooper had spotted him in the Universal later. Dmitri made friends with the barman, Emile, who was a great gossip and told him Nosik was a regular, known as Rossi; he was born in Switzerland and had served in the Swiss army. He owned a house in the Swiss canton of Valais. His mother was Italian and he claimed one of her uncles was a Catholic cardinal. Rossi said he worked for General Motors and visited Switzerland, Italy, Bulgaria and Romania for them. No one knew his real surname but it sounded like de Rue or de Ry. Emile also warned that the man was a cheat and could be dangerous. It was time to make a move.

Dmitri stationed himself at an outside table at the International, sketching quietly and waiting until Nosik/Rossi/de Ry arrived. He heard him order a double whisky, went inside, stood next to him and ordered the same, mimicking his words and gestures to attract his attention. He whispered 'Italian ciphers' into his ear and contact was made. After the way the Russian embassy in Paris treated de Ry in 1928. Dmitri knew he couldn't admit he was a Soviet spy so he pretended he had been commissioned by the Japanese to buy Italian codes, and thus another agent was recruited.

De Ry agreed to get the codes from a corrupt Italian diplomat. KGB records show he was paid at least two hundred thousand French francs. Dmitri would usually meet de Ry in Berlin where he said his contact worked. Dmitri soon found de Ry was as shady a character as the barman had warned, and was selling the same codes to agents of several countries and demanding advance payment for making contact with fictitious agents. There was nothing he wouldn't do for money but he was worth it: he gave Dmitri valuable information about how the international market in stolen codes worked, suggested more possible spies and became known as one of Dmitri's most successful finds.[11]

Dmitri found de Ry in 1930 and soon after de Ry introduced Lemoine. The suave, elegant, fastidious Dmitri was revolted by Lemoine. In his youth Lemoine was a fine looking man, something of a dandy, like Dmitri, wearing cashmere suits, silk socks that slipped into hand-made Russian shoes. Now, almost sixty, he looked 'old, ominous and repulsive'. His shaved head gave him a rather threatening look. In the script for a screenplay, *Generous Hearts*, which he wrote in 1965, Dmitri described the man's profile as if 'cut out of cardboard and daubed with yellow and brown paint'. He looked like a villain in theatre makeup.[12]

Luckily. Dmitri didn't have to deal with Lemoine for long. He gave him the work-name of Joseph and passed him on to 'Walter Scott', an 'American' military intelligence agent. In fact, this man was Ignatii Poretsky, working for Soviet Foreign Intelligence under the cover name of Ignace Reiss. Lemoine was himself, or as much of himself as he ever was: an agent of the Deuxième Bureau. His usual method was to play a sort of Happy Families, swapping foreign code systems, building up his own collection. It should come as no surprise that Lemoine was not above cheating. In May 1931 he handed over a genuine Italian cipher to Walter Scott. Other information, such as that Hitler had made two secret trips to Paris and that the French were paying him and doing all they could to bring him to power, the Russians dismissed as nonsense but they went on paying him through Reiss, who was still posing as an American.

In 1933 Lemoine took his boss, Gustave Bertrand, to meet Reiss; he, too, was given a code name, Orel. Still pretending to be an American officer, Reiss offered to exchange some Latin-American diplomatic codes but Bertrand was not interested in South America. Not long after this Reiss confessed to Lemoine that he was really an OGPU agent. Lemoine had probably guessed. The American alias was likely a trap; once Lemoine had taken Soviet money it would be an easy job to recruit him; either he became a spy or had to confess to his bosses that he had been fooled into taking Soviet money. Was he recruited? Who knows? Lemoine and Bertrand continued to meet Reiss. Bertrand gave Reiss a new Italian code in 1933 and the three were photographed together in Rotterdam in 1935. In a biography of his career published in 1935 by the SVR, the Russian foreign intelligence service, Dmitri is credited with saying, without mentioning names, that he received Austrian, Italian and Turkish material, and even German secret documents, from a member of French military intelligence.

In return, Reiss gave Madame Lemoine a magnificent wild mink coat, smuggled into Paris in the Soviet diplomatic bag.[13]

* * *

Schmidt continued supplying cipher information from Germany as well as information gleaned from his brother, Rudolf, who was now teaching at the *Kriegsakadamie*, war school, in Berlin. He even introduced another informer, the brother of General Erhard Milch, the man who founded Lufthansa after World War l, now Secretary of State for Air who later became an Air Marshal and inspector general of the Luftwaffe; he was the ablest man in the Luftwaffe. His brother, Otto Hartura, was ambitious, homosexual and for more than three years provided information gleaned from his innocent brother about the expansion of the Luftwaffe. Hans's brother, of course, had no idea what his sibling was up to, though he might have wondered how his fortunes had changed; Hans now wore elegant suits and silk shirts and ties and was taking expensive holidays with his wife, partly for fun, partly as cover for his espionage. He also visited the bars and nightclubs of Berlin – alone. Lemoine was afraid that this extravagance would draw attention to the fact that he was living above his pay grade and helped him establish a small soap-making factory next to his house to explain his sudden wealth.[14]

***

The Nazi party came to power in January 1933. Following the Reichstag fire on 27 February, communist and socialist parties and trades unions were banned and anti-semitic attitudes became more open. On 15 March 1933 Schmidt sent a message to Lemoine saying said he had serious news and needed to see him.

On 31 March a Herr von Koenig checked into the Adlon Hotel in Berlin; the Adlon, its address 1 Unter den Linden, was one of those massive hotels built at the beginning of the century when the railways were expanding. As ever, Lemoine chose the best hotel in town. In the 1920s it was the most famous hotel in Europe, frequented by the stars of film and opera. It was surviving Nazism but this was a bad moment, the receptionist told him, for the next day was to be a national day of protest against the boycotting of German goods by Britain and America who were protesting at Germany's treatment of Jews.

He was wakened at eight the next morning by the raucous sounds of a band of fifes and drums. A lorry-load of SA men, the Stormtrooper veterans of the Great War, followed the band, bearing anti-Jewish placards and behind them was a motley crowd carrying similar banners and shouting insults. In the night, posters had been stuck up on shops saying 'don't buy anything from Jews' and the Jewish shopkeepers had pulled down their shutters. The big clothing store, Heitinger, had the word *Jude* painted all over it in big white letters. Police and passers-by took no notice when shop windows were shattered. There was a strange atmosphere.

Lemoine – Herr von Koenig – met Maurice Dejean, the Deuxième Bureau's representative at the French embassy, for lunch in a quiet restaurant in Charlottenburg. It was the same all over Germany, Dejean told him: Jews were banned from working in the civil service, universities and hospitals. They needed special passports to travel abroad. Lemoine wanted to know if he had heard anything from Schmidt. He hadn't but no news was probably good news. He was aware of the possibility of trouble and had devised a way for Schmidt to get in touch with the French embassy in Berlin quickly in case of emergency.

Schmidt came to the Adlon at teatime, understandably ruffled. Things were moving quicker than he expected. Lemoine said he thought the day's demonstrations were the Nazis' way of getting their own back because they blamed the Jews for the boycott. There were at the time eight million unemployed in Germany – a record – five million communist voters and seven million social democrats who were very hostile to the Nazis, whose hold on power was not strong.

Schmidt had told Lemoine six months earlier that Hitler was anxious to know what was going on behind the scenes in the Reich, foreign embassies and the SA The SA, *Sturmabteilung*, or brown shirts, was a quasi-military organisation set up in 1921 and led by General Ernst Roehm, an old friend of Hitler; they had been together since they joined the Nazi party in the twenties. Now Hitler was beginning to feel threatened by his friend and his henchmen in the brown shirts. Apart from a penchant for rough-housing and acting like gangsters, he was afraid they wanted to put socialism back into National Socialism, and that could lead to communism. Hitler had no confidence in the police or the Abwehr (the army intelligence service) and had talked of setting up an intelligence department of his own to keep watch on these groups. The idea came to the surface again in February and now Hermann Goering, in charge of the SS, Hitler's Stormtroopers, was given the job of putting it into action. For the past few weeks he had been holding secret round-table meetings at the Chancellery with service chiefs, Nazi party officials, Heinrich Himmler, Reinhardt Heydrich and two of Schmidt's friends, Paul Korner, who was Goering's private secretary, and Gottfried Schapper; sometimes Hitler turned up.

Reinhardt Heydrich was a very ambitious man and pushed Hitler to let him go to Berlin and set up and run the RHSA, the *Reichssicherheitshauptamt*, which was the overlord of all the interior and exterior security of all the Reich. Hitler was more impressed with his ideas than those of Ernst Roehm.

'Roehm's a brute,' Schmidt told Lemoine. 'He controls a revolutionary army of more than a million veterans – you saw them in action today. Do you know the SA has opened concentration camps where they lock up anyone they don't like?' The SA were out of control.

Schmidt told him Goering's plan would be put into action in the next few days. It involved the creation of a state secret police, *Geheime Staatspolizei*, the Gestapo, in Prussia, where Goering was President. Goering would be in charge with the assistance of Schmidt's friend, Paul Korner. (Korner became secretary of state in the Ministry of State of Prussia on 30 November of that year and stayed in the job until 1942.) The second part of the plan was the formation of the *Forschungsamt*, a secret organisation to be disguised as part of the Air Ministry although it had nothing to do with it. It was to intercept every letter and listen to every phone call that went out of Germany. Hans Schimpf, a friend of Goering and a former naval captain, was to be in charge.

'And,' said Schmidt, 'Gottfried Schapper wants me to join this new organisation. What do you think? And what will Paris think?'

Lemoine thought for a couple of minutes. 'If I understand it, with the *Forschungsamt* the Nazis are going to listen at the borders, open letters, penetrate ambassadorial secrets. With the Gestapo and the concentration camps they are going to get rid of the opposition.'

'Yes, but the *Forschungsamt* will be more important. It will be the source of the most secret intelligence and it will be in constant touch with the Gestapo and, above all, the *Chiffrierstelle*.'

Lemoine reckoned it would take a long time for the *Forschungsamt* to be up and running and they needed to learn more about Enigma from Schmidt in his present job.

'For the moment, don't move,' he told Schmidt. 'See what happens and stay in touch with Schapper. I'll tell the boss about it.'

'Be quick then,' said Schmidt. 'Schapper is pressing me for a reply.' He promised to give him the Enigma code settings for March and April the following day.

'Understood,' said Lemoine. 'Let's eat. Where do you fancy?' They had a jolly evening at La Taverne in Friedrichstrasse and arranged to meet again at five o'clock the next day, before Lemoine left for Paris. Schmidt brought the Enigma key settings and news of his brother's latest promotion, to Colonel, as well as the fact that Hitler had decided that very day on a complete overhaul of the Reichswehr.

Three days later Schmidt received a letter in invisible ink from Andre Perruche, of the intelligence department of the Deuxième Bureau: 'Stay where you are.'[15]

The *Forschungsamt* was formed on 10 April 1933 and the Gestapo on 26 April.

* * *

Bertrand visited his opposite number in the Polish army's cipher bureau that summer. The Poles were anxious to know the Third Reich's political intentions with regard to their country. He passed the query on to Schmidt, who asked for a meeting at Spindlermuhle in Czechoslovakia on 16 September. The year before, with his new wealth, he and his wife Charlotte had spent six weeks travelling in Czechoslovakia (dumping their children at a children's home run by a Jewish couple) and he had liked the small ski resort in the north-west, close to the German border, now known as Spindleruv Mlyn. The nearest German city was Dresden. Lemoine was on holiday so Bertrand and Commandant Guy Schlesser went together. Schlesser had joined the department at the end of 1932 and had impressed with his ability. He spoke German fluently and was now head of the Counter-Espionage section.

They arrived at the Davidsbaude Hotel on the evening of the 15th. It was on the edge of the village, surrounded by thick forest that reached almost to the German border. It was a large mountain chalet style building, *gemutlich*. A huge tiled stove warmed the big sitting-room where four men were playing cards in a quiet corner. But there was no sign of Schmidt. While waiting for him next morning, they strolled up the rocky path that climbed through the woods towards the frontier. Bertrand insisted that they each carry a revolver. About eleven o'clock they were near the crest of a hill when they saw the silhouette of a climber descending. He reached them. 'It's Ashay,' said Bertrand, using Schmidt's work name, rather surprised, for he was quite a sight in full Bavarian rig: long woollen socks, bare knees, lederhosen and studded boots. He wore a dark green jacket and a felt hat trimmed with a tuft of badger tail and he carried an enormous rucksack. A perfect picture of a Bavarian rambler.

The sun was shining and it was hot; a little waterfall ran alongside the path and Schmidt was happy. 'Isn't it lovely?' he said, and suggested a little rest in the cool of the trees. He had driven into Czechoslovakia via Dresden and Hirschberg, left his car near the frontier and walked several kilometres to the rendezvous.

'Not wise,' said Bertrand.

'In the unlikely case of a check, a party card reigns supreme here,' he replied.

Guy Schlesser was astonished at what Schmidt produced from the rucksack. On the mossy bank where they rested he made a list: papers for Bertrand giving daily Enigma key settings for September and October, an enormous study of the German high command, a detailed description of Polish places and their populations. There were battle orders, with relevant maps, details of Polish troops and the air and sea threat that Poland posed to Germany. He also had, from his brother, the 1934 programme of work of the *Kriegsakademie*, which Rudolf was now in charge of and the news that Hitler wanted the number of infantry divisions to be tripled to twenty-one. Schlesser had never known another informer capable of producing, at one time, so much information of real value.

They returned to the hotel about one o'clock; lunch was almost finished. But there was to be no lunch for Bertrand. He had to go to his room to photograph the papers which Schmidt needed to return the same night. He planned to sleep at Dresden where he no doubt had an assignation. Schmidt and Schlesser had a long lunch. After several whiskies, two bottles of Bordeaux and a glass of Cognac Schmidt relaxed his reserve with the new man and talked freely about his work. Schlesser pressed him for exact details of the way the *Forschungsamt* worked. It was nearly five o'clock before

Bertrand rejoined them – he had spent four hours photographing the huge pile of papers. He handed back the rucksack. 'It's a bit heavier than when you arrived,' he told Schmidt in his bad German. He had tucked in ten thousand Marks. 'It's a lot of money,' he said to Schlesser, 'but the information he has given us is priceless.' They walked with him to the path and left him to find his way back to his car in the dusk.[16]

CHAPTER TWENTY-THREE

A Family Christmas

Throughout the spying, the boozing, the gambling, and the constant travelling, it was his family that held Lemoine's loyalty; he always went back to his wife and children and he treated them well. They spent Christmas 1933 and the New Year in luxury at the Hotel Murren, in the Swiss village of the same name. It's more than six thousand metres high and there's no road but it's a dramatic climb from Interlaken by mountain railway. The village attracts a rich, cosmopolitan crowd for skiing and apres-ski and this is where the James Bond film, *On Her Majesty's Secret Service*, was filmed. The Hotel Murren's huge bay windows looked out on to the glaciers of the Jungfrau – so close you could almost touch it – as well as the Monch and the Eiger. The Lemoines liked to sit there at tea-time watching the setting sun bathing the snow in a glorious glow. On 4 January they were sitting there, listening to the pianist gently tinkling out Viennese waltzes and enjoying the warmth of the huge log fire on the stone hearth when a couple of new guests walked in, shivering. They warmed their backs by the fire. Lemoine half-raised an eyebrow in acknowledgement. They two men were Schlesser, tall, thin, elegant in a flashy sort of way, and Bertrand, shorter, plumper and with a more sedate style. They had arrived for a long weekend, Thursday to Tuesday. Like a spa in the summer, a ski resort made a perfect clandestine meeting place: guests came and went, for a weekend or a few days, drank with new acquaintances, enjoyed the conviviality and comfort of a cosy hotel when it was cold outside; they kept the staff too busy for them to take much notice.

Unusually, Schmidt had asked for this surprise meeting, overcoming his customary reluctance about crossing the Swiss border; neutral Switzerland did not like spies on its land. They had agreed in the Deuxième Bureau in Paris that Lemoine should greet him as a friend and invite him to dine with him and his wife. Schmidt was due to arrive the next evening, on the last funicular of the day. Lemoine, waiting in the lobby, was amused by his spectacular entrance: he stepped out of a horse-drawn sleigh, his smart buckskin boots daintily tripping along the cleared path; he wore a large fur-lined overcoat and an Astrakhan hat and a porter carried his expensive deerskin case. Lemoine had to smile, remembering the shabby fellow he had recruited at Verviers two years before. They greeted each other warmly. After settling himself into his room, Schmidt joined Lemoine in a quiet corner of the bar, Madame made herself scarce. Not far away sat Bertrand and Schlesser.

Schmidt was bursting with pride and Lemoine couldn't believe his ears when he heard why. 'Since the first of December,' said Schmidt, 'I have been in charge of liaison between the *Chiffrierstelle* and the *Forschungsamt*. I am responsible for exploiting the interceptions and the decoded messages in western Europe.'

Now Lemoine's spy had really got to the heart of German intelligence. He had already made a decision: the listening post at Stuttgart wasn't big enough, it was snowed under with work and he thought another one should be installed in Switzerland. His superiors agreed and gave him *carte blanche* to pursue it. Then he produced his trump card: he had told his bosses that he was nervous about crossing frontiers so he had been given a permit stamped by the Ministry of Air, with Goering's signature *and* a diplomatic passport. That was why their man had not been nervous about crossing the border.

Schmidt was gleeful, the others were astounded. The champagne flowed, it was nearly midnight. Schmidt and Lemoine and their new acquaintances at the table nearby moved on to the *grand salon* where a few couples danced to the music of a gypsy band. It drowned their conversation. Schmidt produced some thick files he had been hiding under his table napkin all this time. Bertrand went off to his room to photograph the loot. There were the Enigma settings for January and February as well as the 'red button', the code that would signify the mobilization of the army. He could hardly believe it.

Schlesser took shorthand notes while Schmidt told him of the immediate plans of the Nazis: Himmler was to take over the Reich police, Heydrich to be head of the Gestapo, there was to be reform of the penal code with new penalties – up to the death sentence – for treason. The concentration camps at Dachau and Oranienburg would be reorganised to accommodate Jews and political opponents discovered by the *Forschungsamt* listening posts. Himmler took over the Reich police on 20 April 1934, Heydrich became head of the Gestapo on 22 April and the new repressive laws came into effect on 24 April 1934.

Schmidt was never wrong. But his story was not finished. He next produced the 'mission statement' for the *Forschungsamt*, written by Schimpf with the agreement of Goering, a huge document marked *Geheime Reichssache*, state secret. Lemoine and Schlesser studied it: there was no doubt that it was genuine. It was late, the hotel was quiet by now; Schlesser took the documents to bed with him.

The snow was good that year and Schlesser and Bertrand spent the day on the slopes and the 'new' friends met up again at 11 pm for champagne and cigars. Schlesser, always keen for more intel, had composed a long questionnaire for Schmidt to complete. Lemoine was more concerned with his spy's welfare and wanted to know about the progress of the little soap factory that he had added to his house in Ketschendorf as cover for his new wealth. He hoped to move in the following spring and his wife and son and daughter would work with him. 'But it's all expensive, very expensive,' he said, gazing into Lemoine's ice-blue eyes.

Schlesser took the hint. 'Here's your envelope,' he said, 'with ten thousand marks. With what you get every month in Berlin, you should be all right. If it's not enough, tell me. The essential now is to help you to follow Hitler's military plans. I count on you to let us know as soon as possible.' Schlesser inspired Schmidt; he admired his passion for his work and always found him friendly and courteous. He respected and admired Lemoine, too, but he was rather frightened of him. When he left next morning on the first train, he was determined to please Schlesser.

Lemoine was Schmidt's recruiter and handler but more and more Schlesser dealt with him himself. Schmidt had been sending weekly reports – written in invisible ink – about the increasing mechanisation of the army but Schlesser wanted more. Against his boss's advice, he decided to go to Berlin. Lemoine organised an identity card in the name of Saint-Georges, a reporter with *Le Journal*, a French newspaper with an office in Berlin and Schlesser wrote to one of Schmidt's secret letter boxes asking for a meeting on 21 April. They met at La Taverne in Friedrichstrasse, a strange choice as it was a favourite hang-out of Nazi officers. He asked Schmidt if he could get anything from his brother about the rearmament programme.

'Give me forty-eight hours,' said Schmidt, always eager to please. They agreed to meet at 7 pm in the bar at the Adlon on 23 April. 'It's Heydrich's favourite place. With a bit of luck you'll find some pretty girls there.'

Schmidt turned up on time, as always, and he was not at all put out by the excitement in the bar caused by the arrival of a tall, blond young man with a beautiful young woman. It was Heydrich and this was the day after he had been appointed head of the Gestapo. Under his very eyes, Schmidt produced a big envelope with the Enigma settings for April and May. That was not all. He had dined the night before with his brother and his assistant from the Kriegsakademie; he had steered the conversation round to the military teaching in the academy and heard that in 1933 the Reich had made a general plan for re-armament for 1934 and Rudolf had instructions to teach a course based on Hitler's new doctrine of *blitzkrieg* by combined land and air forces.[17]

* * *

In June 1934 Schmidt wrote to Lemoine, warning him of Hitler's coming 'night of the long knives'. He and Goering planned to take action against Roehm, the head of the SA, and his supporters on the night of 30 June/1 July 1934. Hitler felt more and more threatened by his old friend and his brown shirts. Schmidt was hankering after a trip away from Germany for a few days R and R. and suggested meeting in Evian-les-Bains on Lake Leman on 4 July, when he would tell them more.

Lemoine assured Schlesser and Bertrand that a visit to a spa town presented no risk – he regularly took a three-week cure at the Royal Hotel himself – and they wouldn't attract any attention. Grand hotels held no fear for Lemoine: for thirty-odd years they had been his place of work, long before he became a spy. The four men met at 11 am on the terrace of the Royal on 4 July; Schmidt needed a double whisky before he could tell them about the night of the bloody purge. The SA had to be destroyed and the SS, the *Schutzstaffel*, Hitler's personal bodyguards, were to do it. Schmidt was right about the date. It was a long night; in fact, it lasted for seventy-two hours. While the shooting was going on Hitler held a tea party on 1 July to show how 'normal' everything was. Nobody will ever know how many died that night: some say two hundred, others more than a thousand. Ernst Roehm was taken to Hitler who told him he was under arrest. He was put in a cell, given a loaded revolver and told to shoot himself. He refused, so someone did it for him.

'Hitler is now the absolute boss. But the SS won't stop there. I know from Schapper that they are plotting something in Austria,' Schmidt said.

'A Nazi putsch?' asked Schlesser.

'In effect. And it won't end there.'

That was it. He said no more. He had done his job. He changed the subject, said how grateful he was for the work they had given him. He was at last back home with his family and his factory was doing well; now what he needed to do was to get some help with the marketing of the soap. Once again, Lemoine showed he could fix practically anything; he arranged a fake contract whereby a French manufacturer ostensibly paid to use his new way of making soap; this would provide cover for his secret service pay.

'Well done,' said Lemoine. 'But you said you had lots of documents yet you've come empty-handed.'

He explained: his travel documents covered him only for Switzerland, not for France and he daren't take the risk of being stopped by customs or the French police. That's why he was staying at Montreux, on the Swiss bank of Lake Leman, and that was where the photographs were. He was at their service for a few days but he had to be back at the listening post in Berne on the 7th before returning to Berlin on 8th.

After telling them the gruesome news of what Germany calls the *Roehm putsch* Schmidt spent the rest of his day like many other visitors, at the roulette tables of the casino. He broke off at seven pm to meet his handlers, take several aperitifs, eat a huge dinner and discuss his work. At 1 am he took the last shuttle from the casino back to Montreux.

Next day Bertrand and Perruche went to meet him there. Lemoine stayed behind, feeling 'tired', possibly in need of another three-week cure. It was a fine, hot day and they decided to spend it in the mountains. They took the funicular up to Caux, a popular village a thousand metres above Evian, to enjoy the fantastic view – Mont Blanc, the lake, the Rhone valley – spread out below them. They were safely hidden in the crowds of holidaymakers. There was a large restaurant where they probably consumed a large lunch, and a garden where they could work. Schmidt handed over his documents: the Enigma code settings for June and July 1934 and orders signed by Goering in June for creating within two years six bomber squadrons, two fighter squadrons and 21 reconnaissance aircraft, fourteen hundred planes. It was all wrapped up in a double envelope with dire threats – including the death penalty – for anyone who leaked the information. They were all very jolly and arranged to meet again the next day at Evian – between roulette sessions.[18]

* * *

On 1 November 1935 Colonel Rudolf Schmidt was moved from head of 13th Infantry Regiment to the prestigious job of senior adviser to the army's top brass in Berlin. He cleared out his desk – he had amassed dozens of notes, details of manoeuvres, accounts of conferences – and gave them all to his brother to destroy, according to the rules. He burned them in the furnace of his soap factory but not before gutting them. So Hans was able to warn the French in January 1936 about Hitler's plans to invade the Rhineland, which happened two months later. Brother Rudolf was promoted to General on 1 October 1936, and there was another desk to be cleared...[19]

All the time Schmidt was sending weekly letters to 'post boxes', people who would hold letters for him; the interception of mail meant using the postal service was very risky so Lemoine arranged to make Schmidt's payments into a bank account in Berne. Schmidt met Lemoine and Bertrand occasionally, once in Copenhagen but usually in Switzerland, when he had documents to be photographed.

On 2 November 1937 Schmidt's brother, now serving at Weimar where a month before he had taken over command of the First Armoured division, came to Berlin for an army briefing. He had given up his apartment in Berlin so Ashay put him up. For the following two days he took part in a *Kriegsspiel* (war game) run by General Wernher von Fritsch, the head of the army; he was surprised by the subject, which was an offensive against Czechoslovakia. The next day Hitler called a meeting in his private apartment at the Chancellery of the chiefs of the three armed forces. He outlined his future plans for reviving the economy, discussed rearmament and the need for expansion and more land for the German people. He needed iron ore from Scandinavia, wheat from the Ukraine, coal from Czechoslovakia – which meant war. Listening were the head of the army, General von Fritsch, the head of the Luftwaffe, Hermann ·Goering, and the naval chief, Admiral Erich Raeder, the foreign minister, Baron Konstantin von Neurath and the war minister, Field Marshal Werner von Blomberg. The Admiral needed more steel if the navy were to be kept up to scratch; but it was a heated discussion because Goering and von Fritsch were not prepared to give up any of their allocation.

The meeting finished at twenty past four. In the evening Hitler threw a cocktail party in the Chancellery to which General von Fritsch invited the generals who had taken part in his *Kriegsspiel*. It was a good party, attended by about a hundred people, the cream of the armed forces and the diplomatic corps. It started at six o'clock and the champagne flowed generously. Hitler, von Fritsch, Goering, Raeder and von Neurath looked in at half past eight. Among Hitler's party was Colonel Friedrich Hossbach, his *aide de camp*, who had been at the afternoon's conference and was going to write up the minutes. Colonel Hossbach was pleased to find General Schmidt there; they had been friends for a long time and kept no secrets from each other. Hitler's party ended at nine o'clock and the fun continued at a ball. Hossbach and Schmidt didn't go, preferring to dine together. Shocked by the talk at the conference, Hossbach told his friend about it. Just as perturbed, General Schmidt went back to his brother's house and confided Hitler's plans.[20]

At eight o'clock the next morning Georges Blun, a French journalist working in Berlin, was wakened by the telephone ringing. Hans Thilo Schmidt was making his emergency call. Lemoine had given him a routine to follow if he needed to get in touch urgently: he was to telephone Georges Blun and give him the sad news that Uncle Kurt had died. This was the signal that he needed to see him immediately and they both made for the arranged meeting place, the waiting-room in the Charlottenburg railway station in Berlin. At ten Schmidt was sitting there, reading a newspaper, with his white briefcase held between his legs. Blun approached, asked: 'Do you have a message for Uncle Kurt's family?'

'Sure. Would you like to take a little walk?' They left the station and walked along Wilmersdorferstrasse in the direction of Kurfurstendamm. Without stopping, Schmidt slipped an envelope to Blun. 'Take this to your friends quickly. It's urgent, very serious,' he said, then disappeared.

By eleven Blun was at the French embassy in Pariser Platz. He was shown into the office of Maurice Dejean, the Deuxième Bureau's representative, and handed over the envelope without a word. Before putting it in the diplomatic bag, as he should have done, Dejean sneaked a peep. What he saw made him rush to the ambassador. What ambassador Andre Francois-Poncet read shocked him: 'My God, it's not possible. It means war.'

Schmidt's document, an account of Hitler's meeting the day before, outlined his plan for the expansion of Germany over ten years, from 1938 to 1948, starting with Austria and Czechoslovakia. Francois-Poncet couldn't believe it but Dejean assured him, without revealing his informant's name or job, that the man was absolutely trustworthy and provided superb intelligence regularly. The ambassador felt the Foreign Office at Quai d'Orsay needed to know about this immediately, the diplomatic bag would be too slow. Thanks to Schmidt's earlier information, the ambassador already knew the Germans had broken the diplomatic code he used to communicate with Paris. He now had a new one but if they had broken the code once, they could surely do it again. He ignored the danger and sent a telegram, a rather strange and vague telegram. The Germans *had* broken the code and the telegram *was* intercepted by the *Forschungsamt*. It read:

Yesterday afternoon an important meeting took place in the Reich's Chancellery which was attended by a large number of generals and admirals.

The newspapers have not reported it and it is difficult to know what this long meeting was about. I have been told that it was about raw materials and the difficulties which the shortage of iron and steel impose on rearmament... But it would be astonishing if that was all that was being talked about when so many high-ranking officers were summoned to the Chancellery.

The last sentence of the message intrigued the *Forschungsamt*; they felt it suggested that Francois-Poncet knew more and would send the information later by safer means.[21] The diplomatic bag fell like a bomb in Paris the next day at midday. Louis Rivet, the head of counter-espionage and foreign intelligence in the Deuxième Bureau, called a meeting. Schmidt had asked at the end of his report for a meeting at Basle on 15 November and this confused them; for a year Lemoine had been meeting Schmidt in Berlin regularly under the cover of his business trips and collecting information on the Enigma codes, and Schmidt had been posting intelligence reports in invisible ink every week. For him to leave Germany now and carry intelligence documents to Switzerland was almost absurdly risky. It must mean he had something very important to tell them.

Schmidt had used the need to visit the new *Forshungstamt* listening post at Berne as a chance to go to Basle and so the meeting was agreed. Perruche thought it must be so serious that he decided to go himself.

It had not taken long for Schmidt to hear about the interception of the telegram. When he arrived at the Hotel Euler in Basle, the usually smiling and relaxed spy was anything but. Straightaway he started cursing the unbelievable stupidity of the ambassador in Berlin. 'Why did he open the envelope addressed to you? I don't want to have these men as intermediaries. I want to work alone in future. Alone, alone!'

Lemoine, Bertrand and Perruche had no idea what he was talking about. He told them the grim news that the ambassador's telegram was picked up by the *Forschungsamt*, decrypted in less than twenty-four hours and was on Goering's desk on 8 November. 'I leave you to imagine what's going to happen.' It was news to them all. They were stunned. Lemoine broke the silence to try to reassure his precious spy. He told him there was no sign that he was in danger but Schmidt replied: 'You know this game too well not to realise that the Abwehr, the Gestapo and the *Forschungsamt* will unite to trace the source of the leak.'

Fortunately Schmidt had not given the French ambassador everything he knew about Hitler's secret meeting and when Lemoine had calmed him down a bit – 'You've done well' – he replied: 'It would have been perfect but for the stupidity of your ambassador. There is something that I kept to myself, though. Rudolf gave it to me just before he went back to Weimar. Some hours later I heard of the interception of Francois-Poncet's telegram.'

He pulled a piece of paper from his inside pocket and unfolded it. It was a map of Europe. There were dates written on Austria, Czechoslovakia and Poland, dates showing when Hitler planned to invade: Austria, spring 1938, Czechoslovakia, autumn 1938, Poland 1940. A line was drawn across France cutting it in two. General Maurice-Henri Gauché, head of the Deuxième Bureau, was the first to see the map. He later wrote that it was Hitler's plan to take over the whole of Europe between 1938 and 1948, with the exception of the Mediterranean coast of France, which was reserved for Hitler's Italian partners.[22] It caused a sensation in Paris Almost incredibly, it coincided with the *zone libre* later agreed by the armistice of 1940, showing this had long been Hitler's plan.

Lemoine had once tried to get Schmidt to recruit his brother but Hans ruled it right out. If Rudolf knew what he was doing he would have him shot. But Lemoine didn't need to recruit the general; he had become one of the best informers he'd ever had and cost-free. Rudolf was used to protecting his harum-scarum younger brother – he'd paid his debts and found him his job – and he also came to see him as a safety valve, a shoulder to moan on, away from the military politics.

It was Colonel Hossbach's job to write up the minutes of the meeting but he did not do so until five days later, partly from notes, partly from memory, so perhaps General Schmidt, who heard his account on the day of the meeting, had a more accurate report. The colonel's minutes came to be known as the Hossbach Memorandum and were produced as evidence at the Nuremberg war trials in 1945 when their accuracy was questioned, so perhaps General Schmidt and the French did indeed have a truer account.

The intercepted telegram put Schmidt in great danger. He changed his office, moved from the Cipher Office to the *Forschungsamt*, the letter-interception and telephone-tapping organisation, which meant that he could follow the progress of the investigation into his own leak. The French provided some new safeguards: he was never to meet a French agent in Germany, he was given new letter boxes in Switzerland for his mail and he was to use a new sort of invisible ink.

* * *

German intelligence was thrown into turmoil by the discovery of the leak. Admiral Wilhelm Canaris, head of the Abwehr, called a meeting on 9 December to try to find the source. Hitler absolutely refused to believe that any of his personal staff had been involved. Everybody denied all knowledge; everybody suspected everyone else. The best Canaris could suggest was to place the French ambassador under surveillance and check all his contacts with Germans, and put an informer in La Taverne, the bar-restaurant that was a favourite meeting place of journalists, the French and German army officers.

CHAPTER TWENTY-FOUR

The Trap

The intercepted telegram was almost a disaster for Schmidt and French intelligence. But real disaster struck in another place a few months later: Lemoine vanished.

At first Palliole was not unduly concerned; the man had freedom of movement, made his own decisions and often was not heard from for three or four days. But silence for eight days was unheard of. Colonel Rivet was not bothered. It wasn't the first time their man had been in trouble with the German police or any other foreign police. He was very strong, the Germans knew his international reputation from the beginning of the century and were impressed, he could talk his way out of any situation. Paillole had often been wryly amused that the safety of France depended on two Germans, Lemoine and Schmidt; but now he fretted. What if Lemoine had transferred his loyalties back to the land of his birth? Lemoine was the Deuxième Bureau's best recruiter of spies/informers. He was a fine judge of character and temperament, a skill honed during his daredevil card-sharping days. With carefully probing questions he could size up a possible recruit, judge his political feelings, work out what it could cost to buy him and to keep him onside. He knew a huge number of German dialects so that he could talk with people from anywhere in the country. He also had great charm and, of course, a limitless supply of Marks.

A star recruiter needs to recruit. How did Lemoine do it? Simple: he advertised in local newspapers. He placed job ads in newspapers in French and German industrial towns offering work to industrial correspondents and salesmen. He would then interview anyone whose reply looked promising. He had arranged to meet one such possibility at the Dom hotel opposite the cathedral in Cologne on 9 March 1938. It was one of those grand hotels that had sprung up to offer luxurious lodgings to the new breed of traveller that the railways had brought. It was the hotel where, thirty years earlier, Monty Newton received a new Daimler tourer in payment of a gambling debt, the car that took the two of them chasing across Europe after Count Gravich.

Lemoine was early for his appointment; there was no sign of a single man waiting for him. There were two men together; they approached Lemoine, spoke politely, then they arrested him. They were Gestapo officers. His over-confidence had betrayed him. His letters to the would-be recruit were signed 'V. Verdier' (yet another alias); one was intercepted by the *Forschungsamt*. The Gestapo knew that Lemoine had worked for the French secret service since 1920 and kept tabs on him and a sharp-eyed operator noticed that the intercepted letter came from Lemoine's address: 5 rue de Madrid, the brand of paper was the same, the letter heading was the same. So the trap was set.

The two officers took Lemoine to Gestapo headquarters in Alexanderplatz, Berlin, next day for questioning. A big blond, good-natured chap called Lipik interviewed him, then an astute detective, Josef Kieffer, took over. He knew Lemoine's dossier by heart. He even had his *fiche anthropometric* (the record of his physical measurements and attributes) from 1920 in the name of Stallman. The Gestapo knew they had a big prize, a star performer. Should they lock him up, make him reveal his secrets and betray the Germans who spied for him or should they use him, turn him? Lemoine answered the question for them. He didn't bother to deny that he worked for the French but he offered to help the Germans, too. He knew they needed to know about Communist sympathisers in Austria and he could help here. From his dealings with the Russian, Walter Scott/Reiss, he knew the way the Communists worked and, in the anti-Nazi Bodo in the Austrian Embassy in Paris he recruited after that Christmas party at Quai D'Orsay, he had a source of information on anti-Nazi activity in Vienna. It was a perfect deal.

When Lemoine got back to Paris, Paillole was worried that he had been turned. He was interrogated thoroughly and all seemed well but Palliole still couldn't rest: 'There were many shady corners in our relationship with Lemoine.' He called in his friend, a police detective called Jean Osvald, who had specialised in counter-espionage work for ten years. He also knew Lemoine and his team well, particularly Drach, his assistant. Paillole took Lemoine and Osvald to lunch at La Rotisserie Perigourdine in Place Saint-Michel (spit-roasted pork, *confit* of goose on the menu.) Palliole hadn't seen Lemoine for some months and he was shocked at his changed appearance: thin, aged and tired. He was sixty-seven but looked ten years older. Was it the emotional shock of his arrest or the first sign of the illness that killed him eight years later? Both, perhaps.

Lemoine was not at all put out to see Osvald; he knew perfectly well that he was there to judge him. Palliole wanted to know what he had given to the Gestapo to justify his quick release.

'Nothing much, just promises,' said Lemoine, 'An agreement that I can keep or not keep. You know that I met Walter Scott fairly often in Vienna. I made a report for him, [Kieffer] with the names of thousands of communists in the town. I have names in my notebook, others in my head. I also proposed to supply diplomatic codes that I got from Walter Scott. They concerned Hungary, Czechoslovakia and Italy... I knew from Ashay that they [already] decoded the messages of these countries so the gift was not of great value.'

Palliole listened in silence, said nothing but thought hard and long. It was true that Lemoine's reputation as much as his ease and confidence would have impressed the Nazi police. What a Godsend for the Gestapo to turn the most senior and most celebrated of the Deuxième Bureau's recruiters – and right under the nose of the Abwehr, the German counter-intelligence service, whose job it really was. There was great competition between the two so this would be quite a coup.

Lemoine left after lunch and Paillole and Osvald mulled over what he had said. Osvald was convinced Lemoine had not been turned.

'He has shafted them,' he said. 'There's no doubting the truth of his explanation.' Palliole agreed and they decided to forget the whole thing.[23]

It was not until 1945 that Paillole discovered when he interrogated two German officers that *he* was the one who had been shafted. One, Richard Protze, head of section IIIF of the Abwehr in Berlin from 1933 to 1939, told him they knew about Lemoine's recruiting methods, and SS *Hauptsturmführer* Gunther of the Berlin Gestapo said that the 'sparkling success' at Vienna of Lipik and Kieffer later that year – Austria was annexed on 12 March 1938 – was due to Lemoine's revelations and collaboration.[24]

Luckily, Lemoine's arrest in March 1938 was before the Poles told the French that they were reading Enigma messages; this did not happen until July 1939, so Hans Thilo Schmidt was safe. All the same, Lemoine was told never to see him again, to move house, never to leave France.

Andre Perruche from the intelligence department of the Deuxième Bureau replaced Lemoine as Schmidt's handler, who continued to supply vital information about Germany's plans straight from the horse's mouth – his brother. Rudolf Schmidt was enjoying a brilliant military career and was one of the few soldiers whose competence Hitler admired; they even lunched together. He was wildly indiscreet with his brother and passed on details of the growing strength of the German army.

On 9 August 1938 Hans Schmidt went to Paris for a short stay. He was put up at a smart hotel near the Madeleine where Perruche and Bertrand joined him to discuss his future work. Schmidt had been given two months' leave before being posted to an important new job, taking charge of the *Forschungsamt* at Templin, north of Berlin. He would be difficult for the French to replace but he assured them that he had good friends in his old office and would be able to pass on any new information about Enigma. What was more, in his new job he would be his own boss, whereas before he had been just a subordinate.

In the meantime, he wanted to explore Paris – this was his first visit to the city of light – so the next night Bertrand and Perruche took him to the Moulin Rouge. They observed him carefully as he watched the show, entranced. At the interval Schmidt danced with several hostesses. The fifth was a little plump, Bertrand thought. Schmidt 'loved women but he loved money more,' Bertrand observed. He brought one of the girls to their table. By one in the morning Bertrand was exhausted and left. A second girl, a blonde, took his chair. Perruche soon gave up and left the happy trio to drink yet more champagne.[25]

CHAPTER TWENTY-FIVE

Paris Falls

Since 1932 Gustave Bertrand had been becoming more and more impatient at the lack of progress of the Polish cryptographers. 'Be patient,' Gwido Langer told him. He would be the first to know. But he was not. It was not until 25 July 1939 at a meeting at a secret cryptology centre at Pyry in the Kabaty woods in Poland that the truth came out. The meeting was attended by Bertrand and a French cipher expert, Henri Baquenie, as well as Alastair Denniston, head of the British Government Code and Cypher School, and Dillwyn Knox, who had been working on the Enigma machine since the 1920s. Langer told them his team had broken the code seven years before and had been reading the German messages ever since. Why the secrecy is not known; perhaps because the French simply did not try to break the code and the English seemed to think it was unbreakable. It was the prospect of war and the French and English promise of support if Germany invaded Poland that prompted the co-operation.

Dillwyn Knox famously threw a tantrum in the car taking him and Denniston back to their hotel; unfortunately one of their Polish hosts who was in the taxi with them understood English and Knox's outburst has gone down in history. Bertrand, too, was furious at the distrust and deception and the fact that Rejewski apparently had broken the code using the first three sets of documents Bertrand had taken to Warsaw in 1932, which meant that Schmidt had been risking his life unnecessarily to deliver new settings for the Enigma machine. The following month Langer handed over two replica

Enigma machines, one for Bertrand, the other for Britain. Bertrand led the team that guarded it on its journey to London: it was dismantled and put into diplomatic bags by Commander Wilfred 'Biffy' Dunderdale, head of the Paris station of the SIS, for the journey on the Golden Arrow boat train to London. With him were Archibald and Archibald, the two senior partners of a British law firm in Paris, and 'Uncle' Tom Greene, Dunderdale's right-hand man; these three all worked without pay for the good of their country. When they reached Customs at Dover the party fell in with Sacha Guitry, the French playwright and his actress wife, on the way to London for a performance of Guitry's latest hit, *Pearls in the Crown*. Dunderdale knew them, they were his neighbours, and they had piles of luggage which acted as camouflage for the precious Enigma bags. A quick word with Customs meant they were waved through – Madame Guitry's perfume, Sacha's cognac and all, so he was delighted. 'C', head of SIS, was at Victoria station to greet them on 16 August, seventeen days before war was declared. 'Acceuil triomphal,' declared Bertrand after exchanging kisses on both cheeks.[26]

In spite of the advance warning given unwittingly by Schmidt's brother, Austria had been annexed on 12 March 1938, the Sudetenland, the western part of Czechoslovakia, was taken over in September, too. Langer's decryption team worked on in the deepest secrecy – not even their wives knew what their jobs were. They knew the danger they were in and when the invasion of Poland began on 1 September 1939 (Hitler had planned it for 1940 but he had the forces Schmidt predicted –sixty-two divisions and thirteen hundred aircraft by 1939, so why wait?) they were packed and ready to flee. On 3 September Britain and France responded to Poland's call for help but it was 6 September before the decrypters and their families were evacuated. It was a perilous journey: their train was bombed, it crashed into another train. Rejewski was thirty-four by this time and he and his wife Irena had two young children. Roztcki's wife, Basia, had a four-month old baby, and they had to go searching for food for their babies; it took them three days to reach Brest Litovsk, a distance of about a hundred miles. Then the decrypters were told to go to Romania immediately, leaving their wives and children behind. The men went to the French embassy in Bucharest and were given visas and tickets for the journey to Paris. There Gustave Bertrand put them up in the Chateau de Vignolles, north-east of Paris, and established a new section – the equivalent of Bletchley Park – code-named PC Bruno (*Post de commandant Bruno*) although things were never the same between him and Gwido Langer.[27]

One day after war was declared Alan Turing from King's College, Cambridge, arrived at Bletchley Park. He had been appointed a don at the young age of twenty-two, spent two years in the USA at Princeton University studying for a PhD in mathematical logic but when it became clear that war in Europe was on the way, he took up cryptanalysis, probably in the autumn of 1937. He returned to Cambridge in July 1939, bringing with him a model of a machine he had designed that he called a 'universal machine', which could replace words with numbers. The Government Code and Cypher school knew of his work and invited him to take some courses during the summer at their headquarters in Broadway, by St James's Park in London, where the Secret Intelligence Service was also based. The GC and CS was evacuated to Bletchley Park in August and on 4 September Turing left Cambridge and moved to Bletchley. He was assigned to work with Dillwyn Knox, a classical scholar who had broken the Enigma code used by the Spanish and the Italians during the Spanish Civil War but the German code had eluded him since the 1920s. By now the British, French and Poles were working well together after the revelations in the Kabaty forest. Although the Poles were further ahead on the Enigma codes, the British had more money and manpower to throw at the job and things were moving quickly. 'C', Sir Stewart Menzies, head of MI6, was impressed and on 10 January 1940 wrote to Colonel Louis Rivet, by now head of the Deuxième Bureau, asking for Rejewski, Jerzy Rozycki and Henryk Zygalski to make a 'short visit' to Bletchley Park to work on 'certain mechanical devices' that he could not send to France. This was not allowed but a face-to-face meeting was desirable. Dillwyn Knox was probably *persona non grata* so Alan Turing was sent to PC Bruno to spend several days with Rejewski. This was the only meeting between the two and what they discussed led to the design and construction of the first British bombe, a code-breaking machine developed from the bomba

Rejewski had devised. More scientific and technical advances by Turing led to the construction of the first computer, the Colossus. Harry Hinsley, another King's College recruit to Bletchley and later knighted for his work, was co-author of *British Intelligence in the Second World War*, and wrote that the information provided by the Poles was 'invaluable'. [28] Rejewski believed that without Hans Thilo Schmidt's stolen documents decryption would have taken much longer, 'perhaps for ever'. Curiously, Professor Jack Good, who worked in Hut 8 at Bletchley Park from May 1941 to October 1943 wrote: 'My first boss, the famous mathematician A. M. Turing, only once mentioned the Poles and that evasively.'[29]

Marion Rejewski waited years for some recognition of his achievement in devising the bomba code-breaking machine. In 1943, after Germany invaded the *zone libre* of the south of France, he fled to Britain and served in the Polish army as a cryptologist but without any link to Bletchley Park; he was totally ignorant of what they were doing. After the war he returned to his wife and family in Poland, which was then under Russian control. The communists knew nothing of his cryptology work and distrusted anyone who had worked in the west. He was given a middle-management job in industry. He wrote his memoirs in 1967 but it was 1978 before he was awarded the *Polonia Restituta*, the equivalent of the French Legion of Honour. He died in 1980 and in 1983 his, Zygalski's and Rozycki's work in breaking the Enigma code was finally recognised: with a special postage stamp. A small acknowledgement of the work of the three men – by then all dead – who had done so much for a free Europe.

The German forces invaded Belgium and the Netherlands on 10 May 1940 and advanced fast into France through the Ardennes mountains, to the surprise of the Allies who thought their tanks would never get through the thickly forested terrain; the Allies were pushed towards the Channel and trapped on the beaches. Then came the desperate evacuation of the troops from Dunkirk in May and June 1940. As the enemy pushed farther into France, the cryptologists of PC Bruno were again evacuated, this time to Paris to work in the French secret service headquarters in Avenue de Tourville. They were not there for long, but long enough to ask why the French air force put up no defence when Paris was bombed on 3 June 1940, after the cryptologists had told them a week before that the car factories in Paris were to be attacked.[30]

* * *

With the advance of the German army, one of Palliole's first thoughts was for Lemoine. On 9 June he went to his spy's new flat at 9, Boulevard Pershing. Suitcases were piled up in the sitting-room, the ashes of shredded documents smoked in the fireplace. He told Lemoine the bad news: the Germans were at Rouen, the Bureau's files were on the way to the Loire. The total evacuation of the Service must be complete by the morning of 11 June.

Paillole was expecting Paris to fall within the next few days and didn't want to lose Lemoine to the Germans with all his knowledge of Hans Thilo Schmidt and the decoding of Enigma. Lemoine understood the gravity of the situation and had already made his plans. His sons were in the front line and he had had little news of them, so he and his wife intended to go the next day to his daughter's house at La Rochelle on the Atlantic coast together with Frederic Drach, his faithful assistant. Paillole was doubtful about Lemoine's plan but left him to it, warning him not to leave anything behind that could be useful to the enemy. Lemoine pointed to the smoking fireplace and Paillole left to evacuate the rest of his staff.[31]

The Italians joined the war on 10 June and the Germans marched into Paris on 14 June. By six o'clock that evening the Abwehr had taken over the very smart art nouveau hotel Lutetia on Boulevard Raspail and established themselves. They set about searching for anything that could lead to the capture of any of the hundreds of people suspected of spying against Germany. They had a list and two names – Rudolf Stallman and Rodolphe Lemoine – were at top of it. Paris was empty and dead. The government, led by Marshal Philippe Petain, had fled ahead of the German invasion to establish new headquarters in Bordeaux but they left their offices open, with the filing cabinets intact and the Germans found a treasure trove. Georg Wiegand, a captain in the Abwehr, found a list of Lemoine's contacts, agents and dead letter boxes at the headquarters of the Sûreté Nationale in the rue des Saussaies. He searched Lemoine's three addresses, in the rue de Madrid, rue de Lisbonne and Boulevard Pershing and found his diaries for 1938 and 1939 with lists of names and payments made. The sums were mostly small apart from two paid into an account in Basle for 200,000 Swiss francs. Next they broke open a sealed railway wagon at La Charité-sur-Loire and found it full of the secret files of the French High Command. Pleased with their haul, Admiral Wilhelm Canaris, head of the Abwehr, was excited to receive a message at 7 o'clock on the evening of 16 June saying that the Führer wanted to see him immediately. Euphoric after his team's successful searches, he was looking forward to receiving Hitler's congratulations; in the car on the way to Berlin he mused over the various points he wanted to raise with the Führer. Imagine his surprise to find Reinhardt Heydrich, head of the RSHA, the overall security organisation, waiting in the ante-room; like him, he had been called urgently to the Chancellery. A few minutes later, Goering, in uniform, opened the door and ushered them into Hitler's office, without uttering a word. Hitler was standing, his welcome was polite but cold. He was holding a sheaf of intelligence papers. 'Read these,' he said. 'It's very serious. There's a traitor in the house. This must be stopped. We have to find him quickly. He will be punished, however high his position.'

That was the end of the interview. Dismayed, shaken, they were shown out and Goering told them what had happened. He said that the *Forschungsamt* had intercepted and decoded several telegrams from the Dutch ambassador in Berlin to his government and they had also tapped telephone calls between the Belgian and Dutch military attaches. 'It is clear that a traitor, very well-placed, has told them of our plans and the date of our attack on the west,' he said. 'But it's lucky that our organisation is able to read nearly all of the telegrams sent in Europe and they don't know that. Don't forget, though, in spite of that, we still haven't traced the traitor who told Francois-Poncet, the French ambassador, about the meeting on 5 November, 1937.' Hitler certainly had not forgotten that and he wanted to know if the two leaks came from the same source.

Goering, Heydrich and Canaris went through the decoded telegrams together:

2 May, message to Brussels from the Belgian ambassador, Adrien Nieuwenhuys: 'an attack on Belgium and Holland next week.'

3 May, message from the Vatican to the papal nuncio of Holland: 'next invasion of Holland and Belgium.'

5-9 May, a series of tapped phone calls.

9 May, telephone call between Colonel Sas, the Dutch military attaché, and Lieutenant Post, the Minister for War for Holland, in The Hague (this astonished Canaris and Heydrich): 'Post, you recognise my voice? It's Sas in Berlin. I have only one thing to say: tomorrow at dawn. You understand me? Repeat it!' 'I understand. Received letter 210.'

This was code: 200 signified invasion and 10 was the day of the month, 10 May.

A team from the RSHA, the Abwehr and the Gestapo was set up to work out a plan to find the traitor. The Gestapo team included *Hauptsturmführer* Kieffer, the espionage expert who had interviewed Lemoine in 1938 and let him go; he had never forgotten it. Quite quickly suspicion fell on Colonel Hans Oster, Canaris's deputy and an old friend, who was known for his anti-Nazi opinions. He had been a friend of Colonel Sas, the Dutch military attaché in Berlin since 1932 and had met him every day since 1 May. Had he given away the secrets? If so, was it deliberately or accidentally?[32]

It took till the end of June to rule him out. Admiral Canaris decided there was no proof anywhere in the documents they had seized in Paris that Colonel Oster was guilty. They started again, going back to 1937 when they knew the French ambassador in Berlin, Francois-Poncet, was receiving information about what was going on in the German Chancellery.

* * *

On 19 June Henri Navarre, a French intelligence officer, went to Bordeaux looking for news of the evacuees, but all was chaos. Next day he found Lemoine at the door of the police headquarters in a panic about what was to become of him. The Germans were after him and he needed to leave France. He was far from the suave, confident charmer now. Navarre knew it was vital to get him out of the country quickly and he got him a permit to board a ship bound for England. Bordeaux harbour was packed so they were advised to leave from St. Jean de Luz, a seaside resort near Biarritz and off they went. The next day Navarre found Lemoine's car in the courtyard of a seminary in Bordeaux where they had taken refuge. His wife and Frederic Drach were there, looking miserable and surrounded by a pile of luggage. Lemoine explained why they were still in France: he had been to the English consul in St Jean de Luz with his permit who told them to be on the quay at 5 am where a British minesweeper would be waiting. There they found thousands of Polish soldiers ready to board the ship which was due to leave that evening. The captain told them that because there were so many people they could each take only a blanket and an overnight bag. That night, the 21st, they returned to the quay where the Poles were boarding. 'When our turn came, about 10 pm, they showed us to a place near the bridge in the middle of the crowd. I begged an officer to see if he could find somewhere a bit quieter for my wife. I showed him my permit. His response was to swear at me and tell me why he hated the French.'

Lemoine was furious. He told the officer, in plainest English, that he would rather die in France than be insulted in England and stormed off the ship. It was nearly midnight and the trio slept in the car. Lemoine spent the next day looking for a ship to take them to Morocco without success, so he decided to go back to Paillole. On the 23rd, all dignity forgotten, their car tagged on to the line of refugees and retreating troops. They were able to sleep in a barracks when they got to Mont de Marsan and beg a little petrol to continue their journey. They found Paillole at Bordeaux where the government was based after the fall of Paris. Within three days of the fall the government collapsed and Marshal Pétain asked for an armistice. General Charles de Gaulle refused to accept defeat and next day fled to London and broadcast an appeal to the French to fight on, establishing himself as leader of the Free French Forces. The armistice was signed on 22 June; this divided France into two zones, with the Germans occupying the north and the west coast as far as the Spanish border, and the *zone libre* of southern France, just as Hans Thilo's brother, the general, had reported in November 1937.

Its capital was at Vichy, an elegant spa town in the Auvergne, famous for its *art nouveau* buildings. Marshal Petain was head of state. But despite being a hero of the First World War, he collaborated with the Germans, even going as far as passing anti-Semitic laws.

Two days after the armistice was signed, Paillole was in Toulouse to meet Gustave Bertrand and his Polish and Spanish cryptologists who had come by bus from Paris. He organised flights to Algeria for the team and next day was back in Bordeaux where Lemoine found him. He suggested the little party took refuge on the Cote d'Azur – this was much more like it for Lemoine. 'No problem,' he said. 'I have money there and friends. I will report to the gendarmerie and await your instructions.'

Before they left Lemoine opened his case to take out a file to show Paillole. What he saw in the case frightened the life out of him. It was stuffed with confidential documents, the codes of various countries, blank passports for Holland, Sweden, Denmark, blank identity cards, rubber stamps of all kinds; in fact, everything a fraudster could need to pursue his business. Pailllole wrote that he was 'stupefied' and asked Lemoine if he was certain that nothing compromising had been left behind. He said he had been very careful and everything that was not in his case had been destroyed, he just thought these things might come in useful. Paillole was agitated about the safety of Hans Thilo Schmidt and felt that trouble was ahead but he could do nothing but let Lemoine loose. If the Germans caught him it would be the end for Schmidt and the end of the decryption of the Enigma codes – the Germans had no idea that their codes were being read. [33]

* * *

All was not well with the *entente cordiale*. Prime Minister Winston Churchill commented in a cabinet meeting on 24 June 1940: 'Our relations [with the French] might well apply very closely to those of two nations at war with each other.' In fact, the government would have no contact with Pétain because of his collaboration, and General de Gaulle's July meeting with C, head of SIS, was distinctly frosty because thirteen days after the Armistice, Churchill had ordered the scuttling of the French navy in North Africa to prevent it falling into the hands of the Germans; the Vichy government was also angered, and there was a wave of anti-British feeling.[34]

The Cinquième (fifth) Bureau, an extension of the Deuxième, was formed on the outbreak of war as its hands-on branch and Paillole and Bertrand were part of it. With the signing of the armistice, the French secret intelligence services were supposed to be disbanded but by 25 August they were reformed under the cover of the Bureaux des Menées Antinationales. Its staff was paid by the Vichy government and its official job was to protect what remained of the French army from British and communist subversion. Colonel Louis Rivet, old head of the Deuxième Bureau, was chief, Paul Paillole took charge of a unit called Enterprise Générale de Travaux Ruraux, with an office in Marseille, supposedly trading in fruit, vegetables and wine but really aimed at rooting out collaborators and Germany's spies, eighty per cent of whom were French nationals. It also spied on the Allies in France. Marseille was a good choice for its headquarters because Paillole spent some of his teenage years there, knew it well and had friends there. Of course, the port offered a simple escape to North Africa if necessary.

Why spy? The French distrusted all foreign intelligence services operating in France, especially, it seems, the British. 'Germany is number one danger. England is the number two danger,' Paillole said in a lecture to students at spy school in 1942. 'So what is being spied on? What does the enemy seek among us? Everything.'[35]

The Germans needed to make sure the terms of the Armistice were being kept to, to keep their finger on the pulse of the French population, watch for any risk of rebellion, look for any sign of rearmament, check industrial production, even the harvest. The Travaux Ruraux arrested about 2,000 French nationals. Paillole himself became suspected of betraying French resistance workers, even of being involved in the capture of Jean Moulin, hero of the resistance. The problem was that some resistance groups had inevitably been infiltrated by collaborators pretending to be anti-German. Nobody could be trusted. Paillole told his student spies that he did not trust certain resistance groups, particularly Gaullist groups in the occupied zone; he felt they had been infiltrated. He didn't think much of Britain's SIS either, believing it to be run by naïve amateurs – he was right – but he admired German intelligence methods and admitted learning from them.[36]

* * *

On 8 July Gustave Bertrand was given unofficial permission to re-establish his code-breaking business and resumed radio contact with 'C'. Bertrand was still in the French army, paid for by the Vichy government; the left hand truly didn't know what the right hand was doing and if it had come out that Britain was dealing with the Free French *and* Vichy, we could perhaps have found ourselves fighting the French as well as the Germans.

Bertrand bought the remote Chateau des Fouzes near Uzes, 20 kilometres north of Nimes, in wild mountainous country. He spread rumours that the chateau was lived in by communists to discourage the local ladies from calling, and named it PC Cadix. The job of Cadix was to keep the Vichy government informed of German and British activity in France but he continued to work secretly for SIS. He brought his fifteen Polish and seven Spanish cryptographers back from Algeria and by the beginning of September they were sending decrypts to C about German plans, their intelligence, the movements of their armed forces. For the next two years he continued his work; it was, said Winston Churchill, the most extraordinary piece of secret service work carried out under the hostile circumstances of war.

Bertrand did not have the means to tap telephone lines so intercepts were provided by the daring Gabriel Romon, a communications expert in the French post and telegraph service before the war. He was head of technical services at PC Bruno until the armistice and was now working for the Groupement des Contrôles Radioélectriques de l'Interieur, its job to track radio transmissions of the resistance. This organisation was established with the agreement of the Germans under the terms of the armistice. But Romon was secretly working for the resistance section of what remained of the French army and he came to Bertrand's aid. He put taps on the phone lines between France and Berlin and collected Gestapo, army, air force and Abwehr secrets, details of troop movements, secret service activities throughout Europe and the USSR. There was masses of stuff which he sent by airmail, collected by Bertrand from the little Nimes airport not far from the castle, in spite of flights being under Luftwaffe control at both ends. The material was then transmitted by radio to England. There was an enormous amount and the Germans were very good at picking up long transmissions. Although they were based in the *zone libre* Bertrand knew that they could be raided at any moment by Vichy or German forces so there were always three vehicles ready to evacuate the thirty-three people at the chateau if they were discovered.

Before the fall of Paris Bertrand had spare parts for his Enigma machines made in Paris and he needed more now. He had to go to Paris to collect them but the train journey was difficult: as a civilian, posing as Monsieur Barsac, the owner of the chateau, he needed a special pass for the Vichy-Paris train. There was a check *en route* and another before he could leave the Gare de Lyon in Paris. He got the pass by posing as the manager of a perfume factory in Grasse, the centre of the French perfume trade. He said he was taking essences to Paris to be made into scent for the wives of the German forces. The railway police obviously saw this as important war work and Bertrand made a pretty remarkable twenty-six journeys without being stopped.[37]

Meanwhile, in Paris, after weeks spent scrutinizing the captured French documents, the German team was no nearer to finding the traitor. Admiral Canaris became convinced that spymaster Lemoine was the man to lead them to him. 'Find Lemoine,' the order went out on 15 August. He put Georg Wiegand in charge of the operation, the man who had found Lemoine's diaries. He was about fifty, slim and elegant. His chestnut hair was fading and thinning at the front, which managed to give him a distinguished and serious look. He spoke French well, too. Canaris told him to work secretly and to find all Lemoine's contacts in Germany, particularly in the Chiffrierstelle His men watched Lemoine's flat in Boulevard Pershing and intercepted a letter posted by him in Saint-Raphael on 30 August, asking the concierge to send the keys of the apartment to his daughter. Naturally, he didn't give his address but a secret agent was sent to Saint-Raphael, with a photo of Lemoine, to look for him; in vain, for Lemoine had been staying at the hotel Beau-Rivage under another name and by the beginning of September had left. He knew he was safe in Saint-Raphael but he was impatient for action and anxious about not hearing anything from Schmidt, so he went to Vichy in search of information about his colleagues. He tracked down Colonel Rivet and Gustave Bertrand in their hiding-place at the hotel Saint-Mart at Chamalieres, Puy-de-Dome. He told them he wanted to get back to work and suggested going to Spain and Portugal to try to get hold of some Spanish codes.

The interception and de-coding of radio messages between Madrid and Berlin was one of Rivet's preoccupations at the time because he knew Hitler was seriously thinking of attacking Gibraltar. They jumped at the idea and a week later, armed with a diplomatic passport and yet another false identity, Lemoine crossed the Spanish border. He was devoted to his wife and they usually travelled together on his missions but this time the excitement of spying beat domestic bliss at the seaside and Madame Lemoine was left by herself in Saint-Raphael for several months; once or twice she visited their daughter at La Rochelle.[38]

In December 1940, Gestapo man Kieffer, with the agreement of the Abwehr, was sifting through the records of the Prefecture of Police in Paris. He found a huge dossier on Lemoine. 'There was so much stuff you would need a wheelbarrow to move it.'[39] After several weeks' work, he found the transcript of a 1938 interview by the Prefecture of Police of an Italian in an 'irregular situation' in Paris. He was precise in his statement: he said he had a *Chiffrierstelle* code and demanded a large reward for letting the Italian government have it. And he said that it was Lemoine who had offered the code. This was certain proof that there were leaks from the *Chiffrierstelle* as well as the *Forschungsamt*.

In February, 1941 Admiral Canaris called a meeting in his office of the chiefs of the three security services: there was General Erich Fellgiebel from the *Chiffrierstelle*, Heydrich, chief of the Reich main security service, which included the Gestapo, and Prince Christoffe von Hesse, director of the *Forschungsamt*. Canaris asked the three chiefs to secretly check the details of every person who had been employed in their departments since 1 January 1937: their origins, way of life, the company they kept, their state of mind.

By March 1941 Palliole was becoming even more uneasy about Lemoine; he didn't know the result of his work in Spain but his own spies in the Abwehr warned of their growing interest in him, so he was relieved when he showed up in Saint-Raphael again. When Lemoine arrived it was a quiet fishing-port. Far from living a discreet life by the beach, he was up to his usual money-making activities with Drach: selling currency, providing Spanish passports to enable people to cross the border into Spain, black market dealings and so on; in fact, using everything that the contents of the briefcase that Palliole had seen in Bordeaux had equipped him for. He was a brilliant spiv whom Palliole needed to protect and try to control. He asked the Gendarmerie at Saint-Raphael to order Lemoine and Drach to report to the chief of police of Marseille, Jean Osvald, at 2pm on 15 April. Not knowing what was troubling Osvald (this was the old friend who was convinced of Lemoine's loyalty after his arrest by the Gestapo in 1938) the two were surprised to be confronted by Palliole when they entered the chief's office. He wasted no time in getting down to the nitty-gritty.

'You must get out of Saint-Raphael and lie low. Two rooms have been reserved for you at the Hotel Splendide in Marseille from 1 May 1941.' I wonder why he gave them such a lot of leeway – two weeks – during which they could have got up to even more mischief.

Lemoine was happy. The Hotel Splendide really was, another of those grand hotels where he and Monty Newton had passed so many evenings playing cards. It suited him, too, because he knew they would be watched by police, which gave him some sense of security now that the Germans were looking for him. They were not to leave Marseille without Osvald's permission; they must get rid of the false papers and stop trading codes, forget the false beards.

Paillole was not worried about how they would manage: he knew Lemoine had several kilos of gold in his bags, from his concession in the French Guiana gold mine, and hundreds of Louis (twenty-franc gold coins). Lemoine paid Frederic Drach monthly and he surely had savings.[40]

On the day the Lemoines and Drach moved into the Splendide, General Canaris's group met again to compare notes; they were no farther on. Then in June, they came up with a list of ten men who had worked in both the *Forschungsamt* and the *Chiffrierstelle* since 1937; among them was Hans Thilo Schmidt, brother of General Rudolph Schmidt.

Canaris raised his arms to the ceiling in dismay. 'You're looking for trouble! First Oster, now you're blackening the name of one of the most prestigious families of the Reich and of one of our most respected generals. Forget it.'

The Admiral was convinced that the key to the problem lay in France and that Lemoine was the solution. The German intelligence services knew all about his long career with the French intelligence service and they admired his strong personality and his audacity. They respected him more than many of their own colleagues. Canaris remembered his arrest in Cologne, just before the annexation of Austria; he remembered how he had offered to spy for Germany then and he wondered if it would be possible to turn him now and if he would tell them who the spy was. His trading in codes suggested he could have contacts in the *Chiffrierstelle*. His age, his delicate health, his love of the high life, the different situation in France now, all suggested he might be lured back to his homeland.

Captain Wiegand made no more progress than anyone else in tracking down Lemoine and in the end it was accidental. In February 1942 an Italian who was working for the Abwehr arrived in Marseille after a mission in Tunisia. Strolling up the Canebière, the great boulevard that leads from the port to the centre, who should he see but Monsieur and Madame Lemoine, enjoying the spring sunshine! He had known them before the war but he was wary of approaching them and he reported the sighting. Wiegand sent a young German woman who spoke French and knew Marseille. It took her a few weeks to track them down to the Hotel Splendide. She returned to Paris in triumph.

The Abwehr had recruited a villainous bunch of secret agents during the occupation and Wiegand found two, Marang and Marette – they sound like a music hall act – and as luck would have it he had seen their names in Lemoine's notebooks they had found in Paris; Lemoine knew them so it would not be strange for them to renew contact and sound him out, tempt him to change sides and seduce him with the promise that Germany would treat him well. After all, they called him the spy of the century, the *eminence grise* of the Service de Renseignement since the Great War.

Charles Marang was the first secret agent Wiegand used. He was a Dutchman of about sixty who had a business near Paris with his son. Lemoine had introduced him to the Deuxième Bureau in 1939. He was handled by Captain Simoneau (who had been at St Cyr military college with Paillole). He had given him some intelligence work in Holland. which they were pleased with. In July 1941 Simoneau, in need of new agents, looked him up but wasn't impressed by the man: Marang told him that his son had been arrested by the Germans and then released, rather suspicious.

The man seemed old and scared and Simoneau assumed he was being watched by the Germans and decided it would be dangerous to use him. He was quite right. Wiegand saw his name in Lemoine's notebook and interviewed the old man, who convinced him of his loyalty. Like the Abwehr and the Gestapo, who were in competition to catch Lemoine, he, too, would love to be the one who turned Lemoine, so he visited him at the Hotel Splendide in June 1942. He told him that if he returned to Paris the Germans would welcome him and he would be totally free. Lemoine was happy to come out of retirement, looking for new adventures, curious about the possibility of being a double agent, working for the Germans as well as the French. Before giving an answer, he went to see Osvald, the police chief of Marseille and asked what he should do. Osvald said 'under no circumstances'; he had read Captain Simoneau's report on Marang the year before and now ordered him to be arrested immediately. Too late, Wiegand's man had already left the zone. Alarmed at this breach of security, he reported to Paillole, who came to Marseille with Rivet and Perruche at the end of June. Paillole was only half convinced by Lemoine's story and Lemoine could see by the expression on his face that Paillole didn't trust him.

'What do I do now, my commandant?' he asked.

'You must leave France immediately. I order you to go to North Africa.'

Lemoine objected: what about his business, his children, his age, his health? Paillole could see that the man had aged, he lacked energy and was clearly ill, he had long and painful bouts of coughing during their talk. He told Lemoine that he must go; the Germans were very likely to move into the free zone, which would be very dangerous for him and his family. He would arrange for him to go to Spain, on to Gibraltar and then cross into Morocco. Eventually Lemoine agreed to a compromise plan: Paillole said he knew an 'adorable' village, Saillagouse, 1,300 metres up in the Pyrenees and close to the Spanish border. There was a good inn and the chief of the Gendarmerie was a friend. Saillagouse was an old village a few hundred metres from the little Spanish enclave of Llivia. There was a road to the Spanish village of Puigcerda and they had been using this as a crossing point since 1941. The Lemoines arrived at the inn on 30 June 1942 and he soon saw the advantages of the situation.

The couple became a familiar sight, strolling through the village with their little dog, waving regally at passers-by. All the same, it was a long way from the buzz of Marseille.

He soon found an old acquaintance in Err, the next village: the mayor, Barthelemy Lledos. Lemoine knew him before the war in Paris when he had business dealings with Denmark and persuaded him to work for the Deuxième Bureau. He was able to provide information about the Reich economy and German-Russian relations. The mayor found a little furnished house for them to rent, Villa Sainte-Lucie, near the school in Saillagouse. With the help of a village girl they made a comfortable life for themselves. On fine days he would play pétanque with the gendarmes. The evenings were cool up in the mountains and the mayor would come over and they would sit round the fire, chatting about the old days and exchanging confidences. Here the Germans struck lucky again; Barthelemy Lledos, who often went to Paris, made no secret of his admiration for Germany and his contacts with the regime. Lemoine took it all in.[41]

When he sent him up to the hills, Paillole was doubtful about Lemoine's story of the Germans trying to recruit him in the Hotel Splendide, so it comes as no surprise that just after he moved to Saillagouse, a counter-espionage mission called But-Crayfish was supposedly mounted according to one written record by the Bureau Centrale de Renseignements et d'Action, General de Gaulle's intelligence service. A team was to parachute into France, their mission to track down Lemoine and Drach and find out if they were double-dealing. The operation, on 24 July 1942, was led by a French Air Force officer called Dupré. He was accompanied by Francois Rouxin, code-named Guere, and Corporal Jean Orabona, who was unfortunately killed in the drop. The whole thing was fake news from the start because Captain Dupré turned out to be Henri Bertrand, a double-agent. Had he met Lemoine, who knows what might have happened?[42]

In fact, an operation called Crayfish/Bril *did* take place on July 24 1942 but that is about the only thing true about this story. A team set off in an RAF Halifax of Squadron 138 (Special Duties) from RAF Tempsford that night. It was flown by a Flight Lieutenant 'Bunny' Rymills. Squadron 138 was one of the so-called Moonlight

Squadrons; their special duties were to drop equipment and Special Operations Executive agents behind enemy lines on moonlit nights. This time the drop was near Boisset-lès-Montrond in the Loire valley. True, the leader was called Bertrand, but his first name was André and he was the head of the FFI, the French Forces of the Interior; his *nom de guerre* was Benoit, not Dupré. With him were twenty-two-year-old Rouxin, but his first name was Xavier, aka 'B', and Jean Orabona, code name Grimaldi. The three Frenchmen were probably resistance agents returning to France after a briefing in England. This is just one example of how these Resistance stories can become garbled.[43]

Back on firmer ground, Gustave Bertrand's journeys to Paris continued without discovery and in spite of food rationing, he didn't stint himself. One night that summer, while dining at Maxime's in the Rue Royale, then, as now, the go-to place for grandees and gourmets with its crimson banquettes and amazing art nouveau décor, he chatted with a German working at the Berlin embassy; we know him only as Max. How they met, and how they communicated is a mystery, for neither was confident in the other's language and they often had to use a dictionary, but they became firm friends. Bertrand sensed that Max was a high-ranking officer at the embassy but not the Hitler admirer one might expect. Bertrand became such a familiar visitor to the embassy that the guard even presented arms once; Bertrand felt it wise to salute the portrait of Hitler on the stairs. Both men were taking extraordinary risks. Max presented Bertrand with an even better travelling aid: the metal pass of a German diplomatic courier and he became the escort for the diplomatic mail between Paris and the Armistice Control at Vichy, tucking the equipment he had collected for the Enigma machine in with it. Max warned Bertrand that if Britain and the US invaded northern France, the Germans would occupy the *zone libre* in return. Bertrand never identified Max and said he did not know who he was, but the information he handed over shows he was either head of chancellery at the embassy or the head of the German cypher office. Bertrand said he was not another informer like Schmidt and we do not know if he was paid; he remains a mystery man.[44]

Meanwhile, Lemoine's health was improving in the clean mountain and his businesses were doing well – he organized profitable border crossings to Spain, bought and sold black market goods for himself and his friends – but it was a very quiet life and he longed for more excitement, so he was curious when he was called to the telephone box in the village at the end of September. The doorman of the Hotel Splendide hotel was on the line. Apart from Paillole and his children, he was the only one who knew where Lemoine was. He had a message from his Swiss friend, de Ry, who wanted to see him urgently. In earlier days, with the agreement of the Deuxième Bureau, Lemoine had sold German codes provided by Schmidt to de Ry. This sounded like the excitement he sought. Without telling Paillole about this, he was in Marseille the next morning. He found de Ry in a quiet corner of the huge salon of the Splendid and heard his story. De Ry was on the trail of an Italian code called *Impero;* a civil servant in the Italian ministry of war wanted to sell it but demanded a high price. As proof, de Ry produced a photograph of the cover of the code manual and a couple of pages of text.

Lemoine rushed back to Saillagouse, went to see Barthelemy Lledos, the mayor, and suggested that he should sell the code to the Germans for him on his next trip to Paris; they would share the proceeds. Lledos accepted, happy to have the chance to ingratiate himself with the Germans. He was in Paris by 15 October and asked friends there to make contact with the Abwehr for him. On the 20th he had a meeting at the Hotel Lutetia with an intelligence officer. He showed the *Impero* photographs and explained how they had come to him. When he mentioned Lemoine, the officer pricked up his ears, told de Ry to stay where he was and dashed out of the room. An hour later he was in the presence of Colonel Friedrich Rudolf, co-ordinator of Abwehr activities in France, and Georg Wiegand, for some serious questioning.

Ten days later he was back at Lemoine's house. 'Everything went well,' he reported. 'The Germans quibbled over the price but they want the code.'

The Abwehr asked the Lemoines to go to Paris to finalise the deal. Their expenses would be paid and they had nothing to fear. Quite the contrary, Lledos assured him. Lemoine thought about it.

It was certainly tempting but he hesitated; this was the second time he had been invited to Paris by the Germans. If he asked Paillole's advice, as he did the first time, it would show that he had disobeyed orders by trading the Italian code. He mused for two days – could he trust the Germans after working against them for so long? Finally his hunger for intrigue and adventure got the better of him. He went to Err and told Lledos that he accepted.[45]

* * *

Back at Chateau des Fouzes Bertrand was always on the alert for signs of German radio vans listening for the source of the vast amount of material they knew was being transmitted; although the chateau was in the *zone libre*, Germans and Vichy forces were always listening. Early in November 1942 he noticed a van, with crew dressed in the navy blue overalls of radio repair men, visiting a couple of farms in the area. Everybody in the chateau packed and was ready to move out.

On 8 November 1942, British and American forces invaded north-west Africa: Morocco, Algeria and Tunisia, which were controlled by the Vichy government, in preparation for the invasion of southern Europe. In retaliation, Germany invaded the *zone libre* four days later, as Max, Bertrand's informant at the German embassy in Paris, had warned him earlier in the year. During the dark winter nights, Bertrand and his men had hidden all their secret equipment, something they had done so efficiently when they were forced out of PC Bruno at the Chateau de Vignolles in 1940 that the Germans had no idea that the chateau had been the French equivalent of Bletchley Park. Bertrand evacuated PC Cadix on the 9th and the Germans raided it on 12 November. He put up the cryptographers in four houses he had rented in Cannes. It was essential to get them and their secrets out of France immediately – but they were still there four months later. This was partly because of the smouldering animosity between Bertrand and Gwido Langer, partly because of simple inefficiency, partly because of the heavy drinking of Langer (known as Monsieur Beaujolais) and the rest of the Poles. Finally, an attempt on 12 March 1943 to get them in small groups across the Pyrenees into Spain failed: they were betrayed by greedy guides, and arrested.[46] Three of the Poles were sent to Germany as slave labour and two of them perished.

Bertrand and his wife, Mary, went home to their house at Theoule, where he joined the Kleber resistance network. Paillole went back to his fruit and vegetable business in Marseille They did not know what had happened to their men until a month later, by which time Bertrand also knew that Lemoine had been arrested.

Paul Paillole considered the British intelligence service to be amateurish but his own organisation was as bad The French had made serious mistakes in letting Lemoine stay in France and in not evacuating Bertrand and his cryptologists; Lemoine knew the identity of the Enigma spy, and of hundreds more spies, Bertrand knew more about the decoding of Enigma than anyone else apart from 'C', the head of British intelligence, and the cryptologists knew exactly what messages were being read.

Paillole had spent Christmas 1942 in London, called to face Britain's MI6, who had suspicions about his loyalty. MI6 Chief Sir Stewart Menzies was on a secret visit to Algiers on Christmas Eve. He had flown out on hearing that Georges Roninof the Deuxième Bureau, had managed to escape from France when Germany invaded the south; he hoped they could set up a new intelligence service based in Algiers. He was having lunch on a sunny rooftop in Algiers with Squadron Leader Fred Winterbotham, who was responsible for the security and distribution of Ultra – the name given to all the material decoded by the Enigma machine – Ronin and Colonel Louis Rivet, head of the Deuxième Bureau. It was here that they learned of the assassination of Admiral Jean Darlan at his office in the Palace of State a few hundred yards away. Darlan was French naval commander of Vichy forces, a supporter of Nazi Germany and a man who was determined to gain power over France when the war ended. The President of the United States supported him and Britain did not, so his 'removal' solved many problems. Britain did not, of course, give their agents a licence to kill – but Sir Felix Cadogan, head of the Foreign Office wrote in his diary 'We shall do no good until we've killed Darlan.'[47]

Paillole would surely have been seen by Sir Stewart Menzies who was back in London in time for the New Year celebrations;

he was certainly seen by Lieutenant Colonel Felix Cowgill, head of Section V, the counter-espionage section of MI6, who defended him strongly, and by Kim Philby, his deputy, who described him as 'a most attractive character whose anti-Axis feeling was beyond reproach'. Kim Philby, one assumes, would have been a good judge of such things.[48]

Darlan's killer was a young Frenchman called Fernand Bonnier de la Chapelle; he wore British army uniform and was being trained as a Special Operations Executive agent to be parachuted into France to lead the Maquis, the resistance movement that grew in the south after the occupation of the *zone libre*. He was arrested, found guilty on Christmas night and put before a firing squad immediately. There were rumours that Darlan's death was part of a British plot to kill others, including General Dwight D. Eisenhower, the commander of *Torch*, as part of a plan to bring French North Africa into the British Empire. Admiral Sir Andrew Cunningham, Eisenhower's deputy, put out a statement rubbishing these stories and Bonnier seems to have acted alone. His sentence was annulled in 1945 and his civil rights restored posthumously in 1945 on the grounds that Admiral Darlan had been acting against the interests of France and Bonnier had been acting in the interest of the liberation of France.[49]

The odd thing about Menzies' visit to Algiers is that it was secret even from Patrick Reilly, his personal assistant. His described the strange episode:

At the beginning of December 1942 'C' asked me whether I would like to take a short leave. I was surprised at this suggestion for it was the only time he made such a suggestion. I was rather tired and I accepted gratefully and when I went on leave 'C' was at his desk. When I got back, 'C' was still at his desk. I did not know he had been a way on a foreign journey and did not know until forty years later that he had been away and then only when Winterbotham wrote to me and asked me if I knew why 'C' had gone to Algiers. I then saw that the coincidence was remarkable, although I still cannot say that 'C's' journey had anything to do with Darlan's murder, except that 'C' was in Algiers when it took place. I am now inclined to the view that he gave me leave at that time because he wanted me out of the way while he was abroad. Had I not been on leave, I would have been at my desk at Broadway and I would certainly have known that he had gone to Algiers.[50]

Other intelligence workers at Broadway would have known of his trip; I wonder why Patrick Reilly was not in on the secret.

By January 1943 Paillole was back in Algiers, where his *Travaux Ruraux* was now based. He felt certain that Lemoine had escaped into Spain when the south was occupied; that was their agreement and it almost happened. On 10 December the Lemoines had a message from Marseille that the Germans had been looking for them at the Hotel Splendide. They packed up, ready to escape with the help of the gendarmes, but a few days later there was a telephone call from one of their sons, Rolf Guy Lemoine, telling them he had been arrested. To Madame Lemoine, who wrote to Paillole about it in 1946, it sounded as if there were a Gestapo agent at his side; they decided against fleeing, they couldn't leave their son behind.[51]

What Madame Lemoine didn't know was that Rolf was in the hands of Kieffer, the Gestapo man who had interrogated Lemoine in 1938 and now wanted to win the race with the Abwehr to capture him. What she also didn't know was that since Lledos's visit to Paris in October the Abwehr was equally determined not to let him slip through their fingers. On 15 November Wiegand sent his second secret agent to Saillagouse. This was Henri Marette, who had worked for the Abwehr since the end of 1940 under the name of Hubertus. He had known Lemoine well before the war when they worked together in French Guiana, where Lemoine had the gold mine concession that explained his great wealth. Marette had offered to work for the French in 1937 but they didn't trust him; Lemoine had kept in touch, finding him an intelligent and astute man who could be used on jobs that were just this side of illegal.

Wiegand and Rudolf counted on Marette to help them decide how to handle Lemoine: to arrest him or use him as a double agent. Marette went to Saillagouse on 15 November but he didn't report back until February. He had Lemoine in the palm of his hand, he boasted. He reported that Lemoine was friendly with all the military and civilian authorities and was perfectly *au courant* with all that went on in the region. 'Lemoine proves a real and sincere Germanophile spirit and truly wants a German victory.' He underlined this sentence, then said he recorded Lemoine verbatim:

> I hate the English and scorn them. You can't imagine how I detest them. If the field-marshal ordered me to struggle against the English and rally with Germany, I would do so with a big heart and with great pleasure. The Germans have courage which you have to admire and it is deplorable that the pernicious Anglo-Saxon propaganda is blinding the world to the dreadful the menace of communism which only Germany can fight.

Lemoine was anxious to show that it wasn't his fault that the Germans found all those secret intelligence archives in Paris; he and his wife had spent two days destroying documents about their French and foreign agents. The documents they seized were abandoned by the French intelligence service. 'You're quite sure?' asked Marette. 'Absolutely.'

His conclusion was that Lemoine was thoroughly anti-English (his wife, too), thoroughly anti-Bolshevik, and sincerely and truly sympathetic to the German cause. He told Marette about his activities with the Deuxième Bureau and expressed a willingness to tell everything and be useful. Marette ended his report with instructions on how to find the Villa Saint-Lucie, Lemoine's house at Saillagouse, including a sketch map.

At 3 o'clock on 25 February 1943 Colonel Rudolf, Wiegand, and Lieutenant Colonel Reile huddled over Marette's reports. At six o'clock they telephoned Canaris. Admiral Canaris was precise: 'Seize the Lemoines immediately. Treat them with respect and in absolute secret, including the RSHA.' The RSHA was the umbrella organisation for all the Nazi Party's security agencies.

Two days later at half-past four, Wiegand, clutching Marette's sketch map in his hand, drew up at Lemoine's house in his chauffeur-driven staff car. When he was interrogated at the end of the war he described the meeting: 'Our secret agent, [Marette] was in the house. I surprised them in the middle of their conversation.

Lemoine was astonished. He said to me: "I was expecting you tomorrow. You evidently have my photo and you have come from Marseille."

I told him that I did have a photo but I hadn't come from Marseille and I did not belong to the Gestapo.'

The couple was put up in a room at the border Customs house while the house was searched. They found nothing of interest, just their personal papers. The day before they left they found a cash box. They paid the bills in Saillagouse, the rest, about 30,000 francs, was given to the Lemoines to pay their expenses in Paris.[52]

And what expenses they were! They were taken to the palatial Continental hotel in Rue Castiglione, the same five-star hotel where, a short time before, Lemoine had entertained his friends and spy recruits right royally. The Abwehr treated him well, too, more like a guest of honour than a detainee. 'There was no question of an arrest,' said one who was there. The Abwehr had taken over a whole floor of the hotel and the Lemoines were in room 159; it was opulent, with a thick red carpet and lots of gilt on the Empire furniture with a spacious bathroom adjoining. There was a hushed, almost reverent attitude to the couple and if they wanted anything special, Lemoine would send the orderly who served his food to get it from his black market friends. Lemoine didn't go without.

In his usual charismatic way Lemoine drew people to him; they were in awe. He entertained like a king – his work name Rex was very apt – pouring the champagne and the whisky, offering little tidbits his orderly had brought in. There was a glorious glow of goodwill towards the old man.

The next day, 2 March 1943, his interrogation began in the next room. It went on for *nine months*, conducted by Georg Wiegand helped by a Frau Schmiedler, a bi-lingual secretary. It wasn't really an interrogation, more Lemoine telling his story, slowly describing how the Deuxième Bureau worked. Wiegand didn't push him and Lemoine sometimes hesitated. What they really wanted to know was the source of the leaks in Berlin. But the first person he denounced was Drach, his loyal assistant for twenty-odd years.

'Believe me, Herr Wiegand', he said, putting it in a nutshell, 'he worked for the English and was a German Jew *and* a communist', everything that Lemoine now said he hated.

'He hates his own country and has denounced the work of the Third Reich since 1933. His book, *Deutschland in Waffen*, accuses the Reich of secretly re-arming contrary to the agreement of the Treaty of Versailles.'[53]

He even told them where Drach was living with his mistress, Nelly Goujat: on the first floor of No 43 Boulevard d'Arras in Marseille, under the name of Francois Denis with false papers provided by Osvald, the chief of police of Marseille.

Wiegand was delighted. He went to see Henri Marette, his secret agent, at the Hotel Lutetia, and paid him ten thousand francs for his efforts in discovering Lemoine's true feelings during their fireside chats at Saillagouse and told him about Frederic Drach. He gave him another ten thousand francs to find him but he had moved from Marseille and it took Marette until 14 July to trace him to Nimes. He resisted bravely when he was arrested the following afternoon. He was thrown into prison at Nimes where he was found hanged dead at four o'clock the next morning. Suicide or murder?

Lemoine wrote and signed a statement:

I am naturalized French and I have worked for the French secret service against Germany. I believe I can say that I have done my duty towards my country, France. Petain and Laval would honestly like a reconciliation with Germany with a view to integrate into Europe. I can't act against Germany any more as a loyal French person and as an Anglophobe. I, therefore, wish to put myself at the service of the Germans.

Please don't be angry with me if I don't betray my French comrades. I will never do anything against France.

Later he wrote: 'Here are my reasons behind my attitude: I want to be useful to France, with all my strength as I have done since I was thirty-five years old and now that France is allied to Germany. If Germany falls, France is lost.'[54]

His revelations included the names of dozens of agents he had recruited as well as top men in the Wehrmacht: the pre-war German ambassador to London and a fervent anti-Nazi, Leopold von Hoesch, Wirth, an ex-chancellor, Otto Hartura, the brother of air force general Milch, and Bodo, the spy in the Austrian embassy.

At last, on 17 March, after fourteen days of questioning by Wiegand, Protze and sometimes Rudolf himself, alternately friendly and threatening, Lemoine cracked and revealed that Hans Thilo Schmidt, alias HE, Ashay, was the man they were looking for.

He talked for four days, telling everything, from that first meeting in Verviers in 1931 when the hard-up Schmidt came with Cipher Office secrets to sell, to his fabulous supply of information about the Enigma machine, about the OKW (the *Oberkommando der Wehrmacht*, the armed forces' high command), the *Forschsungsamt* and the Abwehr. He told them about Schmidt's womanising, his relationship with his brother, his skill in avoiding all checks and surveillance, how he explained the origin of the riches he had acquired through spying. The Germans were astonished at the scope of the affair Lemoine revealed. That Schmidt's work for the Deuxième Bureau lasted for about ten years; that he left the *Chiffrierstelle* two years before the war to become head of the *Forschungsamt* post at Templin. His wife didn't know about his spying work. He always needed money and Lemoine had the impression that what the French were paying him hadn't been enough in the last few years. He thought he was working for someone else, which was why he considered him dangerous. And he indicated he despised Schmidt. 'His cupidity and venality' was what made Schmidt break off contact with the French in 1939 Lemoine said, because he thought he would get more money by working for the Russians.

Late on the night of 19/20 March 1943 Colonel Friedrich Rudolf came back to the Continental hotel, shaken by the extent of the disaster which seemed to have engulfed the entire German military system: the Cipher Office, the Reich chancellery, the OKW, the *Forschungsamt*, the RSHA (the Reich's security overlord), top civil servants, dignitaries, officers of all ranks, high and low. And worst of all was the passing on of the private thoughts and the records of one of the top men of the Wehrmacht, General Rudolf Schmidt, the innocent brother of the traitor; the indiscreet brother, for he had written devastating letters to Hans from the eastern front where he was in command of the second army, criticising Hitler and the regime.

Rudolf was horrified and probably terrified by the new turn the interrogation had taken. He swore Wiegand to secrecy. No one, and that included his boss Lt Col Reile and his colleagues at the Lutetia Hotel, must hear a word. He ordered him to write up a report, get from Lemoine a signed account of the precise nature of the intelligence given by Schmidt, with his letter boxes in Switzerland and his agents' names and addresses. And he was to make sure there was no doubt about the identity of the leak: was he really the brother of Hitler's favourite general?

He had Wiegand's report by 5 pm on 20 March and at 10 am on the 21st Rudolf presented it to Canaris in his office in Berlin. For hours the two men sat alone, poring over every aspect of the enormous scandal and the huge repercussions that would follow if it became known. Apart from anything else, Canaris was a great friend of General Schmidt and knew how much Hitler thought of him: he had trusted him on 15 November 1941 with the command of the second army. At least, though, it removed all shadow of doubt from his deputy, Colonel Hans Oster, who had originally been suspected of being the leak and found innocent.

(Innocent but how loyal to the regime? He and Canaris were friends and conspirators: after Hitler and Neville Chamberlain signed the Munich agreement on 30 September 1938, which allowed Hitler to take over Czechoslovakia, there was great tension between the German General Staff and the Nazi leaders. The army 'strove unremittingly and courageously to restrain Herr Hitler and were instrumental on at least one occasion in averting an order to march,' wrote Stewart Menzies.[55] When he was unsuccessful General Ludwig Beck resigned as chief of the German General Staff and Canaris and Oster were part of a conspiracy that joined him in December 1938 in an approach to Britain with a deal to avert war; they failed. Canaris, head of the Abwehr, and his deputy Oster carried out their duties in the Abwehr meticulously. They were arrested on 23 July 1944 after the attempt on Hitler's life on 20 July 1944 and hanged at Flossenbürg concentration camp, Bavaria, on 9 April 1945, to the sound of the approaching Allied guns.)

Horrified and shocked, Canaris went to ask Goering's advice the next day; which was to find Schmidt immediately and arrest him. When this was done he would tell Hitler. They found him on 23 March at the flat his daughter, Gisela, had found for him in

Berlin; the marital home was now at Templin but he liked to spend the night in Berlin sometimes, probably with one of his girlfriends.

Schmidt had probably known the danger he was in for a couple of years, since the Germans discovered there had been leaks from the Cipher Office as well as the *Forschungsamt*. The police documents abandoned by the French National Security as they fled Paris could possibly lead to him; Lemoine himself and the Deuxième Bureau men he had met so often were all on the run – and if they were caught and tortured... He was just waiting, so it was probably no great surprise when the Abwehr arrived. They searched the flat, turned everything upside down; they even ripped open the mattress on his bed. Then they took him away and he vanished.[56]

There is no official record of what happened to him. For years after the war Paul Paillole searched the German records but his name didn't appear in a single official document. Family, friends, lawyers, interrogators, none of them would say a word. Paillole assumed he had been shot in July 1943. It was Hugh Sebag-Montefiore who unearthed the facts. He traced Schmidt's daughter, Giselle, who told him she tried to smuggle cyanide into her father's prison cell, but it was found. Her brother did the same and their father was found dead in his cell in the middle of September 1943. Neither church nor civil authorities would bury Schmidt so his brother, who had always picked up the pieces for Hans, did it. He lies next to his mother in a cemetery outside Berlin. It is unmarked. It is as if Hans Thilo Schmidt had never existed.[57] In fact, his identity was not revealed until 1973 when Gustave Bertrand, who had been head of PC Cadix, the clandestine decryption post near Nimes, published his memoirs, *Enigma, ou la plus grande enigma de la guerre*.

When Goebbels told Hitler what had been going on he was devastated, as much by the disloyalty of the great General Schmidt as by the treason of his brother. He sulked, he became paranoid. On 11 April, on Hitler's orders, General Schmidt, now commander of the second army on the eastern front, was sacked, and told to go home. It was not the harshest punishment but Hitler was shattered. Goebbels wrote in his diary on 12 May 1943: '...his best wish was to have nothing to do with them... He no long joined them for lunch at the big table at the OKW. He wouldn't see the generals again... All the generals lie, he said, all the generals are disloyal, all the generals are against national socialism, all the generals are reactionary.'

His friends and colleagues rallied round Rudolf Schmidt: he was innocent and could not be blamed for his brother's treachery. On 22 August 1943 General Schmidt wrote to the Reichsführer, asking to be reinstated. The reply was no. A year later, at the suggestion of the Reichsführer, General Burgdorf wrote to Hitler with the same request and was refused. He tried again on 13 September 1944; Hitler was adamant, no reinstatement for General Schmidt.

* * *

After the debacle of the evacuation of the PC Cadix cryptologists, Bertrand continued his underground intelligence work for the rest of 1943 and became head of the Kleber network in July; Kleber was the secretly re-born SR, the Service de Renseignement, the intelligence-gathering service. Paillole came under a shadow again: in November the British Foreign Office investigated his part in a plot to spirit Marshal Pétain out of France to North Africa, to take over leadership of the French in exile, the position General de Gaulle had made his own. De Gaulle was, understandably, furious.[58]

At the beginning of 1944 Bertrand and Mary, his wife, went to Paris to collect radio equipment sent by 'C' that would enable them to communicate directly – by now the two men were firm friends. Bertrand was to meet the agent with the radio at 9 am on 3 January in front of the statue of St Anthony of Padua in the Sacré Coeur, the huge church with its great white dome high in Montmartre. The meeting went wrong; the man he was to meet did not carry the identifying copy of the magazine *Sentinel*, nor did he respond to the password. The man, who called himself Paul, explained that he had just decoded a message from London but half of it was missing. Bertrand was suspicious but agreed to meet Paul two days later in front of the same statue on the eve Feast of the Epiphany, 5 January. When he arrived at 8 am Paul was not there. Hiding behind a pillar, he saw three men approach the statue; police, he thought, but before he could get away there was a tap on his shoulder. He was taken for interrogation to the five-star Continental hotel where the Lemoines had been held until six weeks before.[59]

This was a disaster. Apart from 'C', no one knew more about Enigma than Bertrand. He also knew about *Fortitude*; this was the plan to fool the Germans into believing that the Allied invasion of France would be around Calais. If he were tortured into revealing this, and if the Germans then tricked the Allies into thinking they were taken in by the ruse, plans for D-Day would be shattered. Bertrand's name was on the Germans' most-wanted list, they knew how important he was. His interrogator regaled him with stories of the water-boarding torture they could use to make him talk; they promised him a house with central heating, (in France, in 1944!), servants, a car, all the petrol he wanted and 200,000 francs a month (he was getting 6,800 from the French) if he would become a double agent. He knew he would not be able to withstand torture so he pretended to change sides and said he would spy for the Germans. They let him free for two days so that he could contact his fellow resistance workers in the south, believing this would convince them that he had not been turned. Bertrand and his wife went on the run.[60]

They were on the run for three months before they could make contact with London. They had a message from 'C' that he was sending a plane to pick them up from a field near Orleans. They missed that rendezvous, waited a month for the next full moon and missed that, too. On 31 May they heard a coded message on the BBC, *Les lilas blancs sont fleuris*: an aircraft would land at a farm with lilacs near Pithiviers. They went to the farm and waited until 1 am when they heard an aircraft approaching. Fortunately it did not see their flashing torch signals because it was a Messerschmidt. They waited until 3.30 am then went back to sleep in a barn. They were finally picked up by a Lysander on 2 June. It was a four-hour, noisy flight before they landed at an airfield near Cambridge at daybreak, to be greeted with offers of a drink: he took a large whisky while Madame chose gin. After a proper English breakfast they were driven to London where Biffy Dunderdale and Tom Greene, his chief of staff, were waiting. Bertrand shaved off the moustache he had grown as a disguise and that evening the BBC broadcast the message *Michel a rasé sa moustache*.

They were taken to Biffy Dunderdale's house in Walton Street at tea-time, where Paul Paillole was waiting. Paillole had been in

London since 8 May, engaged in difficult negotiations with the intelligence staff. 'C' asked Paillole to take Bertrand's report of his arrest and escape; the big question was whether Bertrand had told Abwehr about *Fortitude*. Paillole became convinced he had not but he was worried that Bertrand kept asking him about the date and place for the Allied landings, D-Day (Paillole was the only Frenchman who knew it). Bertrand asked for this information to be sent by radio to his contacts in France, a very risky idea to say the least. 'C' joined the Bertrands at Biffy Dunderdale's for dinner and congratulated him on his brilliant work in the Resistance and told him he was recommending him for the DSO. All the same, Paillole felt perhaps his old friend was not totally reliable and he was kept under a discreet house arrest until after the D-day landings.[61]

CHAPTER TWENTY-SIX

The End

Wiegand's interrogation went on for nine months without a break and he reported on 23 October that Lemoine still refused to give the names of any French officer. Lemoine's capture and questioning were the biggest triumph for the Abwehr, but they had to keep the whole thing secret. They were traumatised by the affair and if anything leaked out, the army, the security services, the German people, would be demoralised.

Finally, on 17 November 1943, General Rudolf handed Lemoine over to the Gestapo; he had refused a request to go back into service and be a double agent. 'You're too late. I'm too old. I want peace,' said the old man and the next day he and his wife were moved from the five-star Continental to the four-star Louvois at 1 Rue Lulli. It was just as comfortable and is now known as the Hôtel des Impôts. They were welcomed by *Kriminallcommissar* Kieffer, the one who had arrested Lemoine in Cologne in 1938. At last he had his man. But there was no gloating. He greeted him warmly and explained that the special commission set up to deal with important cases like his had put Lemoine under his remit. He could no longer be used abroad because the Abwehr had kept him out of action for too long; he could still be of use, though, for there were several cases they could work on together – nothing against France, mind. 'Your advice will be valuable to me,' he finished.

In fact, it wasn't serious work; every so often he would have to go to Berlin with a report and each return became party night: champagne and money flowed. Lemoine took his 'guards' to the good restaurants between the Opéra and the rue de Richelieu.

After Christmas 1944 Kieffer came to the Louvois with a surprising New Year present: his liberty. 'All I ask is that you go on living here and eat at least one meal a day in the canteen.'

Lemoine had fallen on his feet again. The good life continued with more nightclub outings, gifts of jewellery and perfume for the women and bottles of good wine for the men. He was going through money like there was no tomorrow and said he spent a million francs in a few weeks; soon he was running short. He asked one of his sons to go to the south, to the little house at Saillagouse, where he had buried some money. It was what was left of the 170,000 Reichsmarks' worth of gold left by his father. So the good life went on; he lavished favours on all around him. It wasn't all greed and gluttony, though; he was generous with friends who were in trouble with the occupying forces.

This life of luxury was about to end; the Allied forces were approaching Paris and Lemoine had to leave. Wiegand saw him at Chalons-sur-Marne, east of Paris. He was, as usual, in a good hotel with his wife and his Gestapo friends, but they needed to get farther away from Paris and left on 1 September for Frankfurt an der Oder, on the German-Polish border. They put up at the Hotel Prinz von Preusse where Lemoine and the hotel manager soon got the black market going: charcuterie, butter, American cigarettes, silk stockings, all appeared as if by magic. Lemoine never stopped making money; never stopped giving favours.[62]

By February 1945 the Russian army was approaching their little haven in Frankfurt-am-Oder and the group made for Berlin. After a few days in the Hotel Albrecht Lemoine and his wife seem to have been abandoned by the Abwehr, who had their own skins to save, and they moved in with his niece at her house at 22 Wundstrasse, Berlin. (His sister, Anna, had married the man called Wittkop who employed Lemoine in 1891.) They endured the bombing of Berlin and the chaos gave him the opportunity for even more black market dealing.

The Second World War ended on 8 May 1945. The French opened a repatriation office on Kurfurstendam and Lemoine landed on his feet once more. He switched sides again and soon had a commanding position in the new department: his knowledge of Berlin, of the many German dialects, his chutzpah and his flair as a fixer were of great value. In the chaos of Berlin his supreme ease and confidence had a reassuring effect. He took part in screening the French, eliminating the suspects, giving money to the French prisoners released in Russia and on their way home. His wife's return to France was made easy. Everything was hunky-dory; but it didn't last.

The French had not forgotten – he had betrayed his adopted country as well as the land of his birth. To his great surprise, he was arrested on 27 October 1945 and flown to a French counter-intelligence centre at Wildbad in the Black Forest. Colonel Paul Gerar-Dubot and Captain Maurice Dupont were given the job of finding out what information he had given the Germans while in their hands and what responsibility he had for the dreadful results that followed his arrest. They were two of the best operators in the business but they got nowhere. His memory was fading and he was incoherent. They gave up. In spite of what he had done, he was a French citizen and because of his age and his physical state he had to be treated well. He could get any medication he needed, plus coffee, sugar, cognac and so on. He had liberty of movement and, despite his memory problems and his poor health, he was able to indulge in 'certain speculative operations for which he had a particular taste'.

At the end of September 1946 Paul Paillole was Commander of the French occupation troops in Baden. He was often invited to go hunting in the Black Forest and one day could not resist going to see Lemoine in Wildbad. Colonel Gerar-Dubot said he would find him in a pitiable state in the Maison Carola, which was where they lodged people being questioned. But Lemoine just couldn't stop the corruption game. He tried to buy a young officer, believing he could set him free.

'How can he bribe someone at his age, without money and without means?' Paillole asked.

'Lemoine is never without resources, even with one foot in the grave.'

Lemoine had cut open the left shoulder pad of his great-coat with his razor and taken out four Louis, twenty-dollar gold coins and promised the young man that the day he was freed he would find the same in the right shoulder pad. When Lemoine was not freed, he demanded the gold back. The boy wouldn't give it and Lemoine reported him; a betrayer to the end.[63]

Paillole found Lemoine in his bare room at the Maison Carola. He was sitting on the bed in his pyjamas. Unrecognisable, skin and bones, unshaven, his eyes bright with fever. A half-empty brandy bottle stood on the bedside table. He recognised Paillole and tried to get up to greet him but the man stopped him. Paillole asked about his health, his time in the beleaguered Berlin. The old man's voice – he was now seventy-five – faltering at first, gradually became stronger and he became more talkative, jumping from one subject to another. Paillole asked about Schmidt and without the least emotion he said that the Germans knew about his treason. He boasted incessantly about how he had run rings round the Gestapo and the Abwehr.

Paillole was bursting with curiosity; at last he asked: 'How do you explain that you enjoy such freedom while others who have done less damage to Germany than you were subject to worse treatment?'

Lemoine looked at him for a long time then said: 'During thirty years of service for you, I have bought ministers, ambassadors, officers, police, civil servants. For fifty or a hundred thousand francs, sometimes even less, these men risked their freedom, their lives.' He rambled on for a while, not making much sense but he said there were former SS officers among them – why wouldn't they do him favours now, it costing them nothing?

Neither of them said another word and they never saw each other again.

Lemoine didn't get up in the morning. An orderly went to his room at 8.45 and saw that he was ill and coughing badly, so he was transferred to hospital immediately and died the next morning after a violent, bleeding coughing bout.

Lemoine was buried temporarily in Germany. Although his wife had previously lobbied the Government for some recompense for his long service to France, she did not claim the body and in 1949 he was re-buried at the national military cemetery at Les Vallons, Mulhouse; carré E, tombe 75. Madame went back to her maiden name and, known as Marie Renée Lemoine Escalada, died on the island of Ibiza in 1983, aged ninety-eight.

Endnotes

Where a source is noted more than once subsequent mentions are under the author's name alone.

PART ONE

1. Metropolitan Police Services, Records Management Branch
2. L/P&S/11/51 P2324/1919
3. *Our Summer in the Vale of Kashmir,* F. Ward Denys, pub James William Bryan Press, USA. 1915
4. High Court, Dublin, 4 February 1914
5. High Court of Justice, King's Bench, Dublin 1913
6. *The People,* 7 December 1924, p.5
7. *The People*
8. *Our Summer in the Vale of Kashmir,* p.124
9. Oriental and India Office Collection, 1OR R/1.1917
10. OIOC, R/1/ R/1/1/1917. DI (s) 19 May, pp 9-12 and 14-15
11. WO/339/2350
12. OIOC.L/P&S/10/968. File 907.1921. Part 1
13. OIOC.L/P&S/11/151. P2324/1919
14. *Plutocrats of Crime* by Percy J. Smith, p 166. Frederick Muller Ltd, London 1960
15. *The Mr A Case.* Bechhofer Roberts, C. E. Pub Jarrolds, 1950
16. OIOC. Reading Collection. MSS.EUR.E 238/7. Part 1, no 40. PP189-90
17. OIOC. IOR.R/1/1/1476
18. Reading Collection. MSS.EUR.E238. Part 2. No 52. PP 240-2

19. Reading Collection. Part 1. No 42. PP 192-4
20. Reading Collection. Part 2. No 51. PP 235-40
21. OIOC. IOR R/1/917
22. Metropolitan Police Services
23. *My Confessions* by Montague Noel Newton, pub T. Werner Laurie, London 1925
24. PRO. Crim 1/30/
25. Ibid
26. Ibid
27. Ibid
28. DPP/1/77
29. Metropolitan Police Service
30. DPP/1/77
31. PRO. Crim 1/301
32. Ibid
33. PRO. Crim 1/301
34. DPP/1/77
35. Ibid
36. OIOC. IOR/R/1/917
37. FO/371/19735. File 1107/32.pp 192-227

PART TWO

1. National Archives. FO/372.287. File 16929 of 1911
2. Smith, Percy J., *Plutocrats of Crime*, pp 101-07. Frederick Muller1960
3. *The Times*, 27 September 1907, p2
4. *The Times*, 5 October 1907, p 15
5. National Archives WO/339/13427
6. *The People*, 12 April 1925, p5
7. Newton, Montague Noel, *My Confessions*, T. Werner Laurie Ltd, 1925
8. Maillard Eric, *Rudolphe Stallman: Rodolphe Lemoine*. French edition. E-book
9. Maillard
10. Newton
11. Maillard
12. Baden-Powell, Sir Robert, *My Adventures as a Spy*, p 32. Dover Publications, Mineola, New York
13. National Archives WO 339/13427

PART THREE

1. Grafl, Florian, *An International History of Terrorism*, pub. Routledge, 2013
2. McHarg, Farquhar, *Pistoleros, the Chronicles of Farquhar McHarg*, p 252, Christie Books, 2009
3. Grafl
4. Oriental and India Office Collection. L/P&S/11234. File p 2586/23
5. Paillole, Paul, *Notre Espion Chez Hitler*, p 39. Pub. Nouveau Monde, Paris, 2013
6. Paillole, p 36
7. Paillole, p 34
8. Paillole, p 55
9. Hodges, Andrew. *Alan Turing: The Enigma*, p 175. Vintage Books, London 2014
10. Draitser, Emil, Stalin's *Romeo Spy*, p 113-4. Duckworth Overlook, 2011
11. Draitser, p 121
12. Draitser, p 123
13. Paillole, p 149
14. Paillole, pp 104-105
15. Paillole, p 81
16. Paillole, pp 84-88
17. Paillole, pp 94-101
18. Paillole, pp 105-107
19. Paillole, p 120
20. Paillole, p 130
21. Sebag-Montefiore, Hugh, *Enigma, The Battle for the Code*, p 32. Phoenix 2004
22. Paillole, pp 131-2
23. Paillole, pp 146-151
24. Paillole, p 150
25. Paillole, pp 157-159
26. Brown, Anthony Cave, *"C", The Secret Life of Sir Stewart Menzies, Spymaster to Winston Churchill*, pp 207-8. Macmillan Publishing Company, New York,1987
27. Sebag-Montefiore, pp 55-59
28. Hinsley, Sir Harry, co-author, *British Intelligence in the Second World War*, vol 1, p 54. HMS0

29. Stengers, Jean, *Enigma: The Poles, the British and the French, 1931-1940.* Review by Dr Gordon Welchman in *New Scientist,* 7 October 1982, p 42

30. Sebag-Montefiore, p 99

31. Paillole, p 209

32. Paillole, pp 229-233

33. Paillole, pp 212-214

34. Brown, p 286

35. Kitson, Simon, *The Hunt for Nazi Spies,* p 69. University of Chicago Press, 2008

36. Kitson, p 58

37. Brown, pp 402-08

38. Paillole, p 224

39. Paillole, p 237

40. Paillole, p 225

41. Paillole, pp 244-246

42. Miannay, Patrice, *Dictionnaire des Agent Double dans la Resistance,* p 261. Le Cherche Midi 2005

43. www.Tempsford-squadrons.info/index.htm

44. Brown, pp 404-405

45. Paillole, pp 246-248

46. Brown, pp 446-447

47. Brown, pp 447-450

48. Philby, Kim. *My Silent War,* p 127. Grafton Books,1989

49. Brown, p 452

50. Brown, p 452

51. Paillole, p 249

52. Paillole, p 251

53. Paillole, pp 254-256

54. Paillole, p 254

55. Brown, p 193

56. Sebag-Montefiore, p 288

57. Sebag-Montefiore, p 10

58. National Archives. FO 660/149 104/927

59. Sebag-Montefiore, pp 305-306

60. Paillole, p 270

61. Brown, pp 578-582 and Sebag-Montefiore, p 336

62. Paillole, pp 278-280

63. Paillole, pp 281-285

Bibliography

Baden-Powell, Sir Robert, *My Adventures as a Spy*, Dover Publications, Mineola, New York, 2011

Brown, Anthony Cave, *"C" The Secret Life of Sir Stewart Menzies, Spymaster to Winston Churchill*, Macmillan Publishing Company, New York, 1987

Draitser, Emil. *Stalin's Romeo Spy*, Duckworth Overlook, 2011

Grafl, Florian, *An International History of Terrorism*, Routledge, 2013

Hinsley, Sir Harry, co-author, *British Intelligence in the Second World War*, HMSO Official Histories, 2016

Hodges, Andrew, *Alan Turing: The Enigma*, Vintage Books, 2014

Kitson, Simon, *The Hunt for Nazi Spies*, University of Chicago Press, 2008

Maillard Eric, *Rudolphe Stallman: Rodolphe Lemoine*. E-book, French edition

McHarg, Farquhar *Pistoleros! 1.1918*, ChristieBooks/Read 'n' Noir, 2009

Miannay, Patrice, *Dictionnaire des Agents Doubles dans la Résistance*, Le Cherche Midi, 2005

Newton, Montague Noel, *My Confessions*, T. Werner Laurie Ltd, 1925

Paillole, Paul, *Notre Espion Chez Hitler*, Nouveau Monde, Paris, 2013

Philby Kim, *My Silent War*, Grafton Books, 1989

Sebag-Montefiore, Hugh. *Enigma, The Battle for the Code*, Phoenix 2004

Smith, Percy J, *Plutocrats of Crime*, Frederick Muller, 1960

Stengers, Jean, *Enigma: the Poles, the British and the French, 1931-1941*, Revue Belge de Philologie et Histoire, 2004

Index